MW01253093

The Principles and Practice of Crisis Management

The Principles and Practice of Crisis Management

The Case of Brent Spar

Meena Ahmed

160501

First published 2006 by
PALGRAVE MACMILLAN
Houndmills, Basingstoke, Hampshire RG21 6XS and
175 Fifth Avenue, New York, N.Y. 10010
Companies and representatives throughout the world

PALGRAVE MACMILLAN is the global academic imprint of the Palgrave Macmillan division of St. Martin's Press, LLC and of Palgrave Macmillan Ltd. Macmillan® is a registered trademark in the United States, United Kingdom and other countries. Palgrave is a registered trademark in the European Union and other countries.

ISBN 13: 978–0–230–00686–7   hardback
ISBN 10: 0–230–00686–8   hardback

This book is printed on paper suitable for recycling and made from fully managed and sustained forest sources.

A catalogue record for this book is available from the British Library.

Library of Congress Cataloging-in-Publication Data
Ahmed, Meena, 1973–
    The principles and practice of crisis management : the case of Brent Spar / by Meena Ahmed.
        p. cm.
    Includes bibliographical references and index.
    ISBN 0–230–00686–8 (cloth)
        1. Crisis management–Case studies. 2. Brent Spar (Offshore oil platform).
I. Title.

HD49.A36 2006
658.4'77–dc22

2006040955

10 9 8 7 6 5 4 3 2 1
15 14 13 12 11 10 09 08 07 06

Printed and bound in Great Britain by
Antony Rowe Ltd, Chippenham and Eastbourne

For my parents and my husband, Without your love this book would not have been possible

Contents

Acknowledgements

My eternal gratitude for the wisdom, support and friendship of Professor Paul Rock (LSE). I thank all the crisis managers who gave me their time and insight, in particular, Michael Regester, Michael Seymour and Michael Bland. Thanks too to Shell and Greenpeace and for the invaluable comments provided by Professor John Urry (Lancaster University) and Dr Javier Lezaun (LSE).

Introduction

This study examines the new field of crisis management, a consultancy practice embedded within the wider public relations industry. Whereas public relations tends to focus on the construction of desired reputations, the specific task of crisis management is to preserve those reputations at times of challenge or adversity. In particular, crisis management refers quite pragmatically to perception management rather than to the other elements involved in the handling of a crisis. The manner in which crisis management consultants manage perceptions shapes their definitions of 'crisis' and 'crisis management'. Crisis management is thus characterised as an issue in the regulation of adverse publicity:

> A crisis is an event which happens to an organisation which suddenly propels it into the limelight making it the target of unfavourable information and unwanted, potentially unfavourable media coverage (Michael Regester, in interview: July 7, 1997).

Crisis management consultants[1] argue that the most appropriate way to tackle crises is by 'getting your side of the story across' to audiences. The service they sell to public organisations is, therefore, perception management.

This book will focus on the 1995 controversy surrounding the disposal of the Brent Spar, an oil storage and loading facility owned by Royal Dutch/Shell, which has been portrayed by consultants as a powerful illustration of their professional argument and practice.[2] They claim the controversy posed a major threat to the Royal Dutch/Shell Group, a large and hitherto seemingly invulnerable organisation, and that the case of the Brent Spar exemplifies how crises can arise, reputations can be damaged, social reality can be contested, risks can be used for particular purposes, authority can be questioned and crisis management can be deployed as the cure (Regester and Larkin 1997: 63–75).

In 1991, the Brent Spar came to the end of its operational life. The company conducted a series of feasibility studies and consultations to assess options for its disposal and, in 1994, came to the conclusion that the best choice would be deep sea disposal in the Atlantic Ocean. In February 1995, the UK government approved their decision and informed other governments who did not, at that stage, contest it. In April, Greenpeace, a non-governmental organisation focusing on environmental issues, initiated a protest campaign by boarding the Brent Spar and announcing to the world's press that it contained over 100 tonnes of toxic sludge (it later claimed there were 5500 tonnes of oil on board.) Greenpeace also claimed that the sea disposal of the Brent Spar would set a precedent (an idea contested by Shell and the UK government) for disposing of 400 other oil rigs and that this posed a major threat to the marine environment (Rose 1998).

Greenpeace's boarding of the Brent Spar was a secretly planned manoeuvre that surprised all the parties involved. The organisation set up recording equipment on the installation to enable it to transmit video images to the world's television media. Amongst those images were graphic shots of Shell's attempts to prevent Greenpeace's boarding of the Brent Spar by using high-pressure water hoses. Greenpeace's images were used in television news reports, and, according to the consultants, Shell was cast as a Goliath-like bully and exploiter against Greenpeace's heroic David. Consultants remark that Greenpeace had succeeded in conveying its interpretation of reality to the world, whereas Shell had not, and this failure was responsible for the company's later defeat in managing the crisis.

In the end, Shell was obliged to abandon its plan for sea disposal, although it had already spent a considerable sum of money and four years arriving at it.[3] The company had been criticised. Consultants say it had been represented as aggressive and overbearing. There was a widespread perception that it had caused environmental damage and was ethically in the wrong. It even encountered violent protest in Germany, where petrol stations were firebombed.

Greenpeace had succeeded spectacularly well. It had halted the sea disposal of the Brent Spar and had done so by exerting media pressure on, and mobilising public and government opinion against, Shell. Greenpeace's triumph was, however, short-lived. It subsequently transpired that Greenpeace had exaggerated the amount of oil in Brent Spar. Although the organisation was unrepentant about its campaign, it was obliged in time to concede that it had made a mistake (Green-peace News Release: September 5, 1995) (Rose 1998).

This study will concentrate on how crisis management consultants – an emerging profession – construct a particular representation of the Brent Spar crisis to supply parables and nostrums about the new, glob-alised risk society in which they see companies as being obliged to function. I shall turn to theories of symbolic interactionism and the risk society to consider the consultants' reasoning, and will show that consultants also develop their own version of these theories to create and justify their response to crises. In doing so, I shall explore the rela-tionship between professions and ideologies in a hitherto unexamined area of the social world. In short, it will be argued that the Brent Spar incident illustrates perfectly the emergence of a new vision of how the world works.

1

'Crisis Management' – A General Outline

This chapter is an introduction to crisis management, examining consultants' definitions of crises, their accounts of the management of crises and their reasoning as to why crisis management is necessary.[1] It discusses the theories of symbolic interactionism and the risk society, outlines the origins and evolution of crisis management and explores how it is promoted.

Crisis management consultants suggest that crises generally assume one of two guises:

> The Cobra – the 'sudden' crisis. Disaster hits, taking a company completely by surprise, and plunging it straight into crisis.

> The Python – the 'slow-burning' crisis, or 'crisis creep'. A crisis can steal up and gradually crush you, issue by issue (Seymour and Moore 2000: 10).

The Cobra: the case of *Exxon-Valdez*

On March 24, 1989, a 987ft oil tanker, *Exxon-Valdez*, the property of the oil company Exxon, was on its way from Alaska's Valdez to California. It had been navigating through Prince William Sound, an abundant natural habitat, when it crashed and spilled ten million gallons of oil. The disaster became instant news, with pictures of the region's wildlife dying in the oil slick broadcast worldwide.

Despite persistent media inquiries, Exxon pursued a 'no comment' policy for over a week. When the company eventually held its first press conference, the chairman of Exxon attacked the media for their reporting of the situation. He showed no emotion over the environ-

4

mental disaster caused and offered no condolences to fishermen whose income had been destroyed as a consequence (Regester and Larkin 1997: 134–7). The chairman failed, in other words, to represent his company as caring or responsible and gave an impression of arrogance. The immediate consequence for Exxon was that the spill cost the company an estimated $7 billion in clean-up expenses, fines and lost market share. The company slipped from being the largest oil company in the world to the third largest (Regester and Larkin 1997: 134–7). Consultants argue that what was perhaps most damaging for Exxon, however, was being perceived as an insolent and ruthless organisation. This led to anger against the corporation and to a related lack of empathy, resulting in a willingness to apportion a greater degree of blame to Exxon (Regester and Larkin 1997: 134–7).

The Python: the case of Intel's Pentium 1

At the time of this 1994 crisis Intel made nine out of ten of the micro-processors for personal computers. Pentium 1, the company's high-performance microprocessor chip, was known by Intel to fail to produce the right answer in complex division calculations. Owing to the relatively small number of users likely to require complex divisions, the company felt that marketing the chip was an acceptable risk to take and went ahead without having devised a contingency plan should any problems arise.

The crisis arose in July 1994, when Thomas Nicely, a professor of mathematics at Lynchberg College, Virginia, discovered the fault in the chip when calculating complex equations. He contacted Intel for assistance but Intel declined to acknowledge that the error was in the Pentium chip. After several futile consultations with Intel, who continued to deny an error in the chip, Professor Nicely and his colleagues publicised the fact that the chip was faulty on the Internet in September 1994 (Regester and Larkin 1997: 58).

Other Internet users also highlighted the same error in response and an Internet site was set up as a forum, within which Intel came under strong criticism. Media interest and industry concern began to grow, and in October 1994 Intel agreed to replace the chip in PCs – but only if its users could demonstrate that they used their PCs to calculate complex equations. This response exacerbated the situation and provoked further criticism from the Internet news group, the media and the industry (Regester and Larkin 1997: 133–4). The issue became a crisis.

In December 1994, major customers such as IBM and Fujitsu suspended shipments of all products with the Pentium chip. By then there was a perception that the fault in the chip was extensive rather than limited to complex division calculations. Moreover, Intel's initial denial of a fault in the chip encouraged the perception that they were deceiving people. When IBM halted their shipment the New York Stock Exchange stopped trading in Intel shares for several hours. Investor confidence suffered and Intel stock weakened as its share price dipped.

Subsequently, Intel publicly acknowledged an error in the floating point segment of the chip and agreed to replace all chips at huge financial cost (the recall alone cost £306 million) and considerable damage to its reputation (Regester and Larkin 1997: 55–7). Consultants argue that Intel's failure to respond quickly to criticism and admit the error at an earlier stage meant that Intel had summoned the crisis upon itself. Arguably, the widespread *perception* that the Pentium was intrinsically faulty had undermined confidence in Intel (and the chip) (Regester and Larkin 1997).

All consultants interviewed argue that episodes such as the *Exxon-Valdez* and Intel's Pentium 1 have become more salient because organisations operate in an increasingly hostile and volatile environment. A combination of factors – increased scepticism about those in positions of power, growing consumer discernment, the sophistication of pressure groups, the impact of a technologically advanced mass media on public opinion, the quantity and speed of global information – expose companies to criticism and exacerbate situations. The reputations of corporations are exposed to increased risk. Incidents or circumstances can quickly turn into crises in which the extensive criticism levelled at companies gives rise to negative public perceptions of them, undermining public confidence in them, damaging their reputation, and even jeopardising their continued existence.

The argument consultants make is that few companies are equipped to respond with the speed required to handle crisis situations, curtail hostile media reporting and prevent unfavourable interpretations being perpetuated in the public domain, and that 'crisis management', on the other hand, equips companies to influence media representations, control perceptions and thereby manage risks to their reputation (Seymour and Moore 2000; Regester 1987; Regester and Larkin 1997; Green 1992; Bland 1997; Bland 1998).

Consultants' definitions of crisis and its management

Consultants describe 'crisis situations' (i.e. crises of type one and two when they reach crisis stage) as involving the following:

- unexpectedness and surprise
- a disruption to routine
- an escalating flow of events coupled with a sense of losing control
- heightened media interest involving increased levels of media scrutiny, inquiry and speculation
- a widespread view/interpretation of the incident as a crisis (in the media)
- the proliferation of negative publicity[2]

Publicity naturally emerges as the main focus of a consultant's conception of a crisis:

> ... it is usually the publicity that will sink you [i.e. – the organisation], not the damage from the incident itself. Incidents happen all the time. It would be fair to say that most incidents or potential crises you never hear of. For instance, a disgruntled employee sends in a package of documents which could discredit a company with the threat to send it to the newspapers if he is not paid something like three years' salary and a car. It's probably all scandals he has claimed to have unearthed, which if made public could cause a loss of confidence in the company. This sort of thing happens all the time and could become a crisis if handled in the wrong way. Things go wrong all the time, an incident becomes a crisis because the public find out about it and identify the situation in a negative way (Michael Bland,[3] in interview: July 10, 1997).

Given that adverse publicity is such a pivotal aspect of a crisis, the consultant's crisis management approach tends to centre insistently on perception management. The other aspects of a crisis, such as potential loss of life or livelihood for those affected, tend to be submerged, for consultants, beneath a publicity-driven analysis. Indeed, it is the likelihood of adverse publicity that seems to define a crisis. The consultants' definitions of crisis and crisis management are pragmatic and call attention to the areas they consider central and work on. Perception is central. This is evident in Michael Bland's account of an incident faced by one of his clients:

One food company found that one batch of a product was contaminated on a massive scale with salmonella but the salmonella were dead – they had cooked them, they had been killed at the manufacturing stage. So the dilemma was should we announce it and cause panic and loss of public confidence or should we hold our breath and hope no one will find out. My contention is that whatever the situation may be, what counts is people's perceptions about the situation. There was no danger as the salmonella were dead but people would perceive of the situation in a negative way. In this particular incident the company held its breath. I am not saying that is the right thing to do but sometimes realistically it is. The thing to do is to hold your breath and build contingency plans and prepare in case anyone does find out and prepare what to say about not having said anything previously. People do bluff and they get away with it. The problem is that if you do lie and you don't get away with it, you are dead because you face a worse crisis. The best policy is to come out with it and then control the story from the outset (in interview: July 10, 1997).

In the crisis management discourse, ethics tend to be sidelined. The statement above implies that unethical conduct courts unnecessary dangers, and Bland discourages dishonesty by pointing to the harm it could cause a company if discovered. While he does not necessarily endorse dishonesty, it does appear that ethics is submerged beneath a pragmatic imperative driven by the need to protect corporate self-interest. Bland's acknowledgement that bluffing is sometimes a successful strategy also tends to suggest that the approach corporations take, and the advice consultants give, is determined by expediency. And it is the case that the ethical responsibilities of corporations and consultants in a crisis situation differ. For example, in the case where a corporation has caused damage, to the environment, for example, their accountability (ethically and legally) for that will inevitably be more direct and onerous than any accountability a consultant might bear in relation to it. This is not to say that consultants do not bear ethical responsibility consonant with their role, but it is important to bear in mind that consultants advocate a strategic and pragmatic stance and not an ethical one. Radical critics like Pearce and Tombs (1998) argue that what corporations are ultimately interested in is creating rhetorical realities that sell products and ideologies, and they would view 'crisis management' as part of that project. 'Crisis management' has much to do with how businesses improve profits and the measures they use to convince consumers of their viewpoint.

The consultants' emphasis on crisis management as a form of preparation for a possible crisis is supported by their account of what their work involves:

- creating strategic plans for the management of communications should a crisis arise;
- providing training for clients in dealing with crises through mock crisis scenarios;
- advising on how to handle communications once a crisis occurs. In such instances, they counsel on the communications strategy to be employed and put this into operation.[4]

Clearly, consultants promote crisis management as an ongoing effort:

Crisis management is not simply responding to crises as they occur but a preparatory process against crises occurring (Michael Seymour, Managing Director of Crisis Management Burson-Marsteller, in interview: July 7, 1997).

A coherent approach [to crisis management] begins with the identification of potential crises ... [there is a] need to catalogue the areas of risk: to assess the risk parameters (Regester and Larkin 1997: 173).

A crisis is a final instance. Most crises would not be crises if issues management was successful (Peter Sheldon Green,[5] in interview: July 9, 1997).

Consultants view issues management as beneficial both in its own right and to crisis management. 'Issues' are defined as 'social concerns' 'created by discussion, debate or outright conflict of opinions' (Seymour and Moore 2000: 159). Basically, an issue is 'a point of conflict between an organization and one or more of its audiences' (Regester and Larkin 1997: 42). (An example of such an 'issue' is the debate about the health risk posed by mobile phones.) Regester and Larkin argue that issues management affects the handling of crisis and that 'an issue ignored is a crisis ensured' (1997: 63–89). Consultants suggest that crises are preventable through issues management:

To fail to prepare fully is dangerous because every company carries the potential for issues to hit them at any time. Corporate crises are prolonged and complicated when a neglected issue seasons the initial event with outrage. Many crises are eminently preventable, or can at least be contained, if companies tackle those pre-existing problems [in order to] bring issues to the attention of the public on their own initiative, turning issues management into a form of crisis prevention (Seymour and Moore 2000: 161).

Defining crises as creeping events, as well as sudden, facilitates this argument.

Michael Bland observes that, while in the past companies purchased crisis management advice after a crisis, this situation has changed:

> Crisis management, since recently, is changing its nature. It is now more about issues management. The argument made [by the consultants] is that clients have to take account of issues management more in order to limit or manage negative external interest in the company. It is now held that it is no longer good enough to bolt the stable door after the horse has not only escaped but gone on the *Nine O'Clock News* to tell the world what a hopeless rider you are (in interview: July 10, 1997).

Bland relates this change to two factors: consultants publicising the importance of preparing for crisis, and greater client receptivity to that idea.

The consultants' conception of crisis prevention is one that expands crisis management and develops their role. Their formulation of crisis management thus widens the field to include the continual monitoring of 'potential crises', that is, watching and managing issues. They hold expertise in both areas of issues management and crisis management and, given that issues quite possibly arise more often than full-blown crises, their argument may be read as an effort to expand their work and, consequently, earnings. This suggests that how consultants define crisis and its management has much to do with how they would like their field to develop. The practical actions they can take also influence their definitions.

Origins and evolution of crisis management

While crises and their management are anything but new, 'crisis management' is a relatively recent phenomenon and has only existed in the UK since the 1980s. Regester Larkin, the only consultancy specialising in this area, was established as late as 1994. Consultants I spoke to reported a greater demand for their counsel and suggested that crisis management has now shed its neophyte status. My examination reveals that crisis management remains a small, yet commercially successful, specialist area of public relations.

An examination of the Public Relations Consultants Association (PRCA) yearbooks[6] yields an enlightening picture of the origins and development of crisis management in the UK. In 1981, of the 109 members of the PRCA, none listed 'crisis management' as a part of their services. While this does not mean that these consultancies were not providing advice on how to manage public relations during crises, it does indicate that PR companies did not differentiate between counselling on how to handle crises and other areas of public relations.

By 1987 this situation had changed. Of the 113 members of the PRCA, 7 consultancies listed 'crisis management' (1987 PRCA Yearbook). And by 1995, there was a dramatic growth in PR consultancies offering crisis management as part of their portfolio of services. From a membership of 131, 30 consultancies were then providing crisis management (1995 PRCA Yearbook). But, while crisis management had grown since the 1980s and might appear established in the sense that many consultancies listed it, it still constituted a very small percentage of public relations work. For instance, the PRCA membership statistics of 1998[7] show that only 4 per cent of the total consultancy functions on behalf of clients was crisis management. The biggest area of consultancy work on behalf of clients was that of consumer PR, about 23 per cent.

By 2000, 36 companies out of 129 member consultancies offered crisis management. However, I found that crisis management was practised by some consultancies while others merely listed it as a service. It appears that some consultancies developed competence in crisis management and hence gained a greater share of interested clientele. For example, Michael Regester, founding partner of Regester Larkin, told me that his consultancy often received referrals from other PR consultancies whose clients had approached them with an interest in crisis management. The consultancies passed their clients on to them, Regester said, because they felt that they were not as equipped in crisis management as Regester Larkin. Quite a few of Regester Larkin's clients had come via that route.

Initially, crisis management was imported into the UK from the United States in the mid 1980s via large, world-wide public relations consultancies. Kipping and Engwall (2002) observe that highly industrialised countries with large multi-product corporations, particularly those with a high degree of internationalisation, were more likely to exhibit an expansion in consulting than countries with a low degree of industrialisation and/or with mainly small companies. The US has thus contributed significantly to the development of the international consulting industry.

Large international consultancies such as Burson-Marsteller, Shandwick and Hill & Knowlton imported crisis management services into the UK, but certain individuals, such as Michael Regester, in their own small practices, were also active in promoting it. In comparison with the big world-wide consultancies, Regester's firm is small. In contrast to Burson-Marsteller's 190 employees and Hill & Knowlton's 400, Regester Larkin has 15 employees including its founding member.[8]

In the UK, the Institute of Public Relations (the professional body for public relations practitioners) accredits independent consultants and companies, and the Public Relations Consultants Association has certain procedures and codes which its members must follow. However, there are no regulations governing who can set up a company and provide advice on crisis management or any other area of public relations. Consultants say that their reputations, experience and track record enabled them to gain business. Clients would most often know them through word of mouth, conferences and specialist publications such as *PRWeek*, the trade paper for the industry. The whole of the consulting industry relies heavily on reputation and on personal connections to persuade clients of the quality of their services and establish new relationships (Kipping and Engwall 2002).

The emergence of crisis management as a specialist area may reflect a wider tendency within public relations towards a greater differentiation and specialisation of functions. This is evident in the PRCA's multiple categorisation of the member consultancies' services: 'consumer PR', 'financial PR', 'lobbying', 'crisis management', 'community PR' and so forth.[9]

Consultants report that high-risk industries such as the nuclear, oil, chemical, pharmaceutical and aviation sectors tend to have the most elaborate crisis management plans. This is a consequence, consultants argue, of the high risks associated with these industries combined with the level of public, governmental and media scrutiny levelled at them. These industries are also the ones most prone to regulation should crises occur and precipitate legislation. For instance, the Health, Safety and the Environment Act 1974 applied to the companies within these industries and required them to pay a greater level of attention to such matters. It should be noted that such industries are often highly profitable and can afford more extensive services, such as crisis management training programmes.

Consultants say that their clients tend to be large corporations, and this is manifest in the list of consultancies' clients provided in the PRCA yearbooks. While governments and the public sector might use crisis management, consultants mainly target the private sector. This is evident in the way consultants devise their texts on crisis management – the usual presumption is that their audience are companies.[10] In turn, the target market influences how consultants formulate crisis management as predominantly concerning the private sector and big business.

The fundamental principles of crisis management

Following on from their claim that companies must prepare for crises, the literature on crisis management describes the specific activities involved in being prepared for crises. These activities normally include contingency planning that identifies risky areas in a business's operations, testing the efficiency of contingency plans and training clients in handling crises through 'simulations'. However, the fundamental basis of crisis management centres on communication strategy.

The communication strategy the consultants recommend involves assessing and responding to perceptions. Consultants advise companies to view the problem/situation as others are seeing it and to base responses on an assessment of their views. Consultants identify the most important audiences as 'key publics'. As will become evident below, managing communications and relations with them are held to be highly significant in the management of crises.[11]

Key publics

The key publics of a company are its most important stakeholders. These will vary depending on the particular organisation, its ownership, size and structure, product or service market and so forth. Charkham's (1992) study of corporate governance suggests that such stakeholders can be divided into two groups: contractual and community. Contractual stakeholders are those to whom an organisation has a clear-cut obligation. They are said typically to include shareholders, employees, customers, distributors, suppliers and lenders. Typical community stakeholders are identified as the consumers, regulators, government, pressure groups, local communities and the media.

Key publics are important to crisis management in two ways. Firstly, they are seen as vital audiences holding and promulgating views on the crisis and thereby influencing the views of others. Secondly, consultants also attribute a strategic significance to such groups' ability to help control the crisis – their favourable descriptions of the situation can influence perceptions of the crisis:

> While in a crisis the media will be the most vocal and demanding group, executives must remember all those to whom they must communicate ... since many audiences can assist by accurately describing the situation when they are in turn approached for comment (Seymour and Moore 2000: 116).

Building good relations with the key publics of a company can play a beneficial role in bringing a company out of crisis and contributing to its recovery. Equally though, key publics are also in a position to harm or discredit a company.

The media

The media are the most important key public because 'the media are the conduits for other audiences and if you get it wrong with them you get it wrong with everyone' (Michael Regester, in interview: July 7, 1997).

Given that they believe that favourable media portrayal of the corporate view can lend legitimacy to it, consultants seek to 'manage'/control media representations. They identify their objective as being 'to secure total acceptance of your [a company's] point of view' (Seymour and Moore 2000: 166). It is significant that this does not square with the central thesis of the sociology and social psychology of the media: that it is very difficult to predict or manage media effects, and I discuss this in the examination of the Brent Spar case.

There is very little variation in consultants' maxims for dealing with the media and the ensuing recommendations frequently recur in interviews and in the literature on the subject.

Companies are advised to comply with and cater for media requests for information because the objective of crisis management is to control media representations. Consultants believe that if companies do not respond to journalists' demands for information, journalists will inevitably turn to other sources for information. This is undesirable, as the company at the centre of the crisis may not have control over what others say about the crisis. As demonstrated below, consultants advise companies to position themselves as attractive news sources and thereby direct news coverage. This recommendation recognises the importance of sources and the influential role sources are seen to play in the construction of news stories (Ericson et al. 1989; Hall et al. 1978; Gamson and Modigliani 1989; Riechert and Miller 1997; Schlesinger 1991; Anderson 1991). It is instructive, at this point, to reflect on cases consultants cite as demonstrating instances of crisis *mis*management. These cases demonstrate and explain the consultants' reasoning and usefully reflect the tendency of consultants to advance their brand of crisis management by classifying ways in which crises are mismanaged.

Delayed and defensive communications: the case of *Exxon-Valdez*

Consultants argue that speedy responses from the company are especially important. The media will demand information and the company has to position itself as a good news source to curtail hostile representations and prevent negative interpretations being perpetuated. Consultants also argue that it is often the lack of early communication that gives rise to negative perceptions of a company.

Consultants point to the *Exxon-Valdez* oil spill as a classic example of a badly handled crisis:[12]

> It was an environmental disaster that was badly handled from the beginning. The company adopted a defensive posture, decided not to communicate and, in the end, was castigated ... If you allow rumour and speculation to take over, you may never succeed in wresting control back again (Michael Seymour, *Management Review*, February 1995).

Exxon wrongly pursued a 'no comment' policy for over a week, consultants maintain. Communications should have begun immediately. Possibilities for limiting the damage to Exxon were missed by not communicating with, and thus alienating, the fishermen and the media, both of whom were key publics. Admissions of sympathy and regret must be expressed soon after a disaster. Consultants say that companies are often reluctant to communicate because they do not wish to incur liability claims, but suggest that there are ways in which sympathy may be expressed without attracting legal penalties:

> Admitting sorrow does not mean the company is liable. What needs to be said is: 'We deeply regret this has happened and will leave no stone unturned in establishing the cause' (Regester and Larkin 1997: 161).

The point consultants make is that an admission of sorrow is a communication response designed to build community relations and avert negative media coverage as far as possible:

> ... the *Exxon-Valdez* pollution is world famous. But the world outside the US hardly heard about the massive 300 000 gallon oil slick served up on the California beaches a few months later when BP's *American Trader* managed to hole itself. This was because BP visibly went into immediate 'apologise and clean up' mode and ended up being praised by the US coastguard and the media for the speed and responsibility of its response (Bland 1998: 9).

Regester and Larkin argue similarly in saying that the chairman of Exxon should have taken the approach Sir Michael Bishop, chairman of British Midland, took when one of its Boeing 737s crashed a few weeks after the Pan Am Lockerbie crash:

> His response was remarkable. Many people in senior managerial positions, fearful of being misreported by the media ...will not give interviews until they have all the facts at their fingertips ...[But] communication has to begin immediately. Sir Michael Bishop gave interviews when he had no knowledge about the cause of the accident ... lack of information at the outset of a crisis is typical ... faced with this dilemma, Sir Michael focused on expressing how he felt about what had happened and what he was going to do about the situation. He immediately began to 'manage' the flow and content of news to the media ... There was not much 'content' to what he said but he understood and implemented one of the golden rules of crisis communication – begin it at once, from the top of the organization (1997: 148).

Consultants suggest that Exxon's failure to communicate at an early stage was later compounded by misguided and damaging communications. The company's press conference missed, disastrously, an opportunity to express sympathy to the fishermen and to cooperate and communicate with the press (Regester and Larkin 1997: 134–8). In a live interview, the chairman of Exxon, Lawrence Rawls, admitted that he had not read the latest plan for the clean-up operation, stating: 'it is not the role of the chairman of a large world-wide corporation to read every technical plan' (Regester and Larkin, 1997: 136). Consultants accept that this may well be true, but could have been stated differently. The presentational aspects of such a statement, or its diplomacy,

not considered. Moreover, consultants endorse the view that
crisis situations senior managers must be briefed and relieved of
routine responsibilities and give undivided attention to managing the
crisis:

> However accurate the claims of the leanest, meanest, most predat-
> ory corporation may be, the fact remains that it necessarily remains
> locked into normal rhythms of business. The structures work well in
> peacetime, but in a crisis they are severely tested and occasionally
> useless. Wartime conditions prevail; big decisions with a lot riding
> on them must be made in a drastically shorter time than usual
> (Seymour and Moore 2000: 21).

The situation was further aggravated, consultants claim, when the
chairman of Exxon attacked the media for reporting that nothing was
being done. Consultants argue that this was largely due to Exxon's
counterproductive 'no comment' policy.

Moreover, the company should not have retaliated defensively in
response to the anger of fishermen whose lives were badly affected by
the oil spill, or to the persistent inquiries of the press. Consultants
claim that such defensive communications created the harmful impression of the organisation as insensitive and disdainful. In short, Exxon
had failed to represent itself as sympathetic and responsible, which had
widespread consequences. Regester and Larkin observe that new legislation (after the *Exxon-Valdez* oil spill) requiring all new ocean-going
tankers to be built with double hulls proved to be a costly punishment
not only for Exxon but for the oil tanker industry as a whole (1997:
134–6). They suggest that double hulls would not have prevented the
spill and that the new legislation was a 'cosmetic knee-jerk political
reaction' by governments who felt they had to react to the perception
of Exxon and other oil companies as irresponsible – a perception nur-
tured by Exxon's 'appalling communications in the aftermath of the
Valdez disaster' (Regester and Larkin 1997: 137).

Michael Regester insists that events might have proceeded differently
had:

> Exxon acted quickly, been more communicative and co-operative
> with the media at an earlier stage, expressed human concern about
> the damage caused not only to the environment but also to those
> whose livelihood depended on the sea, and had demonstrated that
> the company cared about what had happened and was doing the
> best it could do to alleviate the damage (in interview: July 7, 1997).

These aspects of the crisis have since been recognised by Exxon's chairman Lawrence Rawls, who is quoted in an academic examination of the crisis management involved in the *Exxon-Valdez* incident as having said that he 'has since changed his mind ... if he were to do it again, he says he would go directly to the site and no doubt handle communications differently' (Deppa et al. 1993: 263).

It is notable that the consultants' account of the faults in Exxon's management of the crisis do not comment on the measures the company was taking to clean up the oil spill or ask whether those measures were sufficient. The entire focus is on the company's approach to communications. The consultants' analysis of Exxon's failure in this regard tends to emphasise that crisis management, for consultants, is solely a question of communications strategy.

Contrary to the consultants' argument that this crisis brought criticism of oil companies, Daley and O'Neill (1991) argue that the press reports 'naturalised'[13] the use of and dependency on oil, and withdrew from consideration the pursuit of alternative energy sources. As a result, the press reports directed environmental issues 'away from the political arena and into the politically inaccessible realm of technological inevitability', thereby reproducing 'the political and corporate hegemony of Big Oil' (cited in Allan et al. 2000: 9).

Allan, Adam and Carter (2000) argue that the news media frequently represent environmental crises as event-oriented catastrophes rather than as the outcome of a company's decisions and calculations. According to this view, media criticism of companies during crises *does not always* threaten their existence and may even help their future survival. This is contrary to what is often stated by consultants because the consultants' objective is to argue that a greater communications effort is required.

Dyer et al. (1991), in a study which compared the Associated Press coverage of Exxon Corporation with the company's press releases before and after the *Exxon-Valdez* ran aground, found that Exxon was keen to frame this story in environmental terms, while the Associated Press coverage focused on legal responsibility. Dyer et al. concluded that:

> ... news media do not merely reflect the company line, they play an adversarial role. That is, the news media, in this case, rejected the company position that the disaster should be framed primarily as an environmental concern and insisted on framing it in terms of legal responsibility (Allan et al. 2000: 50).

Perhaps it is true that early communication can ensure the likelihood of a less antagonistic media response. Certainly, Dyer et al.'s study shows that companies may be able to do very little once a dominant interpretation takes hold in the media – an observation that enhances the argument for early communications with the media.

The media's need for a story: the *Braer* incident

Consultants say, in interviews and in their publications, that when a crisis occurs, there is usually a lack of hard information available to the company involved. Internal inquiries will often be undertaken and attempts made to assess what went wrong, but the company is likely to have very little information at the beginning. Simultaneously there is an external demand for information, especially from the media. This poses a number of problems for crisis management:

> ... the media will descend on the site of the accident like a plague of locusts which needs to be fed. If it isn't fed by the organization which finds itself, however inadvertently, at the centre of the crisis, it will feed from the hands of others. And become deeply suspicious of the hand which obviously isn't feeding it (Regester and Larkin 1997: 145).

If a company does not respond to the media's search for comments on the situation, not only will the media rely on the comments of external commentators (whose views may be critical of the company) but may also speculate on the basis of likely factors or rumours in order to fill the information void.

This happened in the case of the *Braer*. On January 5, 1993, the *Braer* oil tanker was carrying 84,000 tonnes of crude oil from Norway to Quebec when it lost engine power and, propelled by 100 mile per hour gale-force winds, went aground in the Shetland Islands. The extreme weather conditions thwarted salvage attempts and, over the course of a week, the *Braer* spilled all its cargo. The spill caused damage to the extensive wildlife in the area and immediate, but not long-term, damage to the local salmon-fishing industry. Fortunately, the high winds that had grounded the *Braer* also rapidly dispersed the oil slick.

Below is Michael Regester's account of this incident and the need to fill the information void. He was managing the crisis on behalf of Ultramar, the owners of the crude oil contents of the *Braer*:

Whenever a crisis occurs there is often an information void because you may know what has happened, you may not know what caused it, and you know something about what is being done to make it better, but then usually there is a communication gap and it is completely crucial to fill the gap yourself, that is, the organisation involved. If you do not fill this gap, the press will fill it from other sources or even to the point where they make it up.

So, there we were in the Shetlands. The weather was dreadful, 100 mile per hour gale-force wind and 500 journalists. Because the weather was so bad people couldn't get on to the tanker to stem the oil leaking, nor could they get the helicopters up there. So essentially nothing had happened. The Shetland Island Council, who were in charge of the clean-up, or those who were acting on behalf of the owners of the *Braer* could have filled the gap with all sorts of things such as stating that the helicopters were on standby or what they could be doing if the weather was not so bad, all positive messages. Instead of which they said nothing was happening. So I overheard reporters talking to editors over the phone and reporting that nothing was happening. I could not hear what the editors were saying but they were clearly saying 'well, make it up then'. Suddenly, what people were hearing and reading around the world was that the island was completely blackened with oil, that the oils contained carcinogens, can get leukemia from breathing it, school kids were being evacuated, sheep were being evacuated, all the salmon fish farms were contaminated and on and on it went. Then one day the media found another story and they went away.

In the Shetland Islands the most important industry is oil, the second most important industry is fishing and the export of salmon to Japan. All the Japanese just stopped importing salmon from the Shetlands because the *perception* was that all of the Shetland Island salmon was contaminated – which it was not, some were, but not all. There is an instance where perception became reality (Michael Regester, in interview: July 7, 1997).

Regester maintains that this instance highlights the problems involved in not communicating in order to fill the communication gap – that it is in the company's interest to provide a story to meet the inevitable media demand for one.

The consultants' main concern is that the company involved must do everything possible to ensure favourable reporting. Sociologists Miller and Riechert, drawing on Vincent et al.'s (1989) observations of different phases of crises, argue that in covering a disaster, journalists need different kinds of information in different phases of the crisis:

Phase 1: This stage of crises involves a disruption of normality. At this stage, the media's preferred sources are eyewitnesses. While companies' statements are listened to, they are treated with scepticism.

Phase 2: This stage is called the 'investigation phase'. The preferred sources are government investigators who are to establish the facts, and experts who can put the facts in context and offer theories as to why the disaster occurred.

Phase 3: This stage is called the 'restoration phase'. It involves attempts by officials to explain how the disaster occurred, and entails assurances that the probability of reoccurrence has been minimised and justice served (Miller and Riechert 2000: 49). Miller and Riechert observe that these objectives have to be met. If not:

... then the disaster itself will slip into the background and news coverage will be driven by conflict amongst stakeholders at which time government officials, stakeholder spokespersons, and the general public become the principal source of news (1999: 49).

In order to secure advantageous coverage companies are advised to call in the help of third parties to put across the company's perspective, a strategy that demonstrates a response to the conditions identified in Phases 1 and 2, i.e. media scepticism towards companies' statements. The consultants' argument that, should a company fail to communicate, perceptions will be governed by other sources and other claims is sustained by Miller and Riechert's observation that conflict exists between stakeholders. If restorative narratives are not employed in Phase 3, news coverage will be driven by that conflict.

Furthermore, consultants claim that once a particular interpretation of the situation has been perpetuated within the media, such a representation may become dominant, entrenched and difficult to reverse. This observation is also made by media researchers who have argued through the analysis of news 'frames' that it is possible for a dominant perception to be propagated in the media.

Miller and Riechert recognise that:

... the ways that news media frame issues can come directly from stakeholders with vested interests. Because news often comes from unexpected events, generally the first journalists who cover them have little expertise and little time to gather background information. They are, therefore, reliant on their sources to provide initial briefings and set expectations ... these briefings can have a powerful effect on the frames set in early news coverage (1999: 50).

They also argue that the initial news frames are likely to be passed on as other journalists rely on observations made by the initial media accounts – in this way, initial frames may become dominant as they continue to be sustained.

Michael Santangelo, a journalist from the New York *Daily News* describing the press reaction to the fatal Pan Am Flight 103 crash at Lockerbie, Scotland, on December 21, 1988 colourfully expressed how important it is for the media to have a story:

> The New York press corps to use the vulgar name – is known as the 'gang bang'. The term 'gang bang' is going out of style now, and it's being known as the 'wolf pack'. It's not much different. I don't mean to condemn myself but you get this sort of – everybody needs to get a story. Until you get a story, ravenous. Somebody gives you a story, you calm down. Then you sit down. You see a lot of people [reporters covering the same story] – we all know each other ... a lot of us are buddies. We talk: 'How ya doing? How's the kid? How's the wife? You get divorced yet? Yeah. Oh you bought a new car ...' It's like a sewing circle. But we can't do that until we've got a story. We're all crazy until then (quoted in Deppa et al. 1993: 123).

Basically, consultants advocate creating useful media representations by exploiting the requirements under which journalists work. Ericson et al. (1989) observe that sources habitually exploit those needs. Deppa et al. (1993), in a study of the Pan Am Flight 103 crash, concluded that 'the development of a working relationship with the media in the face of a disaster is central to any crisis communications plan' (1993: 255). That observation supports the consultants' claim regarding the significance of the media to crisis management.

Managing media representations

Ericson et al.'s argument that 'news is a product of a transaction between journalists and their sources' (1989: 377) also accounts for the significance that consultants place on positioning their clients as a news source.

Consultants would concur with Ericson et al.'s observation that 'failure to control the news media can mean a loss of control over organisational life and serious harms' (1989: 388). Ericson et al. argue that sources assess news organisations in a very pragmatic manner, that all organisations attempt to 'police knowledge' and that such attempts can be 'construed in terms of protecting interests' (1989: 20).

Concepts developed by media studies, such as news values and frames, are ones consultants appear to understand, and apply in the construction of strategies for influencing media coverage. As Ericson et al. observed, 'journalists find a career path from newsrooms to PR work for source bureaucracies' (1989: 7) – a factor that explains why consultants are so knowledgeable about playing to media formats in order to achieve particular ends.

News values and news frames determine how stories are constructed. With regard to news values, researchers argue that they influence what is reported and how this is covered:

> When journalists scrutinise the world looking for news, they evaluate what they see according to news values. These values are criteria for judging what to report and how much emphasis to provide. Nearly all introductory textbooks contain lists of news values which include such things as consequence, timeliness, proximity, prominence and human interest (Miller and Riechert 2000: 48).

Consultants appear to use a similar analysis when advising companies:

> ... a story is subject to the same constraints as any commodity – it has to sell. When you have a problem, or are perceived to have one, your view of the 'facts' is likely to differ from how an editor will see the essential dramatic ingredients needed for a 'good' story. Your message needs to respect those ingredients, without losing its integrity, if it is to be effective (Seymour and Moore 2000: 48).

Thus, companies are advised to format their crisis communications to meet the requirements of the media in order to influence media representations.

What consultants attempt to do in crisis situations is to give 'quotable quotes' (Ericson et al. 1989: 383) and 'to keep reporters preoccupied with things they are bound to be interested in' (Ericson et al. 1989: 18). For example, consultants are aware that the media will want to know the cause of an incident even if the company involved does not have that information. Deppa et al. (1993) argue that journalists are under immediate editorial pressure in this regard:

> It takes investigators a year to find out the cause of a plane crash, but my boss on Long Island wants me to tell them what the cause was two hours after it happens (Howard Kessler, a journalist working for New York *Newsday* who was covering the Pan Am 103 crash, quoted in Deppa et al. 1993: 123).

Such pressure may provoke reporters to offer speculative responses, as Regester noted in the *Braer* case (Regester and Larkin 1997: 138–42). (Incidentally, Regester's critique of the handling of the *Braer* crisis suggests that consultants attempt to control the news in precisely the manner identified above, by Ericson.)

The consultants' claim that during crises there is a greater demand on organisations to manage information is supported by research identifying the media's attraction to situations involving conflict as a news value:

> ... situations involving conflict provide the drama needed to attract audiences and (indicates to the media) that the level of conflict is indicative of the passions participants feel and therefore the importance of the story to them (Allan et al. 2000: 51–2).

Miller and Riechert's observations that 'conflict motivates stakeholders to increase their efforts to influence the public and policy makers' (2000: 51–2) and that by 'capitalising on conflict between stakeholders, those stakeholders also attempt to exploit the imperatives under which journalists operate' (2000: 45–55) demonstrate how news values can be exploited.

The consultants' claim that crises attract a high level of media attention embraces the wider issues relating to the situation. This argument is supported by research revealing that events frequently trigger media interest in subjects that might not otherwise have received coverage. For example, Miller and Riechert argue in relation to environmental risks and the media that:

> Environmental risk abounds in contemporary society, but generally lies dormant until some event drives it onto the public agenda. Whether the triggering event is a natural or human-made disaster, or is due to a stakeholder initiative, it activates contending stake-

holders who seek to win public and policy maker support ... News media participate in the process by accepting and modifying the frames presented to them (2000: 53).

Allan, Adam and Carter argue that this is discernible in a:

> ... variety of instances of news coverage concerned with other environmental disasters during the mid-1980s and since, including the 1984 chemical leak at the Union Carbide pesticide plant in Bhopal, India ... A further instance is the oil spill of the *Exxon Valdez* ... (2000: 8).

The evidence that issues often receive media attention as a result of specific events/incidents lends support to the consultants' contention that issues management can facilitate crisis management. The academic identification of events as activating 'contending stakeholders who seek to win public and policy maker support' is suggestive of crisis management, which attempts to do just that. It also reinforces the crisis management argument that companies need to do more during crisis situations, given that other groups will try and influence media coverage.

Academics also identify news values that consultants say are present in crisis situations: that the story has a strong visual element, exclusivity, identifiable 'goodies' and 'baddies' and an underlying political theme (Chapman et al. 1997). On identifying 'goodies' and 'baddies', Chapman et al. (1997), based on an extensive content analysis of environmental stories, argue that the media often seek to assign blame or responsibility for a situation. With reference to the 1996 *Sea Empress* oil tanker disaster in particular, Chapman et al. observe that the question of blame or responsibility is most often asked in disaster-type crises. Consultants also note these themes.

Media researchers observe that certain situations act as canvasses on which moral and political lessons can be painted. Consultants argue that this increases the demand on organisations to play a role in influencing those pictures when they aim to control how they themselves are depicted. According to media researchers, crisis situations (which frequently have elements attractive to news values) will draw media attention or, more complexly, will be transformed into material which can attract such attention. The notion of news frames explains that process.

Gaye Tuchman (1978), drawing on Erving Goffman's study *'Frame Analysis'* (1974), developed the concept of 'news frames' to describe the way in which journalists process new information. Tuchman argues that: 'an occurrence is transformed into an event, and an event is transformed into a news story'. Consultants make a similar observation. They maintain that it is important for companies to understand that the media will take a particular prescriptive view of events and ask particular types of questions, and that companies must accept and respond appropriately to the news construction process. What media studies call 'framing', consultants tend to characterise as the manageability of perceptions.

Also, given that most people do not have direct lived experience of many of the varied concerns addressed by crisis management consultants, the media play an even greater role as conveyers of information and interpreters of events: 'we are inescapably dependent on the media to comprehend the "world out there" beyond our immediate experience' (Allan, Adam and Carter 2000: 15). Allan et al. maintain that while they 'are not suggesting that there is a "reality out there" that is being falsified …by journalists or other media practitioners' (2000: 13), they are of the view that facts often do not speak for themselves, contrary to what some journalists may insist.

Miller and Riechert examine news media framing in the context of contentious issues and argue that:

… opposing stakeholders try to gain public and policy-maker support for their positions not by offering new facts or by changing evaluations of the facts, but by altering the frames or interpretative dimensions for evaluating the facts (2000: 44).

The notion of news frames reveals how journalists may be presenting information in a manner which appears to be objective yet is not:

Framing allows journalists to focus on facts and still shape discourse – either consciously or unconsciously (Miller and Riechert 2000: 45).

A natural question arising from this consideration of 'framing' is: in whose interest does it take place? There is no clear consensus on this point. Miller and Riechert disagree with researchers such as Entman (1991), Fine (1992), and Hornig (1992), who argue that framing is:

… driven by unifying ideologies that shape all content on a topic into a specific, dominant, interpretation consistent with the interest of social elites. [They conceptualise] framing as an ongoing process by which ideological interpretative mechanisms are derived from competing stakeholder positions (2000: 46).

Certainly, some media studies consider that an organisation's access to the media influences their ability to frame news, but although elites have access, they do not appear to have it all their own way. For instance, Ericson et al. (1989) suggest that the media play an important role in policing elites for procedural irregularities and that 'there is a continual struggle over what is proper procedure for organisations to follow' (1989: 17). Cottle (2000) argues that while news access is an important influence on the creation of definitions, there are other processes at work and that more access does not necessarily mean greater control over media representations.

The idea that framing is commonplace, and that claims making is a strategy available to those interested in influencing both opinion and the formation of policy, is common to media studies and consultants. Crisis management itself is an endeavour that starts with a desired frame/interpretation (that of the company's) and attempts to influence how others perceive (frame/interpret) the situation. Given that other claims makers are also present in this process, companies do need to influence media representations. Ericson et al. observe:

... there are escalating investments in knowledge control because knowledge is so difficult to guard, and because the demand for knowledge is so elastic and insatiable. Policing knowledge becomes an end in itself ... private corporations as much as government bureaucracies are bound to buy into it (1989: 260).

Academic accounts of framing identify a further process – that certain frames become normalised and thus dominant. Deppa et al. (1993) argue that one aspect of the media reporting of crisis events is that the media stories, as time goes by, take on a routine. Stories report similar interpretations of the situation and this story (interpretation) becomes authoritative, as happened in the case of the *Braer*. Ericson et al. (1989) identify a process they call 'pack journalism', where there is a convergence of similar news content across media and markets. This is why consultants encourage interpretations to be managed from an early stage before they become governed from elsewhere and a damaging interpretation gains momentum. They aim to create a 'pack journalism' that is directed by them. Pack journalism, Ericson et al. (1989) argue, arises from various factors, one of which is sources trying to create it:

By restricting reporters to particular times and places, and by enclosing on knowledge, sources can effectively circumscribe news stories so that 'pack journalism' is the only outcome (1989: 29).

Consultants explicitly endorse this type of action.

It is interesting that the media may be aware that claims makers wish to influence their coverage. Indeed, this partly explains the scepticism they display towards the claims made by companies during crisis situations. Deppa et al. (1993) argue that during crises the media now *expect* the organisation involved to have crisis management plans in place – they expect to be briefed, to be kept informed, to be restricted, to be managed and, consequently, the media are on their guard. Consultants, in turn, are mindful of media scepticism, and this is arguably reflected in their concern to build good relations with the media and other key publics who can bolster the company's claims and interpretations of the situation and furnish the media search for additional sources.

In summary, academic research suggests that real possibilities exist for the perpetuation of certain interpretations in the media, and it is apparent that consultants actively encourage the exploitation of opportunities to do so.

Consultants' communication strategy and symbolic interactionism

Although consultants do not refer to symbolic interactionism and disclaimed any knowledge of it when directly questioned, interactionism provides an enlightening theoretical framework through which to conceptualise the consultants' approach to crisis management.

An outline of symbolic interactionism

Comte divided the study of society into statics (structure) and dynamics (change). Interactionists are critical of those who develop the statics aspect of social life, claiming that it produces a theory of people as the 'living dead' and that it does not allow for the active person who defines society and directs self (Charon 1979). Instead, symbolic interactionism, which borrowed from Simmel's Formalism and American Pragmatism, portrays society and the social as a fluid and changeable series of transformations which cannot be described in terms of structure and statics (Rock 1979). Symbolic interactionism sees the empirical world as in a continual state of flux; the Spencerian notion of equilibrium is discounted and the focus is placed upon the processes involved.

Even though their view of society emphasises its dynamic nature, interactionists do not completely discount the existence of an object-ive reality. They 'operate from an assumption that a physical objective reality does indeed exist independent of our social definition, that our social definitions do respond, at least in part, to something "real" or physical' (Charon 1979: 36). Therefore, they do not claim that the world is only a subjective entity, even though the subjective aspects of social life are given a greater emphasis than the idea of the world as an external entity. Yet interactionists see all human action as responding to a social definition of external reality: '...the Symbolic Interactionist man is the inhibitor and creator of a symbolic world in which the existence of language, symbols and gestures enable him to attach meanings to objects and actions in everyday life, to interpret the world around him and to daily create social life' (Plummer 1975: 11). Furthermore, each individual because he sees the world, has an indi-vidual personal reality (Charon 1979). However, we are not wholly free to determine our own course of action. It should be understood that symbolic interactionists primarily see the world as a subjective reality, as process and interaction. Their task is therefore to study the emergent and constantly changing nature of social life.

Symbolic interactionism regards society as a process in which both stability and change inhere in the meanings that individuals develop in interaction with each other and with themselves. Meanings are seen as being modified and constructed through interaction. The focus is upon emergence and negotiation – the processes by which social action in groups, organisations or societies, are continually being con-structed in everyday life.

George Herbert Mead is acknowledged as a central founding figure of the interactionist movement and all modern discussions of the ap-proach give Mead a central place. Mead begins by making a distinction between humans and animals, asserting that what separates these two species is the existence of language or what he terms the 'significant symbol'. Language, states Mead, developed in the course of interaction. Interaction itself is, and was originally, a means of facilitating the achievement of practical results in co-operation with each other. He maintains that shared meanings gave rise to language as it is based on mutual understanding between communicators. Nevertheless, we can never be sure that meanings are actually shared; all we can do is see the outward signs.

Meaning takes a central role in the thinking of symbolic interactionists as it is their contention that social interaction produces meanings and that human beings act towards things on the basis of the meanings things have for them. Thus, we create our world by giving meaning to it. Such meanings change and develop and, as they do, the world changes and develops. The processes of interaction in which we create our shared world take place through language or 'external conversations'. However, meanings are also modified and handled through an internal interpretative process used by each individual in dealing with the signs each encounters. This internal interpretative process is also a conversation between two different parts of the self which Mead identifies as the 'I' and the 'Me'.

Mead recognises the 'Me' as '... the organised set of attitudes of others which one himself assumes' (Mead 1967: 230). This is because the significant symbol, for practical purposes, calls out the same reaction in myself as it does in others; it enables me to view myself as others see me. The second aspect of the self – i.e. the 'I'– Mead identifies as 'the response of the organism to the attitudes of the others ...' (Mead 1967: 230). It is the part of the self that Mead sees as the source of originality and creativity. It is the part that views the self in an introspective manner, but which cannot itself be viewed.

This conception of a partitioned self involves a description of the process of socialisation. It is contended that as a child grows older, he comes to see himself in an increasingly wide context until he takes on what Mead terms the 'role of the other'. The 'other' can be particular or generalised. Mead classifies the 'generalised other' as '(t)he organised community or social group which gives the individual his unity of self ...' (Mead 1967: 220). This enables him to view himself as he imagines the society as a whole views him. Craib pinpoints this process as the individual taking on a 'social conscience' (1992: 88). Taking the role of the other is never an authentic process of knowing how others see the world; it is only a speculative exercise. Finally, Mead states that it is by taking view of the generalised other that shared meaning arises: '(i)t is through the ability to be the other at the same time that he is himself that the symbol becomes significant ...' (Rock 1979: 110).

Symbols are defined in social interaction and are thus conventional: '... they are representative of something else only because people have come to agree that they shall be' (Charon 1979: 41). Many objects can take on a symbolic quality, words are symbols and as Meltzer claims, our acts are often symbols: '(h)uman beings ... respond to one another on the basis of the intentions or meanings of gestures. This renders the

gesture symbolic, i.e., the gesture is a symbol to be interpreted ...'
(Charon 1979: 42).

Language serves for symbol creation and, as Hertzler argues, it per-
forms an important function as it is 'within and by means of the lin-
guistic framework that the ideationally established world exists and
operates. Language is the means and mode of man's whole mental
existence' (Charon 1979: 54).

Interactionists hold that it is through symbolic interaction with each
other that we give the world meaning: 'Meaning ... arises out of the
social interaction that one has with one's fellows' (Charon 1979: 54).
The world is without inherent or intrinsic meaning. Therefore, meaning remains negotiable because it arises through interaction. For
instance, interactionists view objects as social objects because, for the
human, they are isolated, catalogued, interpreted and given meaning
through social interpretation. Thus, objects are assigned meanings.
Meanings vary and 'are not intrinsic to the object' (Blumer 1969: 38).

The self also arises out of interaction and, like all social objects, is
defined and redefined in interaction. Thus the self, like all other social
objects, is continuously changing. As Berger states, it is a: ' ... process
continuously created and recreated in each social situation that one
enters ... Man is not only a social being, but he is social in every
respect of his being that is open to empirical investigation' (1963: 136).
What is of importance is to note that symbolic interaction conceives of
identities as Berger describes: 'identities are socially bestowed, socially
maintained, and socially transformed' (1963: 91). There is throughout
symbolic interactionism an emphasis on process and becoming so that
selves are rarely stable.

Mead argues that taking the role of the other is first; we come to
know the other first before we come to know our selves. However, we
do not really 'know' the other; we only have inferential knowledge
about him/her. Then, with the development of self, we develop mind
and symbols, followed by more complex role-taking, or taking the perspective of the other. Taking the role of the other, asserts Mead, is
important for the emergence of the self because: '(t)he individual
experiences himself as such, not directly but indirectly ...' (Charon
1979: 101). Taking the role of the other is viewed as being the basis of
human symbolic communication.[14]

In contrast to all individualistic theories, interactionism suggests that
it is not possible to understand the distinctly human aspects of social
life unless one examines the part played by others in influencing and
shaping an individual's actions. The importance of others in symbolic

interactionism is featured in its key concepts such as 'self', 'role' and 'reference group'.

The individual's conception of the self is one of the key elements in understanding the social situation in which one acts. Therefore, as Turner points out, the self is not only a 'product of interaction', but it is also a 'determiner of the course of interaction' (Charon 1979: 72). Blumer notes that the active nature of a person arises from self-hood: '... he acts towards his world, interpreting what confronts him and organizing his actions on the basis of the interpretation'. The individual must analyse the situation he is in in order to ascertain what line of action to take, and he analyses action in the situation in relation to the self and adjust his acts accordingly. The 'generalised other' is the individual's standard used to control his or her action. However, that control may be negotiated or resisted. Each situation we enter is different and each, to some extent, demands active participation by the individual in relation to the self. In addition, the human identifies with a number of social worlds (reference groups), learns through communication (symbolic interaction) the perspectives of these social worlds and uses these perspectives to define and interpret situations that are encountered. Each situation is unique to some degree and, to be handled appropriately, demands some definition and some self-direction. Although recurrent action does become unreflective and habitual, action that is purely habitual is dysfunctional in most situations.

We engage in reflective activity throughout everything we do, interactionists argue. Therefore this covert reflective activity, which Mead sees as a 'temporary inhibition of action wherein the individual is attempting to prevision the future', plays a role in overt human activity. Mead's four stages of the act (Impulse, Perception, Manipulation and Consummation) draw attention to the fact that humans are goal directed. That is to say, we plan our acts around our goals. Therefore, humans actively perceive, define and manipulate their environment to achieve goals. When goals change, objects take on new meanings and our action changes direction (Charon 1979).

According to interactionism, we construct action, we define self and situation, we establish goals, we define lines of action toward objects and then overt action takes place. Moreover, all those phases of action affect and influence one another. Action involves a constant interplay between overt and covert minded activity. Each situation is unique to some degree. Goals are not static and lines of action are constantly shifting. Therefore, the relationship between the individual and the environment has a dynamic and interdependent character (Rock

1979). The environment continually changes, and the individual engaging in activity in relation to it is continuously redefining it and self in relation to it. As Warriner remarks, the: ' ... stream of action is complex, manifold, multiplex ... with many aspects, characteristics, features, dimensions and interconnections' (Charon 1979: 112). Hence, action is never static and the direction of it shifts in response to a number of variables such as the meanings we attach to it.

Affinities between the consultants' rationale and symbolic interactionism

The consultants' attribution of a centrality to the role of perceptions and the handling of communications in a specified manner is comprehensible within interactionism. The interactionist description of how individuals communicate is similar to the consultants' recommended method of handling communications, where communications are based on an assessment of the likely perceptions of the various audiences and the actions taken are based on presumptions about how an audience is likely to react. Consultants attribute significance to areas that interactionism also considers central: the importance of symbols, communications, identities, of the ways in which we influence others and others in turn influence us. A major shared theme is that distinctly human worlds are 'not only material, objective worlds but also immensely semiotic, symbolic ones' (Plummer 2000: 194).

How interaction takes place is a major concern for both symbolic interactionists and the consultants. However, while symbolic interactionism outlines the manner in which interaction is conducted, the consultants do not take great pains to state that interaction takes place in a particular manner. They are, however, concerned with achieving a particular outcome (influencing perceptions) by identifying how interaction takes place between an organisation and its various publics. And the recommendations made by consultants are implicitly based on a particular view of the interaction process that is very similar to that proposed by interactionists.

The communications/interaction strategy that consultants recommend is based, like interactionism, on the belief that the attitudes of others can be both presumed and responded to (existing perceptions are firstly established and then directed through communications). In both the academic and the lay account, a central role is attributed to others and their ability to influence the actions taken. Interactionism observes that 'taking the role of the other' is the basis of human symbolic communications, and the consultants advocate a similar communication strategy. The basis of crisis communications is held to be the perspective of others. In that way, the consultants' formula for conducting communications assumes and reproduces the process that symbolic interactionism itself outlines.

Both accounts also share an interest in the nature of meanings and how they arise, and the consultants' identification of the process involved in the construction of meaning is also akin to the description interactionists provide. The importance consultants ascribe to perceptions indicates that they consider the meanings held about a matter (perceptions) to be pivotal. And, as demonstrated above, their advice presupposes that perceptions are malleable and can be influenced. The negotiated nature of meanings is a central postulate of interactionism and is fundamental in the consultants' arguments about crisis management. In both accounts, meanings arise through interaction and are negotiated. Thus, it is arguable that for both accounts the world is without inherent meaning.

Just as meanings are socially generated and changeable through social interaction, so are identities. Interactionism represents the self as arising through interaction and as a determinant of the course of interaction. Consultants take a similar view of corporate reputations or identities and assume that perceptions of organisations arise during interactions. Indeed, that assumption leads to their claim that organisations must pay greater attention to the management of perceptions during crises, as such situations often involve a higher level of interaction between an organisation and its various significant publics/ audiences. Consultants also suggest that the perception held of an organisation can be redefined by managing interactions. The process involved in the redefinition of the self, according to interactionism, and the redefinition of the organisation, according to consultants, is based on the same assumptions concerning the nature of identities. The consultants maintain that redefinition can be carried out through an assessment of the perceptions of others and actions being taken on this basis. Berger's (1963) claim about the nature of identities – that they are *socially* given, sustained and transformed – is assumed and upheld in interactionism and by the consultants.

The nature of relationships between (for symbolic interactionism) the individual, or (for the consultants) the organisation, and the environment in which they exist and operate is depicted, in both accounts, as interdependent. The interactionist view of how social action creates and recreates the environment as well as the self is one which appears to be closely analogous to the consultants' deliberations on the interrelated nature of organisations and their environments.

Mead (1967) argues that we plan our acts around our goals through the selective perception, definition and manipulation of our environment. The relationship between the individual and the environment is seen as being interdependent and dynamic because the environment and the self change as the individual constantly redefines the environment and the self in relation to it. The idea that there is interdependency between an organisation and its various publics is also fundamental to the consultants' case. The notion of significant others is central to interactionist theory and, in terms of achieving certain organisational goals (such as successfully dealing with crises), consultants identify a considered response to the views of those involved in an organisation's environment as being highly significant to the eventual perceptions of that organisation. Symbolic interactionism outlines a reflexive process which precedes goal-directed action. Consultants promote a similar model for the organisational management of crises that draws on similar notions to those that interactionists identify.

What have we learnt about crisis management and about symbolic interactionism? The comparison of claims made by the consultants' lay account of social action and an academic theory about the symbolic construction of the world reveals the kind of assumptions consultants make in advising companies to employ a particular type of communication strategy in order to manage impressions.

Moreover, the two accounts tend to support each other. Interactionists and consultants alike are interested in ascertaining what is involved in interactions, how communication is conducted, the development of meanings and how social reality is created, albeit for differing purposes. The consultants' account of how organisations should manage interactions with their audiences is one that promotes their crisis management method. Nevertheless, their claim that their recommendation is based on observations (of different ways in which organisations have interacted with their significant others with varying outcomes), and their advocacy of a method of interaction (which is also described by symbolic interactionism), suggests that consultants have observed much the same world as that described by theorists. In this respect the two accounts corroborate each other.

Although symbolic interactionism largely deals with the individual and consultants are concerned with the organisation, the finding that there is a confluence between these accounts is a significant one suggesting similarities between how perceptions of individuals and organisations arise.

One clear consequence of this confluence is that the consultants' claim that their method of managing interaction in order to manage perceptions is well informed, is given a degree of academic credibility. In particular, the consultants' belief that possibilities exist for manufacturing desired outlooks through an understanding of how an organisation interacts/communicates with its audiences is borne out by the interactionist observation that meanings are negotiated and created through interaction. The interactionist observation that meanings are mutable supports the consultants' argument that organisations can fashion advantageous views. Further, the consultants' claim that organisations must identify and respond to perceptions is sustained by the interactionist finding that an individual interacts on the basis of 'taking the role of the other', that is, by basing actions on an assessment of what he assumes the other thinks. Interactionism views 'taking the role of the other' as the basis of human symbolic communication and consultants recommend that approach, which they argue is more effective given that the desired goal is to communicate more efficiently and in a manner that is beneficial to the organisation.

My argument that crisis management is in some ways a pragmatic construction is significant to a consideration of the similarities between it and symbolic interactionism. The way in which consultants manage crises is a pragmatic undertaking designed to influence perceptions and prevent risks to reputations. Therefore, consultants must believe, or act on the belief, that companies can control their reputations and influence perceptions, and that these can be directed by organising action in a particular manner. The consultants must assume, in other words, that perceptions are governable and that meanings arise as a consequence of and within the interaction process. The very manageability of crises – according to the consultants' formulation – is conceivable because they believe that there are possibilities for an engineered reality.

What the consultants' viewpoint imparts to symbolic interactionism is an empirical experience that appears to sustain the claims of that sociological perspective with regard to how interaction takes place and how meanings and social reality are constructed.

That crisis management, a new phenomenon, is explicable within an interactionist framework also shows how 'quietly endurable' this social theory is (Plummer 2000). As Plummer argues, it is 'far from dead or obsolete' (2000: 193–223). As he also suggests, the theory can be shown to sit well with the current interest in identities and the media.

Crisis management for organisations also demonstrates that impression management is not exclusive to individuals, and it would seem that organisational efforts are not dissimilar to the way in which individuals manage such affairs. The finding that impression management strategies utilised by individuals and organisations correspond sheds an interesting light on the subject.

It should be borne in mind, however, that the exact method for conducting communications prescribed by consultants is not necessarily that which organisations actually use. In fact, the consultants' criticism of corporate communications is focused precisely on their failure to adopt the course of action consultants recommend. It would be a mistake, therefore, to conclude that organisations actually interact in the manner consultants advocate. Still, the finding that organisations are encouraged to take an approach bearing such evident affinities with symbolic interactionism is intriguing.

In summary, the finding that (despite the existence of differences – most significantly in intentions and the subject of study) the consultants' and the interactionists' views both qualify and supplement each other provides a better understanding of what is involved in directing perceptions.

Why is crisis management here?

The consultants' explanation that crisis management exists because it is now necessary will be elucidated in this section. With reference to the risk society thesis (see pages 40–1), the parallels that account has with other independent, authoritative accounts will also be demonstrated. Beck (1992) and Giddens (1999) would concur with the consultants' argument that crisis management arose because of a need for it in contemporary society.

The consultants' explanation

In interviews and in their publications consultants distinguish two 'trends' which they claim makes crisis management necessary and explains its existence.

The fact that the acknowledged experts of crisis management knew each other and were familiar with each other's work and thinking explains why consultants so regularly and uniformly cited the two trends. It became apparent in interviews that the consultants also had similar backgrounds; for instance Michael Bland and Michael Seymour had previously had military careers. Many consultants also worked in public relations departments of companies before specialising in crisis management. For example, Michael Regester worked at Gulf Oil and Michael Bland at Ford. They subscribed to the same publications (such as *PR Week*), belonged to the same associations (such as the IPR and the PRCA), read each other's books, and attended the same conferences. Michael Regester was also regularly invited by consultancies to participate in their presentations to clients. Worldviews can easily be disseminated and gain currency in the small world of crisis management consultancy.

The first trend is identified as a change in attitudes towards authority. The consultants cite the emergence of consumerism, the increasing presence and power of pressure groups, a widespread mistrust of corporations and a belief that they are only concerned about profit and socially and environmentally irresponsible, as a consequence of a wider societal trend towards the right to question, influence and dispute:

> ... the role of government and corporations in society is being challenged to a much greater degree than before ... We are less trusting of those in authority. [There is] a big increase in activism ... In the past ten years, the proliferation of single-issue groups has outstripped anything in the past ... This vocal and energetic movement is growing in line with corporate unpopularity ... they have the power to inflict long-term damage on companies and, like shareholders and politicians, they need to be factored into corporate planning and decision making (Regester and Larkin 1997: 13–23).

The second trend is said to be the impact of the contemporary media on the corporation:

> The contemporary media are technologically sophisticated and are now more intrusive, and extensive. Corporate and institutional behaviour is under much closer scrutiny. The media are very important audiences ... Ignoring the media is a big mistake (Michael Regester, in interview: July 7, 1997).

These circumstances, consultants argue, give rise to greater scrutiny, litigation and adverse publicity. The two trends are also interdependent, they maintain. An instance of such interdependency is that because of a disposition to question and contest, there is a greater probability that the ubiquitous media are likely to reflect and amplify such views which, in turn, creates a greater threat to the perspectives of those who traditionally occupy positions of authority.

Various commentators view contemporary society as decentered and as giving rise to difference, ambiguity, pluralism and heterogeneity, and have talked about the decline in deference and the proliferation of risk. For instance, Macnaghten and Urry (1998), commenting on the Brent Spar case, argue:

> Greenpeace's campaign to stop Shell dumping the Brent Spar ... related to the globalization of risk and the ability of the NGO to operate globally (1998: 68).

And:

> The role of NGOs is of special significance in a period where they are often trusted more than government, and where industry is trusted hardly at all (Macnaghten and Urry (1998: 73).

Macnaghten and Urry also point to the emergence of new patterns of environmental protest which involve an 'inventiveness in method' (1998: 70), such as the use of new technologies in Greenpeace's Brent Spar campaign.

Further, a central observation of postmodernism is that 'the post-modern condition is one of micro contexts and micro struggles in which a variety of social groups attempt to "wage war" against the totalising and centralising power of the modern state, multinational companies and bureaucratised science and technology' (Swingewood 2000: 223). That is quite central to and supports the consultants' views.

Ericson et al.'s (1989) argument that the media police irregularities in corporate behaviour, and focus on bad news and signs of procedural deviance and wrong-doing, also backs the consultants' claim, as does his observation that: 'managing news is important because meanings are assigned to events, processes or state of affairs' (1989: 377). Ericson et al.'s contention that attempts are made to achieve 'preferred versions' and that 'legitimation work has become a most legitimate expense for organisations' (1989: 18), explains practices such as crisis management and points to circumstances that increase risks to reputations and require organisations to manage media representations.

While there may well be congruence between consultants' claims about the world and other sociological perspectives, I pay close attention to the similarities with the view of society proposed by the risk thesis outlined below because that appears to me to be the most striking and noticeable. An examination of analogous observations made by sociological perspectives illuminates what the consultants expound and, regardless of whether or not what the consultants say is 'true', this examination shows that it does at least chime with other authoritative accounts, and has a plausibility, which is relevant to the question of how the consultants gain credibility and business.

The 'risk society' perspective

The idea of the 'risk society' was proposed by Beck (1992) and seconded by Giddens (1998). They argue that society is now entirely different as a result of a globalisation process involving technological, economic, political and cultural changes: 'There are good, objective reasons for believing that we are living through a major period of historical transition' (Giddens 2000: 1). He, like Beck, is of the view that contemporary society is one that is characterised by risk: 'this apparently simple notion unlocks some of the most basic characteristics of the world in which we now live' (Giddens 2000: 21). For Beck (1992) and Giddens (1999), the rise of the risk society is driven by a process initiated by modernisation. Beck argues that the risk society is characterised by an advanced modernity within which 'the social production of wealth is systematically accompanied by a social production of risks' (Beck 1992: 19). He claims that such risks are a consequence of techno-economic development and are new in terms of their global scope; they present global dangers.

Beck and Giddens identify a specific type of risk: 'manufactured risks', which they define as those which arise from developments in science and in technology, thus: 'they are created by the very impact of our developing knowledge of the world' (Giddens 2000: 26). Because of the unintended and unforeseen consequences of technological development, technological innovations have in reality increased risks, they argue.

They also associate risk with the development and advance of knowledge, which is seen as having created a greater awareness of previously unseen hazards. Thus, there is a greater consciousness of risk and that too is a defining characteristic of present-day society. They also maintain that risk consciousness is compounded by conflicting and changeable scientific and technological information, which is also a new aspect of society. Beck and Giddens view science and people's relation to science as having changed, as conclusiveness in scientific findings is now acknowledged to be increasingly elusive. Hence, risk calculation and our ability to accept scientific discoveries are affected by that new condition. Moreover, that condition also intensifies the problems of trust that they observe.

Other academics examining risk, such as Douglas (1992) and Furedi (1998), contest the equation of technological advances with risk. Furedi (1998), whilst agreeing with Giddens and Beck that the development of knowledge has increased sensitivity to unseen hazards, disputes the view that contemporary society is, in actuality, more risky: 'It is striking that despite the many problems that face humanity, we live in a world that is far safer than at any time in history' (Furedi 1998: 54). He sees the association of risk with technological advances as a symptom of another phenomenon: that of an augmentation in scepticism and cynicism about human intervention and endeavour. Whereas for Beck scientific and technological developments have produced new dangers, Furedi claims that there is a cynical belief that society cannot find solutions to its problems and that there is an exaggeration of the destructive outcomes of human activity.

Risk cannot be defined objectively because what is seen as a risk depends on values held by individuals and groups, maintain Douglas and Wildavsky (1982). Douglas (1992) argues that risks are socially constructed and that risk and danger are culturally conditioned notions – there are cultural differences in what is seen to constitute a risk.

Although there is diverging academic discourse about risk and disagreements on fundamental issues, there is agreement that contemporary society is one which is severely concerned with risk and, as a result, also characterised by it. There is an analogy between the risk society theorists' identification of the fundamental characteristics of society and that which the consultants propose, and it is this identification that is discussed in the following section.

Zones of convergence

The worldviews of academics and consultants meet where both accounts see the construction of risks as active and influenced by power and public trust; view the media as playing an important role in the construction of risks and in contemporary society; identify a greater level of public scrutiny in contemporary society; assert that there is a greater level of scepticism; and describe a greater need for those traditionally occupying positions of power and authority to justify their actions and policies.

Both consultants and risk theorists view risks as emergent and open to social definition and construction. Consultants recognise that the risks claimed to be posed by a particular corporation's action are open and vulnerable to diverse interpretations. It is because of this that groups offering contrary definitions (such as pressure groups) have such significance in crisis management. Arguing that '... new risks emerge, the degree of existing risk changes ... a new perception of risks can occur' (Regester and Larkin 1997: 25) and that communicating about risks can control how risks are viewed, consultants accept that risks are malleable. Their attempts to influence perceptions of risks by managing communications about risks are based on this premise.

The construction of risks is seen as active, purposeful and for particular, desired ends. Which particular interpretation of risks will be the dominant one is recognised as variable by both perspectives. Undisputed by both accounts is the centrality of 'how many people become convinced of a particular interpretation and take action upon this basis' (Giddens 1996: 11). Nevertheless, both standpoints assert that questions of power (who is best positioned to exert the greater influence) and trust (who has the greater share of public trust) take on a central role in their ability successfully to influence definitions. Both versions also acknowledge that the media play a central role in defining risks and knowledge about risks. In order to show these conditions, consultants point to the Brent Spar case, where different definitions of risks were simultaneously made by Shell and Greenpeace but, according to them, one party used a better communication strategy, commanded greater trust and thus was more successful than the other:

> Shell was forced to change course over Brent Spar because certain audiences ... believed what Greenpeace told them. They went on believing the interest group even when it was revealed that Greenpeace's original allegations on the level of contaminants [in Brent Spar] were overestimated (Seymour and Moore 2000: 171).

Both accounts similarly classify the situation that perceptions of risk play a central role in the construction of risks and even determine whether something comes to be seen as a risk. Consultants argue:

> Once a risk is perceived then it is real because the perception is that it is. In communicating about risks it is the perceptions of risk that have to be addressed (Michael Regester, in interview: July 7, 1997).

Beck observes, as do consultants, that there are two issues involved in knowledge about risks: the risks themselves and *public perception of (them)*.[15] Beck argues that 'it is not clear whether the risks have intensified, or our view of them [but] ... perceptions of risk and risk [are] one and the same' (1992: 55) because the issue can be described by the 'well known sociological sentence: if people experience risks as real *they are real* as a consequence' (1992: 77). Therefore, both parties maintain that public perceptions play an influential and determining role in considerations about risks. Consultants argue that public perceptions of issues and risks play a principal and influential part in whether a particular corporate action and/or policy is accepted. Beck's observations on how risks are constructed support the consultants' argument on the matter.

The second area of similarity centres on Beck's and the consultants' attribution of a central role to the media in the definition of risks and in presenting opportunities for influencing the definition of risks. The definition of risks, claims Beck, is done within and through the mass media and is malleable because risks are:

> ... based on *causal interpretations*, and thus initially only exist in terms of the (scientific or anti-scientific) *knowledge* about them. They can thus be changed, magnified or minimized within knowledge, and to that extent they are particularly *open to social definition and construction* (Beck 1992: 23).

Consultants take the view that, because of the analysis of risk being dependent on the knowledge held about the risks, assessments of risk can be influenced by managing information. Consultants recognise that knowledge is mediated and, upon this basis, crisis management initiatives attempt to influence that process. Beck argues that the media present opportunities to influence the definition of social problems, and political spheres can only ignore published opinion at the risk of losing voters and supporters. The consultants encourage companies to influence interpretations within the media and that recommendation is based on the recognition that views aired in the media about a corporation cannot safely be ignored by that entity.

Beck also attributes a further significance to the role of the media in publicising issues. He states that the media also perform an important monitoring function with regard to political decisions:

> ... the legal protection and substantive fulfillment of freedom of the press, which in combination with the mass media (newspapers, radio, television) and new technological possibilities, brings about multiply graduated forms of publicity. Even if these certainly do not pursue the exalted goals of the Enlightenment, but are also and

even primarily 'servants' of the market, of advertising and of con-
sumption (whether of goods of all sorts or of institutionally fabricated information), and even if they possibly produce or exacerbate
inarticulateness, isolation, even stupidity, there still remains an
actual or potential monitoring function which media directed publicity can perform with regard to political decisions (1992: 193–4).

Given this function of the media as well as the power of the media
to structure and disseminate knowledge, Beck goes so far as to state
that the risk society is 'also the *science, media and information society*'
(1992: 46). Giddens too believes that the risk society is also the information society. Consultants, like the risk thesis, attribute a central role
to the media within contemporary society. They do so because of the
monitoring function of the media and because they recognise that
the media have a significant influence on perceptions of corporations
and their activities.

Giddens argues that the contemporary media may create a greater
democratisation, yet he also identifies a significant aspect of the media
which might confer certain dangers to such a democratisation as well
as presenting specific dangers such as hampering the discussion of
complex issues:

On the one hand ... the emergence of a global information society
is a powerful democratising force. Yet, television, and the other
media, tends to destroy the very public space they open up, through
a relentless trivialisation and personalisation of political issues
(Reith Lecture 1999: www.reith.bbc.co.uk/reith 99).

In this way, Giddens identifies a characteristic of the media that consultants also observe i.e. that certain aspects of media reporting of
issues require a greater corporate effort, both to defend themselves
from media trivialisation of matters important to them and to provide
a defence of their actions and policies. Consultants claim that corporations have to work harder to gain coverage and support of their views.

Beck (1992) argues that the media might be used to perpetuate 'institutionally fabricated information', and he sees this as being a problematic aspect of society. Crisis management, which seeks publicity for a
particular corporate viewpoint, may be viewed as a form of such 'institutionally fabricated information'. However, the consultants' argument
that such actions are necessary is also based on their identification that
such practices are routinely present in contemporary society. As we

have seen, the consultants' contention is that corporations must publicise their own perspective in response to, and to curtail, hostile views perpetuated in the media. Hence, both accounts point to similar processes.

The risk thesis identifies the monitoring function of the media as having a variety of consequences. One such consequence also claimed by consultants is the opening up of the political sphere; i.e. a 'subpolitics' emerges and takes centre stage. It is characterised as a new political culture wherein citizens, initiative groups, social movements '... are able to utilize all the media of public and legal control and consultation to protect their interest and rights' (Beck 1992: 185). The effect of such actions, the risk thesis maintains, is that techno-economic development loses its non-political status and becomes sub-politics because:

> [t]he direction of development and the results of technological transformation becomes fit for discourse and subject to legitimation ... business and techno-scientific action acquire a new political and moral dimension that had previously seemed alien to techno-economic activity (Beck 1992: 186).

Therefore, Beck echoes a central claim made by the consultants: a greater level of discourse and debate regarding the actions and policies of corporations, which require them to stand up for themselves. As also maintained by consultants, the risk thesis identifies a new type of pressure developed for business:

> (t)he public gets a say in technical details. Businesses that had long been pampered in a cozy capitalist consensus because of their fiscal benefactions and their charitable creation of jobs, suddenly find themselves on the witness bench, or more precisely, locked in the pillory, and confronted with the kind of questions that were previously used to prosecute poisoners caught red-handed (Beck 1992: 76).

Therefore, both perspectives state that businesses in contemporary society are faced with a new type of risk: a societal disposition to question, criticise and disbelieve their claims.

Both descriptions of society also observe that there is a greater level of public scrutiny that is facilitated by the advances in communications. Giddens points to a central and interdependent role of communications and an increased level of public debates. He argues that contemporary society is 'an age of instantaneous communications which has produced more active and reflective citizenries than had existed before' (The Reith Lecture 1999: www.bbc.co.uk/reith 99). Beck writes that whereas 'in an earlier stage, [the risks of techno-economic developments] can be legitimated as "latent side effects"' (1992: 13), they no longer can be sanctioned as such as they are subject to public discourse, criticism, scientific investigation and achieve a central importance in social and political debates.

Additionally, Beck's claim that there is a greater investigation of economic and technological developments within 'the light of a *new ecological morality* ...' (1992: 77) is parallel to the consultants' argument that there is a greater tendency to hold business socially and environmentally responsible. Moreover, the *consequences* of ignoring this new consciousness are also similarly identified by consultants as by Beck: '... market shifts, political pressures [develop], checks on plant decisions, recognition of compensation claims, gigantic costs, legal proceedings and loss of face [occurs]' (Beck 1992: 77).

The loss of trust which academics point to is also observed by consultants. Giddens contends there has been a death of 'traditional deference and respect' in contemporary society, arguing that politics and business previously depended on a passive form of trust which no longer exists. Consequently, he claims, there is now a greater need for businesses and governments to generate a more active form of trust (The Reith Lecture 1999: www.bbc.co.uk/reith 99). That identification of a new requirement for organisations especially businesses and governments, corresponds with consultants' similar estimation and claim that, given the corrosion of traditional forms of deference, there is a greater requirement now for corporations to defend their stance and create a renewed acceptance and public empathy.

Furedi (1998) also suggests that there is a disposition to distrust those in power and he accounts for why this may be so:

> There is a presumption [about the dangers involved] that what is visible or quantifiable is only the tip of the iceberg. Such conclusions often make sense, since many people expect that those in authority are unlikely to tell the truth. That people so readily expect cover-ups and hidden agendas is in part an understandable reaction to past experience. However, it has also contributed to a climate in which the most extreme claims about virtually any issue can be taken seriously – at least until they are disproved (1998: 34).

Furedi's conclusion that even the most radical claim might now be taken seriously supports the consultants' argument that corporations are now compelled to take a greater effort to safeguard their claims and views.

The higher level of scepticism, Beck observes, is also 'extended to the foundations and hazards of scientific work and science is thus both *generalised* and *demystified*' (1992: 14). Giddens argues that there is a greater recognition that knowledge and, within this, scientific authority is also open to doubt: that 'all claims to knowledge are corrigible has become an existential condition in modern societies' (1996: 42). Furedi (1998) also maintains that there has been a loss of trust in a variety of domains that were traditionally prestigious:

> (t)he loss of trust in authority does not merely pertain to the domains of politics, religion and culture. Many of the professions e.g. – doctors, scientists – have also lost prestige and authority ... Suspicion towards science is particularly intense. Instead of trusting the expert opinion of the scientist, many people are disposed to look for a hidden agenda. Indeed, the loss of public trust in science is one of the most striking expressions of the general erosion of legitimacy and authority. A tendency to mistrust scientific claims has helped fuel public unease about the consequences of technological developments. Many of the panics about environmental and health-related issues demonstrate an explicit rejection of the claims of scientists on the subject. Mistrust of science is one of the most visible elements of the growth of risk consciousness itself (1998: 130).

Contrary to Giddens's and Beck's position that expert systems have lost the ability to command trust, Furedi argues that society has not entirely shed trust in all expert systems, rather that there is a selective relationship with expertise:

> ... what is at issue is not a general mistrust of expert systems, but rather of particular types of expertise ... The recent dispute between Shell and Greenpeace [over the Brent Spar] indicates that certain types of expert can always count on public confidence (1998: 132–3).

Furedi points to a significant risk to corporations which consultants also note: he argues that because there is a loss of trust in those in positions of authority, other claims are taken more seriously than would have been the case if traditional sources of authority still held esteem. Thus, a greater trust in groups such as Greenpeace might be a consequence of a loss of faith in authority, as it is likely that trust might be conferred to those who are often in direct opposition to those in whom the public have lost confidence. Furedi's observation mirrors the consultants' claim that the public and the media may be more sympathetic to the allegations of pressure groups. Further, as there is a loss of trust there might also be a tendency to believe bad news – which companies would wish to minimise – rather than good news, which may be seen as self-serving and exaggerated.

Both consultants and academics observe a greater need for those who have lost public trust to justify their actions and policies, and they interpret that as a contemporary element of society. Beck saw such attempts to cultivate support as now regularly taking place. That is reflected in his argument that 'sub-politics' (a third entity between politics and non-politics) has taken over from politics in shaping society. Such sub-politics, he argues, is 'under the jurisdiction of business, science and technology ...' (1992: 14). Giddens also argues that new responsibilities arise for businesses and governments as a consequence of being subjected to a greater level of questioning, and identifies a requirement for businesses and governments to exercise greater efforts to explain and justify their activities (Reith Lecture 1999: www.bbc.co. uk/reith 99). Not only does that parallel the consultants' case, but also the risk thesis's identification of this feature of contemporary society explains the rise of and the very existence of practices such as crisis management. The main objective of the new field of crisis management is to create public acquiescence. The risk thesis recognises that objective, and the fact that it is necessary, as characteristics of contemporary society.

The conditions of contemporary society that Beck and others describe are similar to those described by consultants, who catalogue those very factors as being central to the management of crises. For instance, Beck declares:

> (a)ccess to the media becomes crucial. The insecurity within industry intensifies: no one knows who will be struck next by the anathema of ecological morality. Good arguments, or at least arguments capable of convincing the public, become a condition of business success (1992: 32).

Beck forsees that practices such as crisis management will arise and prosper. He sees the rise in the role and need for corporate communicators and spokesmen and views this as another aspect of the risk society: '(p)ublicity people, the "argumentation craftsmen", get their opportunity in the organization' (Beck 1992: 32). He says this is a response to the need to achieve public acceptance, which is a condition of contemporary society that both the risk thesis and consultants observe.

The promotion of crisis management

Consultants depict crisis management merely as a coincidental response to an exigency, and the risk thesis shows how there might be a need for it, but one important reason for the existence of crisis management is that consultants actively create a demand for it.

A view of society as requiring crisis management

Although the consultants' description of society is paralleled in other authoritative accounts and has a plausibility, it also serves their interests because their account of society attempts to convince corporations of the existence of threats and to persuade them that there is not only a need to deal with such eventualities but also that the consultants can control identified risks to businesses and know how to go about doing so. Consultants demonstrate that there exists a need for their recommendations and, even if that may well be the case, the measures taken to demonstrate such a need also attempt to create one. That is particularly manifest when what they present is not a mere chronicle of conditions but an argument that a need has arisen and a service to deal with that circumstance is matched to it:

> You are more likely to experience a crisis than the person who last held your job ... Your crisis is more likely now that the world is more demanding about what you do ... the outside world is taking a greater interest in a business's operations ... The most sophisticated management teams have problems appreciating how readily borders are ignored or jumped by media ... In a crisis, communication technology may turn against you. The media, the Internet, the telephone all thunder down the information highway to besiege the company ... And it is what you have to say, and how you say it, that will shape the crisis (Seymour and Moore 2000: xiv).

From the above, we can see that a problem is first identified and then a solution is provided. The solution, significantly, is presented as being a greater communications effort, which is precisely the consultants' area of work. The consultants use a rhetorical argument to produce a demand for their services.

It is curious that most consultants, in interviews, began by citing the two 'trends' mentioned previously (changes in attitudes to authority and the contemporary media). It is debatable whether the circumstances they classify are trends or not, or whether they are the two key directions of and/or the conditions of contemporary society. But these questions are not as relevant for my purposes as the fact that consultants present this as being so. It is the case that the two trends they identify are ones that are not only significant to the practical elements of their work but also to the promotion of their enterprise. The two areas they evoke promote crisis management because they are said to be the reasons why corporations should engage in it. That also explains why they are given such a central position and why consultants begin their case by referring to them. The two trends allow consultants to portray corporations as under siege and it is pragmatically advantageous to them to do so. The excerpt above illustrates this depiction of a dangerous world. It is from the opening pages of a text on crisis management written by one of its prominent consultants and it illustrates my point that consultants routinely begin the presentation of their case by describing circumstances which they claim necessitate their services. Kieser saw this as a customary consultancy practice, arguing: 'consultancies who compile a new management concept also construct the business problems for which the offered solution fits' (2002: 180).

There seem to be three main explanations for why the consultants' claims about the nature of society are so similar to those put forward by the risk society thesis: that risk theorists and consultants are responding to 'identical' events in the same way; that their common arguments are just a coincidence – a matter of serendipity; or that they have influenced one another. Arguably, all three possibilities contributed to the situation, but it is impractical to establish the extent of their influence.[16]

Kipping and Engwall would not find the parallels unusual, as they argue that the three main groups in what they called 'the management knowledge industry', i.e. the media, academia and consultants, although sometimes combative, also have a cooperative relationship and routinely support each other (2002: 9). And, just as the consultants take up academic ideas they, in turn, diffuse those ideas in the course of their work. There are mediated accounts of risk that turn empirical studies into theory and theory into practice. The means of doing this in this case would probably be conferences, journals and newspapers.

Most consultants, however, disclaim any knowledge of the similarities with the academic ideas I discussed. Nevertheless, Regester and Larkin writes that their perspective is like that proposed by the risk society thesis (Regester and Larkin 1997: 24). Although they wrote this in a textbook on crisis management and Regester expressed this view in interview, I cannot say how thorough their understanding of that thesis is. But as it is the case that consultants do not 'operate in a void', it is not so unusual that they are aware of leading discourses of the times (Kipping and Engwall 2002: 5). Beck's 'Risk Society' sold over 60,000 copies worldwide and 'produced significant reverberations, both within and outside academic circles' (Mythen 2004: 11). Also, in one instance I know of, although the consultancy concerned said that such occasions are frequent, Regester Larkin organised an 'informal lunch gathering' where a prominent risk theorist, Frank Furedi, was invited to lecture to a group of their clients on the nature of contemporary society. Kieser observed that consultancies organise seminars because they regard them as 'superb marketing instruments' (2002: 170). The observations made by academics such as Furedi allow consultants to lend legitimacy to their claims and demonstrate to their clients the weight of what they propound. These instances allow consultants to advance their proposals by making use of academic observations and support Kipping and Engwall's argument. Not only does the risk thesis support the consultants' case but the consultants also use such discourses to promote crisis management.

However, consultants also portray their observations as being independently made. Despite writing that their account of society is similar to the observations of the risk thesis, Regester said in interview that this similarity was coincidental, claiming that his description was based on observations of crises rather than being derived from a social theory. He, however, was enterprising in claiming that the existence of similar observations to that made by him, and other consultants in the field, further prove their claims. That statement illustrates how the existence of similar notions might be used to advance a case and a practice.

The citation of cases

This allows consultants independently to create client receptivity to their claims. Their citation of cases, such as the *Exxon-Valdez* and Intel's Pentium 1, has a function in promoting the consultants' proposals as it plays a powerful narrative role in constructing crisis management as a project and consultants as the masters of that project. The consultants' classification of characteristic ways in which corporations mismanage crises proposes a set of ideas regarding what constitutes effective management. By arguing in this way, consultants lay claim to the required expertise to deal with crises and, because of this, the services they provide are presented as imperative to the management of crises.

The cases they cite reflect properties of the 'real' world, and the consultants' identification of ways in which crises have been typically mismanaged show the consequences of different responses to crisis. But such classifications also constitute ways in which their method is advanced. For example, as is apparent from the cases I have referred to, although the cases are complex situations, the consultants reduce their explanation of those incidents to the communications strategies employed and to whether managers take their advice. The factors they isolate reflect the practicalities involved in the areas they wish to tackle, but their account is a selective one that proposes a particular type of explanation which demonstrates the legitimacy of their approach. In their citation of cases, what remains hidden is that companies are urged to adopt the consultants' recommendations and this promotes crisis management.

The consultants' explanation of why some cases are so often cited is that they were high profile, not ongoing (i.e. sufficiently in the past rather than being subject to confidentiality), contemporary and relevant. Those cases that the consultants characterise as demonstrative of a poor approach are also ones where there has been some acknowledgement and admission by the corporations involved that the course of action they took in handling the crisis was misguided. For instance, Exxon and Intel have since declared their misgivings about their approach.[17] For persuasive purposes, what the consultants claim is made more cogent if there is agreement on what transpired. The same cases might be cited again and again because there may be published accounts of those instances and, as they become frequently referenced, they may have become established as classic cases which one can point to, or add to easily without having to go into much detail. However, it is also the case that, even if the consultants do not draw attention to it, they have prepared stories to recount. Cases are cited because they encompass, and more complexly, can be interpreted as encompassing, what consultants wish to underscore because a primary objective of citing cases is to promote their reasoning and approach.

By pointing to cases consultants portray the efficiency of contingency plans for the management of crises as being dependent on the incorporation of factors they hold as important: communications that address the perceptions of audiences. Although this characterisation flows in part from what public relations people can do, it also helps the consultants' case. This is not to imply that their case is unwarranted. Academic analyses of crises and their management have also pointed to the importance of paying attention to communications. Deppa et al.'s analysis of the Pan Am Flight 103 disaster[18] and the company's response to the crisis, concluded that Pan Am had paid insufficient attention to communications in the preparatory stages of their plans to manage any forthcoming crisis:

> Prior to Lockerbie in 1988, the most recent run through of the entire Pan Am [crisis] plan was 1982, although exactly one week before the bombing of Flight 103, Pan Am had been the participating airline in an emergency exercise at London's Heathrow airport [however] like so many corporate efforts in crisis communications, the emphasis in mock scenarios at Pan Am tended to be on the operational response (i.e. rehearsals of putting fires out, evacuating passengers, caring for the injured, routes to the nearest hospital), while ignoring a critical element of disaster management: communication of information to key audiences in the outside world (Deppa et al. 1993: 251).

Michael Bland described that tendency as the 'King Kong' syndrome:

> So named after the Bob Newhart sketch in which he plays a janitor in the Empire State Building as King Kong is climbing up the outside. Nowhere in the janitor's manual does it give instructions on what to do about a 40 foot gorilla sticking its toe through a 12th floor window. This is exactly how most organisations prepare for crisis – trying to cover every possible contingency and ending up with a vast crisis manual which is completely impractical and which in any case doesn't contain the instructions on gorilla's toes – which is the one unthought of crisis that actually strikes (in interview: November 4, 1997).

Pointing to the significance of communications in crisis preparedness, consultants bolster their method of crisis management. They give a specific explanation of past crises which presumes the existence and availability of an efficient formula and ignores problems. For example, in the Intel Pentium 1 case consultants assume that Intel could have predicted that the issue would escalate into a crisis and therefore should have prepared for that eventuality, but ignore the circumstance that it may not be possible accurately to foresee and identify crises at an embryonic stage. As we have seen, the consultants themselves define crises in terms of their unexpectedness and rapid development[19] – these are qualities that are difficult to anticipate. There are genuine problems in predicting whether a certain situation will develop into a crisis. One could argue that Intel took a minor risk in marketing Pentium 1 (the fault in the chip was not extensive and just limited to complex division calculations), that risk-taking is normal within any business and that there are innumerable calculations of risk that do pay off. Furthermore, despite the existence of contentious issues, according to the consultants' own admission, many of these do not result in crises (Regester and Larkin 1997: 73). Therefore, predicting which issues will develop into a crisis is largely an inexact exercise but *is easy to do in hindsight*. Consultants often make this type of *ex post facto* identification by referring to past crises, such as the Intel case, and in doing so they create realities that fit the offered solutions.

Regester candidly divulged in interview that he cites and invokes cases for the purpose of furthering his arguments. However, consultants, including Regester, give the impression that they cite them for illustrative purposes only but they are, in effect, useful parables that allow consultants to uphold certain types of responses to crisis as better than others. It is the consultants who specify and define; the cases do not speak for themselves. The citation of cases not only illustrates but also distinguishes the consequences of pursuing particular courses of action. Therefore, the cases serve the additional purposes of sanctioning the claims made by consultants and advancing their proposals.

There are also more obvious ways in which consultants promote both themselves and their practice. Although consultants accept that 'a lot of the principles involved in crisis management have on occasions been used to great effect by people who have done so instinctively ...' (Michael Bland, in interview: July 10, 1997), they discourage companies from relying on the 'instinctive'/self-application of crisis management principles and explicitly stress the importance of external consultants. Michael Seymour argued that 'good managers are often not good crisis managers' (in interview: June 30, 1997) and described not turning to consultants as one way in which companies might be 'heading for crisis' (Seymour and Moore 2000: 17). Companies were warned:

Crises cannot be managed on the cheap, or on the wing. Outside consultants with a wider perspective on the crisis are a necessity (Seymour and Moore 2000: 27).

The suggestion that not asking for the advice of consultants is courting disaster is a blatantly obvious illustration of self-promotion. It quite clearly facilitates the advancement of crisis management and the consultant, and is an example of how self-serving consultants' definitions of mismanagement can be.

Seymour also described 'individuals and teams trying to go it [manage crises] alone' as asking for trouble:

> ... the Chief Executive Officer may try to take personal charge of all crisis operations. This is a fine principle but often risky in practice ... A crisis has broken out when the mess becomes too big for chief executives to clear up alone (Seymour and Moore 2000: 22).

Although consultants said that a team effort is necessary and often extolled the virtues of CEOs personally taking charge of a situation, the above shows that it is not just a team effort that is advocated but a team that includes consultants as a crucial component. And while CEOs may be welcomed for their role in giving a high profile to the matter within the corporation, and appreciated for providing a public figurehead for the company, their value in crisis management is clearly expressed as limited. By creating the impression that their concepts, if implemented with their help, will have a beneficial effect, consultants make their role indispensable.

That argument also downplays routine problems with the implementation of strategy. Despite conceding the influence of organisational culture on actions taken to handle crisis, consultants give the impression that organisations can implement their crisis management strategy by simply hiring consultants and taking their advice. However, in their study of corporate strategy Johnson and Scholes (2002) argue that strategy development is not as simple as that. They contend that, in practice, strategy is driven by the organisational culture, 'an organisation will lean towards those strategies that best fit its culture' (2002: 236), and that strategy emerges rather than being selected. Therefore, even if an organisation has had exposure to the advice that crisis management consultants give, this in itself does not mean that their strategy would be adopted. The 'organisational paradigm', or the set of assumptions held relatively in common within an organisation, is consequential on strategy. Even when faced with pressures for change – such as a crisis – Johnson and Scholes hold that the influence of the 'way we do things around here' paradigm means that 'managers first try and improve the implementation of existing strategy' (2002: 79). Johnson and Scholes also maintain that even when managers know intellectually that strategy change has to occur, and know how to make that change, organisational assumptions and routines will constrain them. Johnson and Scholes's analysis points to the fact that the handling of crisis might have more to do with the way in which particular organisational cultures shape certain responses to crisis than with whether or not organisations act purely on consultants' advice.

Conclusions

This new phenomenon, crisis management, does not involve overseeing every aspect of a crisis, as might be assumed; it is primarily about managing impressions. The consultants' definition of crisis as a consequence of antagonistic publicity quite clearly reveals that crisis management is a special construct and creation of consultants who are concerned, in part, with the kinds of practical activity a crisis entails for them. 'Crisis management' is influenced by what consultants see as important to the management of crises and is propelled by the pragmatic need they identify: to guide and influence perceptions through communication strategies. One could argue, as consultants do, that since a company relies for its existence on consumer perception, the role of the consultants *inevitably* focuses on those aspects of a crisis. In short, it could be argued that it is simply not the consultants' role to be concerned with the broader aspects of the crisis, and that to imply criticism of them on that basis is misconceived. The strategies they uphold are for the purposes of ensuring that a desired perception of a crisis and the company involved can be achieved. It is in this way that consultants view crises as being 'managed'. Others would disagree with this interpretation but this is what crisis management refers to. We have seen that consultants emphasise the notions of risk and trust but, important as these are, crisis management is not just about such issues; it is very much about the advantageous positioning of companies and influencing views of them in order to create perceptions that benefit them.

With the aid of symbolic interactionism, the assumptions and the reasoning that underpin consultants' proposals have been outlined in this chapter. The consultants spell out a communications strategy that has an affinity with symbolic interactionism's description of the process involved in interaction, and the two approaches have many parallels. Not only is symbolic interactionism expedient to describing crisis management but it also illuminates the consultants' case.

What might help these consultants to advance their case and line of work? The sociology of the professions suggests that professionalisation is a distinct process with identifiable characteristics. One important feature is that a central objective of all professional accounts of action is to demonstrate the validity of a certain sanctioned course of action above others, and that professions in the making try to cast their knowledge and practices as expert (Macdonald 1995; Haskell 1984; Abbott 1998; Gerver and Bensman 1995). Crisis management, as an area of public relations, benefits from the authority afforded to public relations. Nevertheless, that authority is not secure (White and Mazur 1995; L'Etang and Pieczka 1996). The public relations industry is young, not entirely established, and has self-consciously sought professional status in an effort to distance itself from perceptions of propaganda at first and then, later, 'spin doctoring' (Ewen 1996; Grunig 1992; Cutlip et al. 1994). Yet the consultants' claim that they are the best equipped to deal with communications is buttressed by the expertise of managing communications being traditionally held by public relations. That consultants said in interviews that, even though management consultancies such as McKinseys have started to advise clients on managing crisis communications, clients will still approach them because they, rather than management consultancies, are seen as the public relations/communication experts demonstrates this. So their association with public relations helps consultants to gain support for their case but, as I have demonstrated, there are other avenues by which consultants independently further and seek legitimacy for their proposals.

Given that much consultancy work in various fields involves creating client receptivity and countering client resistance, it is not surprising that the crisis management consultants promote their ideas and their area of work with these issues in mind. Client resistance, Johnson and Scholes (2002) and Kipping and Engwall (2002) argue is considerable:

... consultancy firms face quite an uphill struggle when it comes to putting their knowledge into practice. They certainly try to exploit the uncertainty of managers and their need to justify themselves with respect to their peers, and succeed to some extent. At the same time, they have to convince managers and other stakeholders in companies of the value they might add ... Often ... they have to overcome considerable reluctance, resistance, and cynicism, particularly from lower levels of management and or workers (Kipping and Engwall 2002: 8).

The consultants market crisis management as a way of managing risks to reputations, which, they say, are quite extensive. That in itself exploits and speaks to the uncertainty of managers, raises the level of anxiety in companies and makes them more receptive to their offers of assistance. Kieser (2002) argues that consultants routinely play to clients' sense of fear and insist that they can generate a greater level of control. The claim that potential crises are perennially present (the dormant, creeping crisis) also seeks to create insecurity and thereby solicits investment in crisis management. This claim also shows how the consultants' construction of crisis and its management is very obviously potentially lucrative to the consultant. The consultants' argument about a proliferation of risks also helps them to sustain their construction of crisis management as necessary whether crises are there or not.

The notion of risk continually arises in the crisis management discourse. Both the illustration of typical ways in which crises are mismanaged and the classification of characteristics of society involve an invocation of the risks involved. Whilst it is useful to consultants and to crisis management to depict the world as presenting extraordinary dangers and hazards, a depiction that makes strategies to control and minimise risks desirable, this also reveals how the notion of risk can be commercialised and indicates why risk management has become so marketable. Beck's and Giddens's analyses show how crisis management might resonate with current preoccupations with risk and risk management. Indeed the very marketability of risk is determined by a wider concern with it and with its control.

With reference to symbolic interactionism, the risk thesis and cases I have suggested that the consultants' recommendations are consistent with processes seen as occurring in the world. I have demonstrated how the consultants' claim about the symbolic construction of the world is explicable within symbolic interactionism, and how the risk thesis corroborates their claims about the nature of contemporary society. There is a correspondence between what consultants and other commentators say about the world, and these parallels provide intellectual support for the consultants' worldview and lend greater weight to their recommendations.

According to the risk discourse, crisis management appears to be very much a part of the modern scheme of things, and the very existence of that discourse provides opportunities for the promotion of crisis management. As Foucault (1977) argued in relation to particular approaches to criminal justice, wider structures and ideologies provide external support for and, hence, assist in the advance of specific approaches. Garland (2001), in a historical study, also showed that responses to crime and crime control are directed, in part, by the dominant beliefs and rationales of the time. In addition, the consulting industry as a whole is highly 'faddish' (Kipping and Engwall 2002), and crisis management consultants might be positioning themselves to take advantage of the current popularity of risk management.

I have shown that consultants are certainly not alone in identifying similar characteristics of society or in arguing that, in response to these conditions, corporations ought to behave in a specific manner. But have these types of discourse brought a greater corporate awareness of the identified societal conditions? The answer is yes.

The power of pressure groups to shift public opinion against a company and its products is now widely acknowledged by heads of corporations. For instance, Monsanto, a company involved in the production of genetically modified foods, stated that Greenpeace had contributed to the backfiring of its promotion of genetically modified foods in the UK through its campaign efforts, which gained considerable media coverage (*Financial Times*, April 13, 1999: 14). Lezaun (2004) observes: '... the United Kingdom was the first market where genetically modified foods failed, on a massive scale ... the explosion of public debate and consumer resistance took place in the United Kingdom at a critical moment in the commercialization cycle of the new products' (2004: 190).

On the basis of the 1996 MORI *'Business and the Environment'* survey, which sought the opinions of 'captains of industry' (of whom 74 per cent were Chairman, Managing Director and/or Chief Executive Officer) from a sample taken from the 'Times 500' largest companies, MORI concluded that captains of industry:

> ... increasingly realise that green pressure of legislators presents a challenge that they will likely be responsive to, [and] that many captains of industry in Britain and elsewhere are acutely conscious of a long-term decline in public trust and confidence in business organizations that represents a drain on the well of goodwill that all companies strive to conserve.[20]

Corporations recognise that their reputations are valuable assets, Sklair (2000) argues, maintaining that the contemporary level of monitoring corporate activities is historically unprecedented, and that corporations themselves as well as their opponents are attentive to the issues of global corporate citizenship.

There is some evidence to suggest that big business is aware of the conditions that consultants identify, and this is beneficial both to the advancement of crisis management and to creating receptivity to the claims consultants make; the consultants' citation of a problematic environment may thus be sympathetically received by those who are inclined to believe it. However, as Garland (2001) and Giddens (1999) note, the notion that we are now encountering an immensely different world remains controversial. Even so, the argument that consultants and others make is phenomenologically consequential, i.e. it has an influence, even if it might be wrong – it is significant in the advancement of the consultants' proposals and significant in explaining how crisis management can be sustained.

It seems plausible that this area of work evolved in response to a growing concern with risks and risk management, as consultants have suggested. Yet it is also the case that its development cannot be explained simply as a response to external societal conditions; it is also a consequence of active promotional work by the consultants. Amongst other things, the examination of the Brent Spar incident and its handling in subsequent chapters will contribute to an analysis of why crisis management is here and what might sustain it.

2

Brent Spar – Setting the Stage and the 'Emerging' and the 'Immediate' Phases of the Crisis

The following three chapters reflect, in relation to this case, on the nature of crises and the consultants' formulation of crisis management.

This chapter deals with the two phases to which consultants limit their account of this case, but because Shell, engaging crisis management consultants, continued to manage this crisis beyond these stages, my case study will examine what I classify as the three phases of the crisis, i.e. the events leading up to the crisis situation, that situation itself and what happened afterwards. I was curious as to why the consultants' rendition of this case disregards Shell's use of crisis management principles after the crisis and why they do not call attention to the company benefiting from their advice.

An introduction to Shell and Greenpeace, the two main parties involved in this case, will be provided here. Their actions prior to the crisis, the claims they made about the situation and the consultants' account of this case will also be described. A descriptive and analytical account of events follows, focusing on how the situation regarding the disposal of the Brent Spar became intense. The area explored in this chapter is particularly significant to the examination of the consultants' main argument that Shell could have prevented this crisis by managing issues early on.[1]

On the different conceptualisations of this case

Like the consultants, Shell also views the crisis as having two phases but differs in their classification. Shell amalgamates the two phases the consultants identify into one, and calls this the first phase of the crisis. The second phase, according to Shell, started after the abandonment of sea disposal:

The first phase of the crisis started from Greenpeace's occupation of the Spar and continued until Shell decided to abandon deep sea disposal. The crisis then moved on to a second phase. Within that second phase, Shell had to deal with the repercussions of the first phase of the crisis (John Wybrew, Director of Public Affairs, Shell UK, in interview: November 18, 1999).

Was this case a 'sudden' or a 'creeping' crisis? The view that it was of the first type is supported by Shell, as the company claims to have been unaware that a potential problem existed until Greenpeace occupied the Spar and thereby initiated its campaign. That Greenpeace induced the crisis for Shell is demonstrated in my analysis as opposition followed rather than preceded Greenpeace's protest.

Although consultants also maintain that Greenpeace provoked the crisis for Shell, they claim that the crisis was of the second type. They argue that the situation was one where Shell's lack of attention to a potential problematic issue (sea disposal) precipitated a crisis situation as Greenpeace simply raised an issue that already had the potential to become problematic. It is interesting that this view favours the consultants' claim that the best way to manage crises is by early management of issues. And, by ignoring the efforts Shell later made and what effects such efforts might have had, consultants can represent this case as confirming their argument. My analysis of this case demonstrates this, particularly the attention I give to the aftermath of the crisis.

An introduction to Shell

Royal Dutch/Shell Group[2]

The Royal Dutch/Shell Group was formed when two companies Royal Dutch and the Shell Group, merged in 1907. The motive was to survive and prosper against the price-cutting of Standard Oil in the Far East (Greene 1985). The three equal partners were Marcus Samuel's Shell, Deterding's Royal Dutch and Paris Rothchilds, who supplied Russian kerosene to Shell and Royal Dutch (Greene 1985). Greene argues that the alliance in 1907 enabled Royal Dutch and Shell to merge their interests while keeping their identities separate. He also maintains that Royal Dutch/Shell is a group of companies and not a corporation, as commonly perceived, and that the Shell Centre in London and the offices in the Hague are its central offices, and not corporate headquarters (Greene 1985). This is primarily because the operating companies are coordinated, but not managed, by the central offices. The operating companies, located in more than 130 countries around the world, are responsible for the management and performance of its own operations. Nevertheless, they can draw on the Service companies, whose main business is to provide advice and services to other Shell companies (http:www.shell.com).

The Royal Dutch/Shell Group consists of two parent companies: the Royal Dutch Petroleum Company and Shell Trading and Transport Ltd, which hold stock in a 60:40 ratio in two holding companies, one Dutch (Shell Petroleum NV, Netherlands), and the other British (Shell Petroleum Company Limited, UK). According to Shell:

> ... as parent companies, the Royal Dutch Petroleum Company and the Shell Transport and Trading Company plc do not themselves engage in operational activities ... The parent companies directly or indirectly own the shares in the Group Holding Companies but are not themselves part of the group. They appoint Directors to the Boards of the Group Holding Companies, from which they receive income in the form of dividends (http:\\www.shell.com).

Shell Petroleum Inc. USA is a separate concern dealing exclusively with the USA. Shell Petroleum Company Ltd UK and Shell Petroleum NV, Netherlands hold all shares in the Service companies and, directly or indirectly, all group interests in the operating companies other than those held by Shell Petroleum Inc. USA.

Shell described the activities of its operating companies worldwide as: 'finding, producing, transporting, refining, and selling oil, gas, and petrochemicals. Some are involved in mining, transporting and selling coal, as well as renewable energy businesses and forestry' (http:\\www.shell.com). The operating companies are largely independent and responsible for their own management and performance, and for ensuring the long-term viability of their own operations.

A Committee of Management Directors (CMD) is responsible for the overall Group policy and strategy. The Committee normally comprises six members who are individually responsible for the different areas of business of Royal Dutch/Shell and collectively responsible for its strategy and policy. The CMD is also finally responsible to the 600,000 shareholders of Royal Dutch and the 273,000 shareholders of Shell Transport and Trading.[3]

The companies within Royal Dutch/Shell are relatively autonomous as long as the financial results are satisfactory. As Greene argues in an analytical and historical study examining the strategies and policies of the 'Majors',[4] Royal Dutch/Shell is decentralised in comparison with the other 'Majors' but quite centralised in comparison with other multinationals 'like Unilever and Nestle' (Greene 1985: 211).

Greene argues that Shell's decentralised structure is its strength:

> The considerable effort at Shell in diplomacy required to coordinate and preserve national identities has yielded an advantage in political acceptability and therefore long term viability ... Its diplomatic style of management and the indigenousness of its local subsidiaries are greater strategic investments in political acceptability, if lower in profitability, than other Majors have chosen to make it ... It is the United Nations of oil companies, as that body wishes it could function (1985: 212).

While that is an enthusiastic account of Shell's decentralised structure, the difficulties Shell had, during the crisis, in preventing contradictory statements being made by its executives shows how decentralisation has its drawbacks. A direct consequence of the crisis faced over the Brent Spar was a centralisation of communications and crisis management within the corporation (John Wybrew, in interview: November 18, 1999). Shell's later strategy was to encourage individual companies to refer immediately any likely controversy to the Corporate Centre, which is operated by the Service companies. The aim was to manage problematic issues better by centralising communications and by developing an overall central strategy for that end.

Although Greene argues that historically Shell was unlike the secretive and closed organisations that oil companies were perceived to be, this opinion was not generally shared in the 1990s. Greene maintains that Deterding's (Chairman of Royal Dutch/Shell in 1907) practices stood 'in contrast to Standard's [Standard Oil] secrecy, secret companies and secret deals', that the corporation's annual reports were 'models of lucidity and candor [and] openly [stated] Shell's intentions and policies' (1985: 223). But confidential opinion polls conducted by MORI in 1995 and then again in 1998 on behalf of several oil companies, showed current opinions to be very different.

The poll tested UK oil and energy journalists' views of the oil companies.[5] The MORI survey of 1995, which took place after the Brent Spar incident, reveals that journalists did not perceive Shell to have an open communications policy and that it was precisely Shell's communications that journalists identified and criticised as having exacerbated that crisis. Robert Corzine, a senior oil and energy journalist working for the *Financial Times*, had this to say about Shell UK's media relations:

As a journalist, if you wanted to question them, you couldn't just call them. You would have to write to them with a letter from the editor of the *FT* and then it would go through the company – it is very bureaucratic – and then finally you would get a reply saying that an interview could not be given at the time, perhaps next year etc. So media relations were very bad (in interview: October 26, 1999).

The 1995 MORI poll shows that Shell was not, at that time, viewed as being open.

Shell UK and Shell Exploration and Production

Shell UK was the Royal Dutch/Shell company at the centre of the crisis. Its main oil and gas producing subsidiary, Shell Exploration and Production (Shell Expro), was the operating company in charge of Brent Spar. Shell Expro itself was a joint venture between Shell and Esso, so Brent Spar was 50 per cent owned by Esso, a division of Exxon. Nevertheless, throughout the crisis Esso and Exxon remained out of the situation by claiming that, as Shell Expro was the operating company and the legal owner, Brent Spar was its responsibility. Therefore, Shell UK and Shell Expro dealt with the crisis.

In 1994, Shell Expro was responsible for approximately one quarter of all UK oil and gas production. The situation in the 1990s was that the production of the giant first generation North Sea fields, holding billions of tons of recoverable oil and gas reserves, was starting to wane. Moreover, gas production had taken over from the production of oil as being the major concern for operators in the North Sea. A study of the Brent Spar case argues that:

> The ageing facilities (in the North Sea) had become costly to main-tain and the few newly found reserves were increasingly located in small fields which were difficult to exploit economically (in 1995, a barrel of oil was one third its 1980 price in real terms). Additionally, gas production had gained more importance and platforms in the North Sea were being modified to produce gas rather than oil (Winter and Schweinsberg, *'The Brent Spar Platform Controversy'*, International Institute for Management Development 1996: Section A: 2–3).

Shell Expro had over the course of three years contracted a number of feasibility studies for the disposal of the Spar and had consulted a number of not-for-profit organisations and five different commercial fishing associations. All of them had accepted the position of Shell UK, i.e. that deep sea disposal was more favourable than land disposal in safety, cost and environmental terms.

Brent Spar

The Brent oil and gas field is located in the northern North Sea and was discovered as an oil and gas producing site in the early 1970s. Since the discovery of the site, Shell and Esso had spent an approximate £7 billion on development and operation. In 1995, they were investing a further £1.3 billion to redevelop the field. This redevelopment involved changing the management of the reservoir so that the field would increasingly produce gas rather than oil, which meant that Shell Expro's three production platforms in the Brent field required extensive alterations. The disposal of the Brent Spar, an oil storage and loading facility, was a stage in the process towards the concentration on gas rather than oil in the North Sea. The Spar was to be decommissioned as it had been made obsolete by the Brent pipeline. It was also old, having been installed in 1976; it was in operation until 1991, when it was decommissioned and plans were initiated for its disposal.[6]

Although oil companies had previously undertaken sea disposal of derelict structures, the sea disposal of the Brent Spar was the first time that an installation of its size was to be disposed of in such a manner.

Shell's description of the Brent Spar emphasised its size and uniqueness:

> Like an iceberg, most of its bulk, mainly the six segmented storage tanks, is beneath the water's surface. At 14500 tonnes, the Spar weighs about the same as two thousand double-decker buses, and with a height of 141 metres, it is longer than a football field floating on its end. Its huge tanks displace 66500 tonnes of water – a capacity that means they could hold the equivalent of almost four Big Bens. Apart from the waters to the North of Shetland, most of the North Sea is too shallow to accommodate it. The Brent Spar...acted as a tanker loading facility for the whole of the Brent Field (Shell UK *'Frequently Asked Questions'*, internet site: http://www.shellexpro. brentspar.com).[7]

The company's description of the Spar countered Greenpeace's claim that it would set a precedent for disposing of other redundant structures in the North Sea. Moreover, because of the size of the Spar, and as it was in waters deeper than 75 m, it did not, according to national and international regulations, need to be removed in its entirety. 'The Troll', the largest oil storage buoy in the world at the time, was owned by Norway and weighed a million tonnes. It was Norway and the UK, the only countries with structures in waters deeper than 75 m, which strongly defended sea disposal and a case-by-case approach. Greenpeace wholly rejected this stance; for Greenpeace, the sea disposal option was totally unacceptable in any circumstance.

When Shell again had to review other options for dealing with the Spar, after the sea disposal plan was relinquished in June 1995, the Norwegian government gave Shell permission to moor it in their waters. The Brent Spar was towed to and remained in Erfjord, north of Stavanger in the Rogoland county of Norway, from 1995 till 1999. In January 1998, Shell Expro announced that a re-use solution proposed by Wood – GMC, an engineering company, was the preferred Best Practicable Environmental Option (BPEO).[8] The plan was to cut the hull of the Brent Spar into slices and use these as the foundation for a new quay at Mekjavik in Stavanger, Norway. This plan went ahead without disruption and the deconstruction of Brent Spar was completed on July 10, 1999, when the last cut and cleaned ring sections of the buoy's hull were placed on the seabed to form the base of the quay.

The cost of the dismantling project carried out by Shell/Wood – GMC was £41 million and, 'taking into account the cost of the original aborted deep sea disposal project ... the total cost of decommissioning Brent Spar amounts to £60 million' (Shell Expro Press Release: September 1, 1999). The decommissioning of Brent Spar had taken a total of eight years to complete and a sea disposal project originally anticipated to proceed without interruption had exerted a pecuniary cost as well as damage to relationships and reputations. Events had not proceeded according to plan and an environmental campaign, that subsequently became renowned for its efficiency, was largely responsible.

Greenpeace and its campaign

Since its establishment in 1971, Greenpeace had cultivated a reputation as an altruistic guardian of the environment, and as a force to guard against corporate and governmental activities that could harm the environment.

In 1995, Greenpeace had 40 offices worldwide and employed approximately 900 people. The national organisations were autonomous and were linked to Greenpeace International, Greenpeace's headquarters based in Amsterdam, through a licensing agreement. Winter and Schweinsberg (1996), in an academic examination of this case, argue that decision-making in Greenpeace was concentrated within a small group of elected representatives; for example, the German organisation's steering committee consisted of 40 voting members, in contrast to its country-wide membership of 507,000.

Through its environmental activism, Greenpeace had experience of how to gain publicity for its views through dramatic direct actions:

> From its 'Save the Whales' campaign to its protests of French nuclear tests in the South Pacific, Greenpeace members were seen – via television and newspapers – selflessly and bravely putting their lives on the line for environmental causes. With virtually every campaign, they gained public support and credibility (Winter and Schweinsberg 1996: Section A: 6).

Winter and Schweinsberg's argument is that Greenpeace knew there was a direct relationship between media coverage of its protests and the amount of contributions it received; in 1995 Greenpeace was experiencing a lull and therefore stood to benefit from a campaign that could attract publicity, and it was for this reason that Greenpeace campaigned against the Brent Spar disposal.

Greenpeace, since the campaign, has directly taken issue with this interpretation, stating that it is:

> ... one of the most widespread myths of the Brent Spar ...[that] it was a good photo opportunity for an organization faced (in some countries) with a decline of its membership and its visibility (Rose 1998: 40).

Nevertheless, Greenpeace accepts that 'the Brent Spar campaign is the single most obvious Greenpeace success of recent years' (Rose 1998: 18). That the campaign was beneficial to Greenpeace need not deny Greenpeace its claim that it campaigned on the basis of a principle that was very important to the organisation: not using the oceans as rubbish tips.

Still, Greenpeace decided to campaign on the basis of careful consideration of whether a campaign would be successful. The Director of Greenpeace Germany in 1995, Thilo Bode, explained how he made the crucial decision to initiate the Brent Spar campaign:[9]

We have a checklist at Greenpeace that helps us evaluate potential campaigns. There are fifteen possible requirements and the Brent Spar fulfilled all of them. There was a clear goal with a feasible solution; the issues were easy to understand; the Spar was a powerful visual symbol; the protest would destroy the image of the opponent; and so on ... .[10]

From the outset there were plans to conduct this campaign visually and dramatically with the aim of attracting media interest and, in particular, television coverage. The very existence of a checklist, which lists the qualities desirable for efficient campaigns as ones that seek to attract media coverage, demonstrates how media 'savvy' and media-centred the organisation was. It was decided that the campaign ought to be run from the Spar because this would be sensational and would provide a platform from which Greenpeace could air its views. The occupation of the Brent Spar by Greenpeace was considered to be more effective than other strategies:

> By getting there before Shell started moving the 'Spar, and stopping them, we could hope to challenge and expose ... in a way which was impossible in the melee of White Papers, green TV debates and earnest reports on environmental auditing (Rose 1998: 9).

Greenpeace's Brent Spar campaign director, Chris Rose, recalls how the occupation plan came about and his decision to send video pictures digitally from the Spar to television studios:

> A proposal to occupy it [the Brent Spar] for as long as possible with an 'Antarctic- style base camp' came first from Rick Le Coyte, a campaigner in Greenpeace UK, and Gijs Thieme, a gentle giant Dutchman...They wrote: 'Rationale: Essentially a sea-dumping issue. The proposed dumping represents a dangerous precedent for the disposal of 60 other UK North Sea off-shore oil and gas installations and approximately 40 Norwegian installations.' I wrote on my copy: 'Looks great to me – can I come? Who's going to pay? Does the logistical capacity exist?? How about turning it into a TV station by putting the squisher on it?' (The 'squisher' compresses video pictures for satellite relay) (Rose 1998: 10).

Greenpeace's plan was to direct media attention to the planned disposal, and they succeeded in doing this.[11] Shell had announced its disposal plan on February 16, 1995 and this had received some media coverage which mainly announced, not criticised, what Shell intended to do. It was not until Greenpeace began its campaign that the media reported the sea disposal plan as problematic. Extensive media interest in the Brent Spar followed rather than preceded Greenpeace's action, which demonstrates what often precipitates crises, especially for organisations such as Shell. The media had not initially considered the disposal to be a worthwhile story. Chris Rose admits this to have been the case:

> Even though environmental correspondents who were 'experts' in their own domain had decreed that it [the disposal of Brent Spar] was not an issue, the public campaign [initiated by Greenpeace] had created the largest environmental issue for years (Rose 1998: 138).

Greenpeace, in effect, 'created' the story as a consequence of its action in boarding the Spar. For instance, the day after the 'occupation', the British press and television news reported that move, head-lining Greenpeace's action.[12] Moreover, Greenpeace planned to remain on the Spar for as long as it took to change Shell's decision:

> The Greenpeace 'Spar Crew'...[had] set up a radio room and a wind generator ... and imported tomato seeds and compost in prepara-tion for a long stay. After a few days I left the Spar for the diminut-ive *Moby Dick*, which served as the Greenpeace support vessel. From there we could talk to the world ... (Rose 1998: 13).

Talking to the world was the central concern in a campaign which intended to make Shell's plan problematic and, in doing so, put pres-sure on Shell to relinquish it. The media were essential for Greenpeace because they could publicise its claims and gain support for its views and, as a pressure group with experience of campaigning tactics, Greenpeace was proficient at gaining media interest and responding to media requests for information.

The campaign was consciously media-directed and the pressure group was also aware that their campaign techniques would work with the media, a sentiment expressed by Thilo Bode: 'Many media like sen-sation. They like the spectacular side of our work.'[13] Thilo Bode admits that Greenpeace is an organisation that works with 'pictures, images and emotions'.[14] Greenpeace is also aware that their campaigns exert pressure on corporations, and claims that it intends to attack a company's image and mobilise public opinion against it:

> Corporations are very susceptible to public opinion and vulnerable to consumer pressure. Companies face a trade-off between the cost of addressing an environmental issue and the cost of damage to their image if they do not. Our interest is to make image a very expensive issue.[15]

Greenpeace focused its campaign on Shell rather than the UK government, perhaps because it was perceived to be easier to influence a company than a government. Additionally, even though the campaign was publicised worldwide, Greenpeace focused its campaign efforts on the UK and Germany. In both countries, the main claims discussed below were the basis of the campaign. However, Winter and Schweinsberg's (1996) analysis of this campaign argues that Greenpeace emphasised different elements of the claims in the UK and in Germany. They maintain that in the UK the level of toxicity within the Spar was the angle taken and scientific studies were cited to refute Shell's case whereas in Germany the campaign took the line that the Spar was a figurehead of 'today's waste society' (Winter and Schweinsberg 1996 Section B: 2). The authors argue that Greenpeace took strategic decisions in choosing the targets for their campaigns.

Firstly, they contend that Greenpeace targeted Germany because of its accurate deduction that the German population was sensitive to environmental issues and, in particular, favoured recycling, which meant that in Germany Greenpeace's case would gain a sympathetic reception. This view proved correct, as it was in Germany that consumer boycotts and protests were most visible, and the German government was one of the first to support Greenpeace's views.

A second strategic decision that Greenpeace made, Winter and Schweinsberg argue, was the targeting of Shell Germany because it considered Shell Germany to be a good ally which could influence Shell UK. Shell Germany had a limited involvement in the production and distribution of oil and gas products, while also being an important organisation in the Royal Dutch/Shell Group. Therefore, Greenpeace calculated that Shell Germany could and would exert pressure on Shell UK to abandon the sea disposal of the Brent Spar, ultimately the responsibility of Shell UK. That too proved an effective strategic decision.

As I have indicated, Greenpeace made other strategic decisions in order to ensure that the campaign was a success. The decision to conduct a visual campaign by using technology to relay images from the Spar to TV studios, for instance, was one such tactical decision that would prove to be influential. The organisation also used seemingly every communication medium. By publicising their claims on 'Greennet', the worldwide database used by Greenpeace, Friends of the Earth, WWF and other groups, it enabled every activist in the world to have access to the issue and campaign quickly. Aboard the Brent Spar, Greenpeace Press Officer Desley Mather kept a diary of the occupation and the daily entries were accessible to anyone on the Greenpeace website. Greenpeace pursued publicity because this is a routine, and indeed a central, component of campaign procedure; the success of a campaign is directly contingent on the amount of favourable publicity that can be gained for it (Wilson and Andrews 1993).

Claims and counterclaims: An outline of the claims made by Greenpeace and Shell

Both Greenpeace and Shell had their own interpretations and each sought to frame the issue accordingly.

Greenpeace's campaign was based on the following arguments:[16]

- the method of disposal was unacceptable; the ocean should not be used as a dumping site for oil industry installations, which was an act akin to littering;
- there were other available ways of dealing with the Brent Spar on land and that the other options were not properly considered by Shell because of concerns about costs;
- in choosing the sea disposal method, Shell had taken the cheapest option and, therefore, had put cost considerations above environmental considerations;
- the sea disposal of the Brent Spar would set a precedent for the disposal of other decommissioned installations in the North Sea, which would result in mass contamination of the oceans;
- no independent investigation was made into the contents of the Spar and, because of this, the environmental impact could not be properly assessed.

Additionally, as the campaign progressed, Greenpeace maintained that its samples from a storage tank, taken during the Spar occupation, showed that the Spar contained 5500 tonnes of oil which would be sunk along with it. Greenpeace also stated that the Brent Spar contained toxic materials which would damage the marine environment.

Shell responded to each of these claims by stating:

> Shell UK ensured that the Spar disposal would be carried out in the most responsible way possible by undertaking careful analyses of the options – some 30 studies, many of them by independent third parties, over three years. These studies concluded that disposal of the Spar in deep water was the best option on all considerations – environmental, safety, occupational health and economic.[17]

Therefore, Shell's riposte to Greenpeace was that:

> As with other Shell decisions concerning the environment, cost was not the determining factor. Although deep water disposal would indeed be cheaper, the other factors (environmental, safety, occupational health) all favour deep water disposal.

In all of its communications Shell emphasised that the disposal would take place in 'deep water'/'deep sea'. That was because the depths of oceans determine the type of marine life present, their resilience to the effects of the disposal and hence also the extent of environmental damage.

Secondly, Shell claimed:

> It is not the case and never has been that the Spar should set a precedent. The Brent Spar is a most unusual installation – arguably unique; there is no comparable structure elsewhere in the North Sea. The vast majority of North Sea structures will be completely removed, brought ashore and dismantled.

Shell also drew attention to the regulations governing disposals, thereby defending its stance and countering Greenpeace's suggestion that the Spar would set a precedent:

> All but 50 of the 220 installations in the UK North Sea are in less than 75 metres of water and, in accordance with international guidelines, are required to be totally removed. The remainder of the installations in deeper water will be approached on a case by case basis – looking at environmental, health and safety and cost considerations. The majority of these will also end up on land.

Shell's claim that the disposal of Brent Spar would not set a precedent was backed by UK government regulations. However, Greenpeace continually stated that sea disposal of the Brent Spar would set a precedent. It was a powerful contention that stressed the damage that could result from allowing the disposal of the one instance of the Spar.

Thirdly, Shell disputed Greenpeace's claim that the Spar contained vast amounts of toxic substances and oil:

> ...Greenpeace claimed that the Spar was 14500 tonnes of toxic litter (14500 tonnes is actually the weight of the Spar and its ballast), contained 5000 tonnes of oil (what company would throw away oil worth half a million pounds?) and was to be sunk or blown up in the North Sea. None of these statements are true (*Brent Spar*, WWF 1995: 9).

Furthermore, Shell argued:

> All the studies on the Spar were carried out by experts in their field, including independent scientific institutions. An extremely detailed inventory of the Spar's contents was prepared, containing hundreds of individual items. It was submitted in full to the UK government and detailed information from it has been widely publicly available.

While Shell had compiled an inventory of the Brent Spar, following Greenpeace's sampling and claim that the storage tanks contained a certain amount of oil, Shell could not credibly provide the evidence to dispute this claim without having an independent party re-check its inventory and the contents of the Spar. That subsequently happened but, at the time, Greenpeace's claim about the amount of oil in the Brent Spar assisted its case.

In response to Greenpeace's allegation that the disposal would damage the marine environment, Shell claimed that the environmental impact would be negligible, predominantly because of the depth at which it was to be sunk:

> It is known (through scientific research into deep sea biology) that enormous natural disturbances occur in the deep oceans, far greater than any disturbance likely to have been caused by the sinking of the Spar. Many experts agree that creatures of the very deep ocean are able to deal with environmental disruption on a vast scale compared to the impact the Brent Spar would have caused.

Shell's position was that the environmental impact of its plan would be 'negligible, localised and inaccessible to the food chain' (Shell Expro Press Release: May 31, 1995). In this way, Shell was not denying that there would be an environmental impact but was justifying its action as one that would make minimal impact. Greenpeace too used the issue of how much of an environmental impact sea disposal would have in order to further its case against the disposal. But Greenpeace also maintained that the issue of what the impact would be was not as important for Greenpeace as its position that it was wrong, in principle, to discard unwanted structures in the seas (Rose 1998).

Still, and as a consequence of the campaign being fought on the grounds of environmental impact, Shell showed that other methods of disposal might be more environmentally harmful. In particular, Shell pointed to problems with what Greenpeace proposed, i.e. disposal on land:

> Onshore disposal would mean that the Spar, which is longer than a football field, would need to be rotated to a horizontal position. This would involve the risk of breaking up under the strain and causing a more damaging environmental impact in shallow waters full of marine life. Waste materials would only be buried in landfill sites. Recycling the metal would require a great deal of energy – such as to offset any saving of natural resources. The Spar is minute in relation to the Atlantic Ocean [the site of the planned disposal] – it would be like placing a pin head in a football stadium!

Shell wanted to persuade people that its chosen route was not only the best option but also of little environmental impact; for persuasive purposes, that argument was sometimes couched in metaphorical terms, as the above citation indicates. At the crux of Greenpeace's campaign, however, was that it found sea disposal to be unacceptable *in principle* as Ulrich Jurgens, Director of Communications, Greenpeace International, argued:

> I don't care about scientific arguments. I don't care if there are ten or thousand tons of hazardous waste on the platform. The question is, how does our society cope with their waste? And our message is: don't litter![18]

But it is not true that Greenpeace was unconcerned about the scientific estimations of the environmental impact of Shell's plan, as Jurgens suggested. That issue was consistently raised. However, by not focusing only on the environmental impact of the disposal of the Spar itself, Greenpeace made a sound strategic decision as it provided the organisation with more criticisms than the purely scientific arguments about the level of environmental impact the Spar's disposal would cause. Greenpeace cleverly anticipated that, as Shell had commissioned scientific impact studies, the company could and would find scientific support to counteract Greenpeace's claims about the environmental impact. Yet, it was very much the case that Greenpeace used a 'dual strategy of producing scientific evidence in favour of disposing of the oil rig on shore, and in mobilising public opinion' (Macnaghten and Urry 1998: 79).

Greenpeace also created certain impressions that benefited its case. It consistently claimed that Shell was showing 'arrogant' disregard for the environment by 'dumping' the Brent Spar. By using specific terminology such as 'dumping' to describe Shell's project, Greenpeace, as Shell also did, tried to frame the issue in an advantageous manner. The impression Greenpeace cultivated was that Shell was wantonly and clandestinely throwing away its waste. This is manifest in Chris Rose's statement:

...here in the northern North Sea was the Government[19] slipping through the gate at the end of the national garden, and conniving with Shell to dump the 'Spar at sea rather than re-use or recycle it – behaving for all the world like a couple of bad neighbours who creep out at night and craftily wheel a rusty old car into the village pond (1998: 9).

The language utilised and the impressions created were evocative and attempted to direct perceptions in a manner favourable to the campaign.

It is for this reason that Shell took issue with Greenpeace's terminology. In doing so, the company also intended to promote its own interpretation:

Dumping (throwing away without care or thought) would be unacceptable, as is throwing litter on the street or abandoning an old car. Responsible disposal means carefully managed disposal after looking at different alternatives, making the best overall choice and then carrying out disposal with due regard to health, safety, environment and cost. There are no simple solutions to managing waste materials whether on land or at sea (*Brent Spar*, WWF 1995: 9).

Greenpeace's allegations were to have a vital impact on Shell's efforts to manage the crisis. The allegations not only questioned Shell's case but were also damaging to Shell's desired reputation for being environmentally responsible.

Consultants' claims about this case

I pay close attention to the case made by Regester and Larkin (1997: 63–75), although other consultants also argue in the manner they do. They have a published critique of this case and their consultancy, the only company in the UK specialising in crisis management, advises many oil companies; prior to the Brent Spar crisis, it also advised Shell UK on crisis management (but, as Michael Regester and John Wybrew said in interviews, the consultations that took place were not in specific relation to the Spar disposal).

Although the consultants credit Greenpeace with instigating the crisis for Shell, they cite two main impetuses for the crisis: Shell's failure to prevent the crisis through issues management and Shell's failure adequately to handle developments during the crisis. A dominant view that consultants frequently volunteered in interviews, which is also found in Regester and Larkin's analysis of this case, is that Shell would not only not have encountered a crisis, but also that its management of the crisis would have been more efficient, if the company had followed their recommended courses of action.

The main argument is that there was no early management of the issue of sea disposal, and that this precipitated the crisis and exacerbated its handling. Regester and Larkin's description and critique of this case argue that this was an instance that indicates that 'an issue ignored is a crisis ensured' (1997: 63–75). Consequently, the consultants' account of this case is one that quite neatly ties up their claim regarding the value of issues management and their promotion of crisis management as an ongoing effort, necessary whether or not a crisis is present. Furthermore, the above argument places much of the responsibility for the crisis on Shell. This outlook also favours their stance that organisations can take action to prevent and handle crises better.

The general observations the consultants make are as follows:

Regarding Greenpeace, consultants argue that Greenpeace's objections, expressed in a sensationalist way, made Shell's plan problematic. Greenpeace was more successful than Shell in gaining media coverage for their claims. The media coverage given to Greenpeace's claims and activities eclipsed that given to Shell's perspective and, thereby, affected Shell's ability successfully to gain support for its case. Greenpeace's campaign gained the support of the media, general publics and politicians.

Regarding Shell, the consultants claim that the company managed the crisis inefficiently because the factors they identify as crucial to the successful management of crises were ignored and neglected. Shell, they allege, did not comprehend public perceptions, mismanaged its communications and thus could not successfully make its case to a wider audience. According to them, Shell had been ignorant of the societal conditions they identify and thus could not respond effectively. For instance, Shell wrongly assumed that because it had complied with regulations, and because its plan was lawful, problems would not be encountered. Shell had not planned for the eventuality that the mode of disposal might be disputed.

All these observations deal with and draw attention to matters they customarily highlight, that is, communications and perception management, because the consultants' portrayal of this case aims to gain support for their argument. They repeatedly suggest that this case illustrates the importance of following their recommendations, but what I find pertinent is that consultants do not view the sorts of problems Shell encountered as irresoluble. My case study asks: is the handling of crisis as straightforward as consultants present it as being?

The emerging crisis

Shell's activities prior to the protest

During September 1991 Brent Spar ceased to operate and in the following month Shell initiated decommissioning studies. A year later in, September 1992, Shell UK began discussions about the disposal of the Brent Spar with the UK regulatory authorities. During 1993 the decommissioning studies continued, and in February 1994 an Aberdeen University study endorsed deep sea disposal as the best option. On the basis of this study, Shell conducted formal consultations with the UK government, conservation bodies and fishing interests in the UK. In October 1994, a final draft of the BPEO and Impact Hypothesis was submitted by Shell to the UK Government's Department of Trade and Industry. In February 1995, the UK Government announced its intention to approve deep sea disposal and notified the other 13 contracting parties (12 nation states and the European Union) who were signatories to the Oslo Convention covering the protection of the marine environment. On the announcement of the decision for the sea disposal of the Brent Spar to European Union governments and the media, no objections were raised, no countries protested and dissent was not expressed. Why then did Shell face a crisis?

I have suggested how consultants answer that question and, given the importance they attach to this period, its investigation is particularly crucial for judging their claims.

How Greenpeace discovered the campaign

In January 1995, Gils Thieme, a Dutch Greenpeace activist, discovered the Shell-commissioned Aberdeen University study. Thieme approached Tim Birch, who was coordinating the Greenpeace involvement in the North Sea Protection Conference. That conference was the fourth of its kind. The conferences had begun in 1984 and were concerned with the environmental protection of the North Sea. While they were primarily for environment ministers of the countries bordering the North Sea, four non-governmental organisations were also included, one of which, from 1987, was Greenpeace.

Thieme tried to persuade Birch to take up the disposal as an issue for protest and told him:

> We have to do something here. This will be a big story for the summer. It has everything you need for a real scandal: visually exciting, symbolic and a strong opponent.[20]

Birch did not consider the disposal of the Brent Spar as deserving much attention and chose instead to focus the protest on chlorochemical dumping in the North Sea, note Winter and Schweinsberg. Chris Rose states that, in meetings on drafting the Declaration that ministers were to sign at the North Sea conference, Greenpeace had proposed that it should address problems of the offshore industry, but ministers had not shown any interest:

> This proposal had met with very little support indeed; as late as April 1995 the draft Ministerial Declarations to protect the North Sea (a region with approximately 600 offshore installations!) did not make any specific reference to the offshore industry (Rose 1998: 44).

Not only was there little political interest in the disposal of oil installations but Greenpeace too had initially shown little interest in this
type of operation. At that time Greenpeace had focused its campaign
efforts elsewhere, despite being concerned with the wider 'ocean
dumping' campaign which, it maintained, had been an ongoing concern since the summer of 1978 when a Greenpeace ship intercepted a
radioactive waste dumping vessel in the Atlantic (Rose 1998).

Despite his initial failure to create interest in the disposal of the Spar
within Greenpeace, Thieme remained convinced that this would be a
good issue for protest and made a series of trips to Greenpeace offices
in London, Amsterdam, Copenhagen and Hamburg seeking support for
a protest campaign. He found such support in Thilo Bode, Director of
Greenpeace Germany, who decided to take up the issue. Chris Rose,
responsible for determining campaigns in the UK, recalls his sentiments when he was first shown the plans of the Brent Spar and Shell's
decision for sea disposal:

> My reaction was simple incredulity: 'They can't be serious – they
> can't be going to dump something so vast.' It simply beggared
> belief, after a decade of ever tighter international agreements against
> dumping all sorts of waste at sea, that Shell, the 'Better Britain'[21] oil
> company, was going to commit the world's biggest act of littering.
> At that point our idea was simple: get onto it and thereby stop them
> from sinking it. [There were logistical problems.] Even so, I felt a
> strong urge to go there. The idea of simply stopping this extraordi-
> nary gross act just by being there had an attraction and simplicity
> ...' (1998: 8–9).

On April 30, 1995, nearly four months after Greenpeace had first
heard about the plans for the Spar, and three months after Shell's
public announcement, Greenpeace activists accompanied by some
journalists boarded the Brent Spar.

Events

February 16, 1995

Outlining the manner in which the company had reached the decision
to opt for sea disposal, and stressing that this was the best available
option having considered for environment, cost and safety, Shell
issued a news release announcing its plans for the Brent Spar. It is

worth quoting from this news release at length because it is Shell's first public communication about the disposal and illustrates the initial stance taken by the company:

> Disposal of the Brent Spar ... has been the subject of extensive discussions between Shell UK Exploration and Production and the Department of Trade and Industry for many months. During that period a range of disposal options has been considered ... Shell Expro has now received from the DTI approval for abandonment[22] of the Spar, which will involve ... a clean-up operation, and towing it to a designated deep water site in the North East Atlantic for disposal ... Preparations are in hand to enable the plan to be put into effect in the summer of 1995.
>
> One possible option, which was investigated closely, was onshore scrapping. However, it was concluded that this approach, involving reversing the installation process, would be technically complex ... would give no environmental benefit compared with deep-water disposal, and would involve a significantly higher cost than the approved option.
>
> Relevant parties, including environmental and fishing interests, were fully consulted.
>
> The detailed environmental impact analysis for the deep-sea disposal option ... shows ... [a]ny environmental impact of deep sea disposal would be negligible ... This method of disposal has been supported by independent evaluation.
>
> Balancing safety, environment and cost factors, deep sea disposal is the best practicable method of disposal (Shell UK Ltd, News Release: February 16, 1995).

The above shows that Shell considered it important to emphasise that land disposal was 'closely' considered and that 'independent evaluation' had judged that the environmental impact of 'deep' sea disposal would be 'negligible'. In doing so, in my estimation, and contrary to the consultants' claim, Shell addressed perceptions of sea disposal as wrong even at this early stage.

At the time of this announcement Shell did not encounter any opposition.

April 30

Heralding the start of its campaign, Greenpeace occupied the Brent Spar.

The Press Association in London announced that 'Greenpeace protesters board disused oil platform'.[23] A consequence of the media coverage of the direct action Greenpeace took (boarding the Spar) was a concomitant coverage of claims that questioned what Shell intended to do. That was a situation that had not previously existed.

May 2

Greenpeace Germany held its first press conference on the Brent Spar situation, publicising its intention to protest at the upcoming North Sea Protection conference.

May 5

The UK Government granted the formal disposal licence to Shell UK. In February the government had informed Shell UK that the licence would be issued.

May 6

Media reports started to link the North Sea Conference (scheduled to be held in June) with the disposal of the Brent Spar.

May 9

The German Ministry of the Environment protested against the disposal plan, sending a note to its British counterpart stating that the land disposal option had not been adequately examined, and citing prominent German scientists who cast doubt over Shell UK's studies of the environmental impact of sea disposal (Winter and Schweinsberg 1996). The reason for this sudden protest, as previously no opposition to the plan had been voiced, might have been Greenpeace's protest and boarding of the Spar. Greenpeace concedes that this was the case:

> On 24 March 1995, at the third meeting of the working group to draft the Ministerial Declaration, the offshore industry was off the agenda ... none of the countries' representatives showed an interest and the meeting ended. Not long after, a fourth preparatory meeting was held in Denmark, and in the meantime the occupation of the Brent Spar had started. The mood had suddenly changed. Several delegates had been instructed by their ministers to push for the inclusion of a section on the offshore industry in the Ministerial Declaration, and to demand – specifically – that the dumping of

decommissioned offshore installations be prohibited (Rose 1998: 44).

Given that European environment ministers had not shown much interest in this issue until after the Greenpeace protest on the Spar, it can be concluded that Greenpeace had raised political awareness of this issue and made ministers question the legitimacy of the sea disposal.

Although there was media interest in the story at this time, Greenpeace was unhappy with the extent of the coverage and uncertain that its campaign would be a success:

> Bode was not comfortable with the amount of media interest that Greenpeace's protest had received. Everyone on the platform was bored; Bode wondered if the activists would need to stay out on the platform until bad weather in the autumn necessitated calling the action off. The support provided to the protesters was expensive, and financially he doubted they could hold out that long. As it was, he feared that the up-front investment was lost [it had cost DM 2 million just to get the activists onto the Spar] (Winter and Schweinsberg 1996: Section B: 3).

May 12

1. Shell assisted two Aberdeen sheriffs to board the rig; they carried a court injunction for the evacuation of the protesters. At this stage the court injunction did not require the sheriffs to remove the activists physically. But the injunction required the protesters to leave and to identify themselves, and required vessels providing provisions to the activists to stop doing so. Shell's first response to the situation was to take legal measures against the activists. I asked John Wybrew, Director of Public Affairs, Shell UK, why this route was chosen. Why, for instance, did the company not speak or negotiate with Greenpeace? He replied:

> Negotiation was not considered because at the time we strongly believed that this was the best strategy – Greenpeace's action was illegal (in interview: November 18, 1999).

From the outset, Shell's press releases would compare the legality of all its actions with the illegality of Greenpeace's. In doing so, the company suggested that the chosen plan for the Brent Spar was the right one, whereas all Greenpeace's actions and claims were wrong.

2.   The activists remained on board.

3.   According to Shell's chronology of events, outlined in its Internet site on the Brent Spar crisis: 'Several independent UK scientists begin expressing support for deep water disposal as a balanced decision.' Shell, in fact, asked many of the scientists involved in the Aberdeen University study, which was the basis of Shell's decision for the disposal, to comment on the situation and, in doing so, lend legitimacy to the company's case.

4.   The Danish government condemned Shell's plans for the sea disposal.

5.   Greenpeace urged the British government to withdraw the licence 'to dump'.

May 15

Shell Germany sought the advice of their public relations consultants. According to Winter and Schweinsberg the company concluded that:

> ... the situation did not necessitate a campaign to counteract Greenpeace's activities. While surveys showed some negative consumer reactions, they were interpreted as being neither representative of the public at large or presenting a significant danger for the company. The (PR) agencies recommended that Shell support the British (scientific) studies and prepare material for Shell employees and service stations (1996: Section B: 4).

These conclusions would soon prove to be wrong and while they seem to have recognised that the service stations may have become a possible target for protest, although perhaps not a target for violence, the recommendations made soon proved to be ineffective. I would suggest that this situation, as with most, shows how difficult it is to predict developments. At this time, it was not anticipated that things would get worse or that protests would escalate.

Consultants argue that if Shell had taken an offensive stance *at this stage*, events might have proceeded differently and to Shell's advantage. My examination of Shell's press releases supports the consultants' allegation that the company counteracted Greenpeace allegations as and when they arose, a reactive policy that placed them in a defensive position. Shell also chose to attack Greenpeace's strategy as 'alarmist', 'sensational' and involving 'misinterpretations', at a late date and only at the immediate crisis stage. Consultants claim that, had Shell gone on the offensive at an earlier stage, it might have succeeded in framing the issue rather than surrendering to Greenpeace, who triumphed in providing the frame within the media coverage of this dispute.[24]

A second aspect of Shell's communications strategy that consultants criticise is that the company concentrated on reiterating the soundness and objectivity of its scientific studies. They suggest that this might have been advantageous as it demonstrated that Shell had conducted independent and objective analyses, but that nevertheless the strategy was wholly ignorant of the subjective and ideological dimensions of the sea disposal method. Those, they argue, Greenpeace utilised with success.

My analysis of Shell's news releases show that the company did indeed emphasise that its plan was based on scientific analysis and that independent scientists had arrived at the decision that the sea disposal was the least environmentally damaging option. In doing so, Shell justified its plan by evoking the legitimacy and authority afforded to science and independent scientific opinion. Consultants argue that the communications employed by Shell were unsuccessful in influencing perceptions because protest against Shell was due to an 'emotional' response to the sea disposal method. They assert that, by contrast, Greenpeace's campaign actively addressed and mirrored those subjectivities.

Greenpeace's campaign did indeed focus on the use of the ocean as a garbage dump for the oil industry's installations in the North Sea, and the terminology used within the campaign was intentionally highly evocative. It appears that Shell also was, to an extent, attuned to the effect of language as Shell had initially used the term 'abandonment' (as is evident in the first news release), which was subsequently replaced by 'disposal'. The observations of Mary Douglas (1966) are helpful in understanding the situation where the form of communication used by Greenpeace could have been more successful than that used by Shell. Douglas (1966) suggests that responses to risks are shaped by accepted ideas of purity and danger. Greenpeace both appealed to and evoked these notions, whereas Shell did not.

Both parties sought to attain dominance of their own interpretation over the other, but, unlike Shell's communications, Greenpeace's resonated and spoke to people's ideas about what was pure (oceans) and impure (unwanted and possibly contaminated oil industry equipment 'dumped' in the oceans).

May 16

Shell issued a press release in response to the UK Labour Party's (the opposition party at the time) criticism of the company. This is the first press release of its kind, as it addressed many of the criticisms made of Shell, and is therefore worth examining in depth. The above observations regarding Shell's description of the disposal are also illustrated therein.

In that press release, Shell replied to the criticism made by Frank Dobson, the Shadow Environment Minister:

> Shell UK strongly refutes the Labour Party's claim that the Government-authorised plan to dispose of the Brent Spar ... compromises accepted environmental standards for short term economic benefit.
>
> ... disposal in the deep Atlantic, some 150 miles from land and at a depth of over 6000 feet ... has been independently assessed as the best option from an environmental point of view, and in terms of several other considerations including health, safety and economic efficiency.[25]

The press release also addressed a number of criticisms made by Greenpeace. Shell devoted more attention to this than it had before as dealing with these criticisms also addressed those of other critics.

In an extensive 'Notes to Editors' Shell explained how the plan had been arrived at. In doing so, it tried to influence journalists' and editors' understanding of the process of decommissioning and, in that way, attempted to direct their representation of the situation. In this press release, Shell not only defended itself against the criticisms that were made but also attempted to sway media framing of the issue.

Firstly, the company stressed that the Brent Spar was 'not typical of offshore petroleum installations' and that it would not have set a precedent as Greenpeace alleged.

Secondly, Shell described the decommissioning process, implying that the process it had followed was routine, that it had acted in a responsible manner by consulting external interests (who had given their support), and that the company also had the authorisation of the Government.

Thirdly, Shell stressed the amount of preparatory work it had done to find the best disposal option, and the scientific considerations involved in reaching the decision for Brent Spar:

The Government endorsed the plan for the Brent Spar after several months careful consideration of the options and more than three years of painstaking analysis by Shell, the completion of fifteen separate studies on their environmental and engineering aspects, taking independent surveys and advice into account, and the careful weighing of all the environmental, safety, health and economic considerations.

Fourthly, Shell stated in the press release that it had gained governmental approval and had followed all the legal requirements:

Every aspect of UK law and regulation has been followed to the letter and to the spirit. The Government is entirely satisfied that it is also complying with the relevant aspects of international law and conventions.

All this attempted to lend authority and legitimacy to a plan that had by then become contentious.

Furthermore, the press release also responded to Greenpeace's claim that the disposal of the Spar should be dealt with on land, by maintaining that scientific studies had shown onshore disposal to be more environmentally risky:

The independent analysis of disposal options ... has shown that onshore disposal would increase the risk of an accident or an environmentally damaging incident by order of six times. Much of the waste material would end up in landfill. The options would cost four times as much, but this has not been the sole consideration. The environmental effect of the proposed deep water disposal ... where the water depth is more than 6,000 feet – is independently assessed to be negligible and very localised. There is in any event very little fish life at this extreme depth.

Shell addressed the criticism that sea disposal was chosen because it was economically attractive in order to counter the impression given by Greenpeace.

Responding to Greenpeace's claim that the Spar contained environmentally damaging substances, and that it posed a risk to the marine environment, the company also told the media about the contents of the Spar and the extent of environmental damage that those might cause:

> Before tow-out ... the structure will be stripped of almost everything on board, and the residual sources of contamination will be minimised. The irreducible sources of possible contamination left before disposal will consist of the paints and sacrificial anodes on the structure itself and up to 100 ... tonnes of sludge, consisting of 90% sand and 10% oil residues ....

Moreover, the account Shell gave minimised and made relative the environmental risk involved in the sea disposal:

> Altogether these represent such low levels of radioactivity that they fall many orders of magnitude within international standards. The level of radioactivity, for example, will be no more than would emanate from a group of granite buildings in a city such as Aberdeen.

The ample 'Notes to Editors' included in this press release supplied a defence of Shell's plan by presenting background briefings and, in providing this account, Shell sought to influence media representations of the company and its (by then, controversial) plan. But this is the first instance where Shell's communications actively addressed the media and sought their help in getting the company's messages across.

At this stage all public relations activities concerning the Brent Spar were still being conducted from Aberdeen and not from the central office in London, indicating that Shell did not conceive that the situation required a new response. Matters were left in the hands of Shell Expro (the legal owner of Brent Spar) to handle in a very routine way. At this time, Shell did not centrally control communications or launch a coordinated offensive action, possibly because the company did not envision that the situation could heighten. But protest grew and the situation worsened.

May 18

Shell UK returned to the Court of Session in Edinburgh, seeking a court order for the Greenpeace activists to be evicted.

May 19

The Scottish Court granted the order for eviction, ruling that Shell had the right forcibly to remove the protesters from Brent Spar.

May 23

1. Shell workers and the police removed Greenpeace activists, accompanying journalists and other protesters from the platform.
2. Greenpeace Germany organised protests across Germany and the German media provided extensive coverage of the protests and of the claims made by Greenpeace.
3. In the Hague, Greenpeace expressed its opposition to the plan and blocked the entrances to Royal Dutch headquarters.
4. Shell Germany asked Shell UK to move its public relations operation from Aberdeen to London in order to manage the situation better, and so that Peter Duncan (Chairman of Shell Germany) and Chris Fay (Chairman of Shell UK) could take further decisions based on their daily informal contacts.
5. The German Environmental Minister, Angelika Merkel, condemned Shell's plans.
6. Shell UK issued three press releases during the course of the day.

The first stated that at 06.07, Shell had 'reoccupied' Brent Spar and that the 'illegal occupiers' were being removed 'in a safe and controlled manner' on to the Shell vessel *Stadive* which had been due to start the final preparations before the disposal (Shell UK News Release: May 23, 1995).

The second press release announced that, at 17.00, 20 people had been removed from the Spar and two remained. It also responded to allegations that violence was involved:

> In fact it was very peaceful ... There was no real resistance just passive obstruction (Shell UK News Release: May 23, 1995).

The third and final press release of the day confirmed that all protesters had been removed from the Brent Spar 'after a team of workers gained access to a heavily barricaded area in the lower decks' (Shell UK News Release: May 23, 1995).

May 24

1. Greenpeace's petition in London for a court injunction against the sea disposal was unsuccessful.

2.   Calls for a boycott of Shell service stations started in Germany, initiated by the Junge Union (the youth organisation of Germany's ruling conservative party), and several other organisations followed suit.

May 29

Winter and Schweinsberg record that:

> Angelika Merkel [the German Environmental Minister who had previously condemned the sea disposal which the UK government supported] endorsed the British decision. After some discussion with her British counterpart John Gummer, she stated that the decision had been made according to international law. She added that she would be happy if the decision was reversed, but nevertheless she publicly accepted the British position (1996: Section B: 5).

This endorsement of the British government's and Shell's position that the decision was according to international law on this matter, as it stood at the time, was a possible result of political pressure applied by the British government to other European governments publicly to acknowledge the legality of the disposal.

May 31

Shell issued a news release expressing its rejection of all the accusations Greenpeace had made in a letter to Shell and, in doing so, aimed to persuade critics and the media that the company was following a legitimate, normal and responsible course. That was, once again, reiterated:

> The disposal plan has followed on every count the procedures, principles and standards of best international oil industry practice, within a UK regulatory regime which is amongst the most scrupulous in the world.
>
> The disposal options have been analysed with care, rigour and independence.
>
> The environmental, safety, health and economic considerations have been responsibly balanced ... The disposal plan has not become public knowledge because of a Greenpeace protest; consultations were held in 1994, the independent analyses supporting the Shell proposal were made publicly available, and all governments party to the Oslo Convention were notified months ago.
>
> The Shell reply rejects all the assertions made in the Greenpeace letter ... (Shell UK News Release: 31 May 1995).

The company restated all of the above in order to counter Greenpeace's suggestion that the disposal plan was a cheap and inconsiderate judgement. Again, Shell emphasised the greater environmental and other risks of onshore disposal. But, for the very first time, Shell also strongly attacked Greenpeace and its strategy, denouncing Greenpeace's campaign tactics as alarmist and its objectives as simplistic:

> Dr Chris Fay, Chairman and Chief Executive of Shell UK Limited, has replied to a letter from Greenpeace International which makes a number of incorrect and unjustifiably alarmist assertions ... Specific Greenpeace statements about the contents of the Spar are overstated and irresponsibly alarmist ... Dr Fay's letter concludes:

> 'I unequivocally reject your assertion that Shell UK is prepared to treat the environment with "contempt". Such a comment ignores the facts relating to our careful and positive environmental management. It also highlights the contrast between those of us who are engaged in the painstaking process of seeking responsible balanced solutions and those, like yourselves, who focus only on the problems' (Shell UK News Release: 31 May 1995).

Those statements indicate Shell's more combative posture as the company alleged that Greenpeace had distorted, manipulated and impeded accurate interpretation of its disposal plan, which it continued to defend. This is a more proactive position, and one that consultants consider to be a good manoeuvre, but Shell took this position only at a late date. By the time Shell attacked Greenpeace's campaign, Greenpeace's allegations had been widely publicised.

June 1

Greenpeace Germany's Director, Thilo Bode, and Shell Germany's Chairman, Peter Duncan, met to discuss the situation. Winter and Schweinsberg (1996) observe that Duncan congratulated Greenpeace for the physical agility shown by those Greenpeace members who boarded the Spar. Duncan also conveyed to Greenpeace that he had no influence over Shell UK and had no say in Shell Expro's decision to dispose of the Brent Spar. Bode is said to have replied that Greenpeace was not responsible for Shell's corporate structure and suggested that Duncan speak to Chris Fay, Chairman of Shell UK, as Fay was refusing to speak to Greenpeace Germany.

Bode conveyed to Duncan that Greenpeace would continue its protest for several weeks and, was not about to back down. He outlined what this protest would include: demonstrations at Shell service stations, letter-writing campaigns, advertisements, and that Greenpeace would accompany the Spar as it was towed towards its site of disposal (a ten-day journey from the North Sea to the Atlantic). Bode also showed Duncan a Greenpeace-commissioned survey in which 85 percent of German car owners said that they 'would support a boycott of Shell'. (Greenpeace never officially called for a boycott – but then there was no need to as one had already begun.)

Duncan stated that he would convey the contents of the meeting to the Hague and London, but he also explained that he would not act against his colleagues or make controversial statements in public (Winter and Schweinsberg 1996). Peter Duncan's statements to Greenpeace have been viewed as illustrating an empathy he felt with Greenpeace, a sentiment which he was later to make explicit in a series of public expressions of 'understanding' the position of Greenpeace. Duncan's comment about how he commiserated with Greenpeace conveyed to Greenpeace, and to a wider audience, that Shell was divided over the disposal. This may have given Greenpeace greater confidence that the disposal plan could have been forsaken if Shell Germany could convince Shell UK to do so. It seems to have been for this end that Greenpeace continued to exert pressure on Shell Germany. Furthermore, as the boycott had gained momentum in Germany, strategically Greenpeace was in a better position to apply pressure to Shell Germany rather than Shell UK. Duncan, however, was at a later date reprimanded by Shell UK.

Additionally, as the consultants argue, Shell appeared uncoordinated. The situation over Brent Spar did not, at this stage, suggest to Royal Dutch/Shell that a coordinated response was needed between the Shell companies, especially between Shell Germany (the country where much of the protest took place) and Shell UK (the owners of Brent Spar). The traditional structure might have suggested to Royal Dutch/Shell that it was sufficient for Shell UK to handle the situation. As we have seen, Greene (1985) views the decentralised structure of Royal Dutch/Shell as its strength, but in the situation with the Brent Spar its structure appears to have hindered its ability to act efficiently and coordinate its strategy at an early stage. This did eventually happen during the crisis stage but not at this time.

June 3

Shell UK announced that it would not take any legal action against the protesters who had boarded the Spar.

June 6

The boycott of Shell in Germany continued to gain momentum.

June 7

Greenpeace tried to reboard the Spar, while Shell took action to repel this attempt by using water cannon. Consultants argue that this event gained extensive media coverage worldwide as it provided visually dramatic footage (in the case of television) and (for the press and TV news) was an event that symbolised the conflict.[26]

Shell's press release once again upheld its position and branded Greenpeace's claims as 'alarmist and incorrect' (Shell UK News Release: June 7, 1995).

June 8

1. The North Sea Protection Conference, attended by environment ministers of the countries bordering the North Sea, began in Esbjerg, Denmark amidst considerable media attention.

As intended from the start of the campaign, Greenpeace used this event to publicise its protests against Shell and even constructed a replica of the Spar at the entrance to the conference. Despite having earlier failed to influence the conference agenda, Greenpeace in effect set the agenda of the conference as it was entirely devoted to the Brent Spar. The official conference agenda was to have focused on the pollution of rivers.

While Greenpeace was very visually present protesting at the conference, and was also attending the conference, Shell had to rely on the UK Environment Minister to argue the company's case. The conference was a governmental forum and, unlike Greenpeace, Shell had not been invited to participate.[27]

Greenpeace's campaign gained a crucial footing at the conference and Bode, Director of Greenpeace Germany, later remarked:

> It was astonishing the effect we had at the conference. Usually it is boring with a sad routine – the proceedings wouldn't even make the newspapers ... [Greenpeace] showed that such conferences can and *have to be* influenced (Winter and Schweinsberg 1996: Section B: 6).

2. Shell Germany's Board of Directors met with employee representatives and trade unions to discuss the controversy surrounding the

Brent Spar. The Royal Dutch/Shell CEO, Cor Herkstroter, did not want to engage in open dialogue about the situation (Winter and Schweinsberg 1996). The Board debated whether Shell should engage in a more proactive public relations campaign that criticised and made problematic the nature of Greenpeace's campaign:

> The second half of the meeting's agenda focused on the possibility that Shell Germany should begin a proactive PR campaign against the Greenpeace protest – or at the very least should change its strategy from a reactive campaign to a more offensive counter-campaign. Shell could publish a position statement and urge a more reasonable public debate. Shell Germany could also focus on the sensational nature of Greenpeace arguments against Shell Expro's original scientific studies. At the end of the meeting, however, the Shell directors decided that it was too late to begin a major media campaign and that the company should continue as before (Winter and Schweinsberg 1996: Section B: 6).

However, as I have demonstrated above, for some time before this Shell UK's press releases had taken a more aggressive tone, in particular the news releases on May 16 and 31. Therefore, there is some indication that, although Shell Germany might have officially decided that it was too late for a major media campaign, Shell UK had to some extent begun to criticise the nature of Greenpeace's campaign and its assertions.

June 9

1.   Greenpeace disclosed a confidential study conducted in 1992 (as part of Shell's commission of scientific investigation into the best disposal solution) which advocated land disposal as the least expensive method for the Brent Spar.

2.   Shell countered that the study was outdated and meaningless.

3.   On the second and final day of the North Sea conference all states except for the UK and Norway (who were the only countries to have large North Sea installations in waters deeper than 75m and, as a result, were allies in this matter), agreed that all future disposals should take place on land. Greenpeace had gained governmental support for its position and many European politicians appealed to the UK government to change its mind and revoke the licence for sea disposal.

June 10

1. Shell prepared to move the Brent Spar to its disposal site which was expected to take ten days to reach. Greenpeace activists tried to prevent Shell from separating the Spar from the anchors which had held it in place.

The consultants observe that these activities, once again being visually dramatic, gained extensive media coverage. Television coverage was virtually guaranteed, they maintain. In addition to the tugs, three Shell security boats, two of which were supposed to prevent Greenpeace from boarding the installation, surrounded the Spar. The third Shell ship had the sole objective of observing *Altaire*, Greenpeace's ship. A Royal Navy vessel monitored marine traffic in the area. Shell's two security boats hosed the Spar and surrounding areas with water cannon in order to inhibit Greenpeace's attempts to board the installation. According to Shell, water cannons were used only as a measure of self-defence, to protect their property. Consultants argue that Shell, in taking the decision to use water cannon, did not appreciate the symbolism of this action because, visually, it suggested a 'David and Goliath' combat which created compassion for Greenpeace and portrayed Shell as hostile. 'Whatever the reality of the situation, Shell found itself floundering on the shoals of worldwide media perception', argue Regester and Larkin (1997: 134). They maintain that this was because 'one image was left with many viewers', the television and newspaper pictures showed water cannon being sprayed at Greenpeace, who were consequently portrayed as 'brave', 'determined' and 'bullied' (1997: 134). It was the symbolic nature of what happened, and the importance that consultants place on the effect of symbols that make this a central aspect of their criticism of Shell's handling of the crisis:

> Emotional symbols – water cannon jets aimed at Greenpeace activists ... aerial shots of the [*Exxon Valdez*] oil spill in Alaska, the cloud hanging over Chernobyl, debris floating in the water off Long Island following the crash of TWA flight 800 ... can overwhelm and *totally negate scientific fact* (Regester and Larkin 1997: 28, original emphasis).

Consultants argue that the symbolic imagery of this event surpassed the company's presentation of its case. They criticise the company's lack of attention to others' interpretations of its actions, and the creation, however inadvertently, of damaging impressions. Winter and Schweinsberg observe that 'the responsibility for the transport was assigned to Shell UK in London, where a number of engineers were responsible for handling the crisis' (1996: Section B: 7), engineers who may understandably have been ignorant of the symbolic and presentational elements of actions taken in a situation with such extensive media coverage.

2.   Shell UK announced that the disposal would take place according to schedule.

June 11

1.   As the Spar continued its journey to the Atlantic, two Greenpeace boats carrying 30 activists and journalists followed. Shell warned Greenpeace that attempting to cut the towing cables would imperil the ships towing the Spar.

2.   In Germany media coverage of the situation was becoming increasingly sympathetic to Greenpeace's viewpoint (Winter and Schweinsberg 1996).

3.   Shell service station owners in Germany voiced concerns about the safety of the stations, as well as concern for their own personal safety.

4.   A meeting of the Oslo-Paris (Ospar) Commission, an intergovernmental organisation responsible for the prevention of marine pollution in the North Sea and the North Atlantic, met in Brussels and supported a moratorium on sea disposal of decommissioned offshore installations. One purpose of the North Sea conference was to decide what the Ospar Commission would address. The UK and Norway again opposed the recommendation for a moratorium. Under the terms of the Ospar Commission, unanimous approval of a proposal was necessary in order to bring it into law.

June 12

1.   In Germany, interest groups, politicians, religious groups and one automobile association called for a nationwide boycott of Shell service stations.

2.   Peter Duncan appeared on several television programmes to defend Shell's standpoint. He claimed to have been disappointed by the many public figures who called for a boycott without having any information on the issues and without fully considering Shell's case.

3. Media reported that Esso owned 50 per cent of Brent Spar. Esso appeared to distance itself from the controversy surrounding the disposal, as its sole response was that 'every action taken by Shell is according to law' (Winter and Schweinsberg 1996: Section B: 7). According to Esso, as the Brent Spar was operated by Shell Expro it was that company's problem. It has been suggested that fearing a rerun of the situation the company faced over its *Exxon-Valdez* oil spill in 1989, wherein the company came under criticism, Esso chose to remain out of the public eye:

> One could argue that, whereas Shell completely mismanaged the Brent Spar crisis, Esso managed that crisis very well – the company stayed out of it. Shell came out of it with damage to its reputation but Esso was untarnished (Geoffrey Hyde, Director of Crisis Management, Burson-Marsteller, in interview: August 9, 2000).

Esso quite rightly pointed out that Shell Expro was the operating company legally responsible for the Spar, but that company was a joint venture between Shell and Esso. And here was the reputation of the whole of the Royal Dutch/Shell group of companies taking a beating while Esso, and Exxon, escaped criticism and managed to do so by putting the spotlight on Shell. In any event, Shell took the heat.

4. Bomb threats were made at Shell Germany headquarters and several service stations. A letter bomb arrived at Shell Germany headquarters addressed to Peter Duncan.

Events had reached crisis point. Media attention increased worldwide as neither Greenpeace nor Shell retreated (Regester and Larkin 1997) (Winter and Schweinsberg 1996). Criticism of Shell intensified.

Over the course of the period described above, Shell seemed to be fighting a lone battle, although it had scientific backing and the support of the British and Norwegian governments. The impression conveyed within some sections of the media was that Shell was stubbornly and selfishly plodding ahead without any support for its sea disposal plan.

That period also saw the greatest amount of protest against Shell coming from Germany (where boycotts appeared to have effect as Shell Germany admitted losing sales), which would also be the situation during the immediate crisis.

Peter Duncan and Thilo Bode were in frequent contact. Duncan was convinced that Greenpeace would not back down and Bode believed that Duncan had met with Chancellor Kohl, who had told him that he would not defend Shell's position (Winter and Schweinsberg 1996: Section B).

The German government had complained to the UK government. Bode was not sure whether Shell UK would back down. On June 20, while Shell was deciding whether to abandon its plans or not and:

> ... as the Royal Dutch/Shell [Committee of Managing Directors] meeting was starting in The Hague, Bode called Duncan's office in Hamburg. Duncan returned his call and again asked for his patience and assured him that they would soon find an acceptable solution. Bode, who had received the same promises over the previous twenty days, was somewhat sceptical. In addition he was very worried about the possibility of Shell using violent methods against the protesters. He urgently appealed to Duncan for Shell to stop its show of force. Bode recalled: 'nearly every day for two weeks, I had spoken with Duncan. Almost every day, our conversation was the same. Duncan would be upset about the situation in Germany and I worried about use of violence against the protesters at sea. He would assure me that Shell would find a solution' (Winter and Schweinsberg 1996: Section B: 10).

Peter Duncan was also in daily contact with Chris Fay. However, communications between Shell UK and Shell Germany were often lacking.

For instance, Shell Germany's Director of Corporate Communications, Klaus-Peter Johanssen, learned of the Greenpeace occupation of Brent Spar the day after the event, when he was asked to comment on the situation by a television journalist. Peter Duncan found out about the events from the television. Shell UK had not informed Shell Germany of the previous day's events. All this demonstrated a lack of an overall communication strategy. Another instance was that, while Greenpeace was asserting that the sea disposal of the Brent Spar would set a precedent for future disposal and was occupying the Brent Spar, Shell Germany was not only unaware of this but had also just launched a high profile media campaign about its concern for the environment. It contained the message 'Shell Wants to Change Something'. This was a dangerous message to issue when Greenpeace was arguing that the disposal of the Spar would set a precedent.

Greenpeace's protest campaign against Shell seemed to be effective. Consultants argue that the effectiveness of the Greenpeace campaign was largely due to Shell's incompetence in anticipating possible Greenpeace protest activities. Greenpeace's occupation of the Brent

Spar had attracted media attention, as had its demonstrations and picketing of Shell petrol stations in Germany. Indeed, what may have retained media interest on the topic could have been the other activities carried out by Greenpeace, rather than just the occupation of the Spar (Hansen 2000).

A significant instance that demonstrates both Shell's inability to predict Greenpeace's protest activities and Greenpeace's targeting of sites other than the Brent Spar, in order to publicise its views, was the protest at the North Sea Protection Conference at Esbjerg. There, as we have seen, Greenpeace's protest was phenomenally successful.

The events preceding the crisis situation contributed to the heightened momentum of the events during this time. It is also a period characterised by the emergence of troublesome issues, as consultants observe.

The immediate crisis: June 14–20, 1995

During this week events took a dramatic and cumulative turn and Shell faced widespread opposition and protest, which all contributed to a crisis situation for the corporation.

June 14

1. Two gunmen fired at a Shell service station in Waldorf, Germany.

2. In the Netherlands, Shell initiated an advertising campaign in which the company focused on the minimal environmental impact of the disposal of Brent Spar.

3. Shell began an internal discussion about strategies for handling the difficult circumstances it faced. One possibility discussed was the option of aborting the project. However, this was not publicly stated, as Shell continued to maintain that it would go ahead. Additionally, there were differences of opinion within the various operating companies in the Royal Dutch/Shell Group as to the best method of handling the disposal. For instance, Shell Germany and Shell Netherlands, which were of the opinion that the sea disposal should be halted, tried to persuade Shell UK to stop its contentious disposal plan. Shell UK was immovable, backed its plans and publicly reprimanded Peter Duncan for saying that he 'understood' Greenpeace's position. However, the internal uncertainty within the corporation created internal confusion and complicated the corporation's ability to coordinate its response to the crisis.

June 15

1.   The German press reported that Cor Herkstroter (Royal Dutch CEO) was personally taking charge of the situation. Herkstroter scheduled confidential meetings with representatives from the UK and Germany. The meetings took place over the coming weekend.

2.   At the G7 meeting in Canada, Chancellor Kohl pressed John Major to stop the sea disposal.[28] Major defended Shell's decision, stating that all its actions complied with regulations and treaties, and that the disposal would go ahead as planned because this was the best possible environmental option.

3.   Greenpeace claimed that a disposal report commissioned by Shell (the Smit Report) showed that the Brent Spar could be scrapped on land for £10 million.

Shell issued a press release refuting this 'allegation as untruthful and irresponsible' (Shell UK News Release: June 15, 1995). The press release stated that the Smit Report was an earlier study which had not considered various critical factors (safety, environment etc). Shell said that such factors were considered by later studies, such as the Aberdeen University study, which demonstrated that deep water disposal was the best option. Also, Shell again asserted that the Aberdeen University study was the basis for its decision.

June 16

1.   In Hamburg a Shell service station was firebombed. 'The attackers wrote "Shell to Hell" on the wall of the station – a slogan Shell remembered from the 1980s, when it attracted widespread attention for its business proceedings in South Africa' (Winter and Schweinsberg 1996: Section B: 8).

2.   In a press conference, Thilo Bode condemned the firebombing.

3.   In Germany, politicians, religious groups, unions and small businesses endorsed a boycott, while the German press reported the enthusiasm of boycotters across Germany (Winter and Schweinsberg 1996). That was also a subject extensively reported by the British press and television reports.[29]

4.   Shell gave statements to the effect that Shell Germany had lost market share. For instance, a *'Newsnight'* programme broadcast by the

BBC on June 15 showed Peter Duncan stating that there had been a decline in business as a direct result of the Brent Spar controversy. He said: 'In terms of tangible business effects, we have very significant measurable losses of business not only with our service stations but with many of the other small businesses within which we work'. On a *Channel 4 News* programme broadcast on June 20 (following Shell's repeal of its contentious plan), John Toalster of SGST Securities, a brokerage firm, speculated how much money Shell might have lost. He argued that the loss of business was quite insignificant in terms of the total earnings of the Royal Dutch/Shell Group of companies:

> Their finances are quite strong with the group having £8 billion in cash on deposit and Germany, of course, is not particularly important in world terms as far as gasoline sales are concerned – very low profits. We could assume perhaps they might have lost about £20,000 a day, which would work out to about £7 million a year. So if [the boycotts] continued for a whole year, [losses] would be very modest in group terms but the main cost [of the incident] has been the loss of prestige, status ....

That view echoed Peter Duncan's statement on the *Newsnight* programme, where he argued that, in addition to loss of business, loss of public confidence in the company was a further and equally damaging result of the dispute over the disposal of the Brent Spar (*Newsnight*, BBC2: June 15, 1995).

5.   In response to the escalating boycott of Shell in Germany, Greenpeace Germany threatened Shell Germany with its intention to make a further financial impact:

> Bode informed Duncan that if Shell did not call off its [disposal] plan immediately, Greenpeace would communicate that Shell was also present in the heating oil market [of which Shell Germany had 35%]; a market that had so far not been affected (Winter and Schweinsberg 1996: Section B: 8).

Although Greenpeace never called for a boycott of Shell, its campaign made maximum use of the boycott that came into effect, as can be witnessed by the above quote.

6.   In a Shell Germany press conference, Duncan again expressed a certain amount of sympathy for the protesters – a sentiment Shell UK

had already reprimanded him for expressing. Duncan also incorrectly declared that the sea disposal would be postponed for some time. Shell UK denied Duncan's remark and stated that the sea disposal would take place as scheduled, on June 22. Duncan later claimed that he had been stating a personal view that it should be postponed. This instance illustrated that the different companies within Royal Dutch/Shell Group had diverse opinions about how best to dispose of Brent Spar. While Shell UK claimed to be confident about its plans, there were many instances where Shell Germany publicly questioned Shell UK's plans for the Brent Spar and appeared to agree with Greenpeace's position.

Instances such as this very starkly demonstrate not only that Shell was not a unitary body with a single voice – it is unreasonable to assume that it would be – but also that Shell had difficulty representing itself as such.

Winter and Schweinsberg (1996) note that the German media criticised Shell for its lack of coordination as contradictory information was reported. At this time, British press and television news reports also frequently represented Shell as divided.

So Shell did not present itself as speaking with one voice, a condition consultants claim is vital for handling crises. Subsequently, however, Shell attempted to adjust this situation. A direct consequence of the disparity in communications displayed that day was that Shell Germany, acting on the advice of Shell UK, stopped issuing its own press releases on the Brent Spar and from then on issued only Shell UK press releases.

7.   Greenpeace, chartering a helicopter, airlifted two activists on to the Brent Spar.

8.   Greenpeace cameramen filmed Shell security boats using water cannon in an attempt to prevent the helicopter from landing on the Spar. This was an image that television studios frequently used.

9.   Cor Herkstroter, Chris Fay and Peter Duncan scheduled a Committee of Managing Directors (CMD) meeting for June 20, two days before the scheduled date for the disposal. Herkstroter wanted to come to a final decision on the day. Should the CMD decide to abort the plans to sink the Spar, he would need the approval of the Chairman of Exxon, Lee Raymond, as Esso owned 50 per cent of Shell Exploration and Production (Expro), the legal owner of the Brent Spar. It did not, however, seem that this approval would be difficult to obtain as, throughout the crisis, Esso had left matters in Shell's hands and publicly stated that position.

The decision to hold this meeting indicates the very real internal dissension on this matter and also that, internally, the disposal plan was being re-examined and the possibility of termination was being considered. Publicly, however, Shell reported that it was confident of its stance, and press releases (such as the one cited below) continued to report this. Although the impression Shell wanted to create was that the corporation still resolutely backed the disposal, public inconsistencies of opinion that arose, most evidently between Shell Germany and Shell UK, damaged that effort.

10. Shell issued a press release which stated that the company remained committed to going ahead with its plans. The press release, once again and as others would also do, emphasised that the plan was legally right, would not set a precedent and had been scientifically proven to be the best option:

> Shell UK Ltd. remains convinced that the sinking in the deep Atlantic is the most responsible way of disposing of the Brent Spar ...
>
> In compliance with all the related national and international regulations ... independent analysis [shows] that in these special circumstances the deepwater offshore disposal option represented the most responsible balance of environmental, safety, occupational health and economic considerations (Shell UK News Release June 16, 1995).

An additional press release commented on the criticisms of various governments and prominent individuals and stated that, as a consequence of such criticism, Shell had reviewed the results of the scientific studies, re-examined its decision and remained confident about its plans. While this, previous and subsequent press releases reiterated that Shell had objectively carried out independent, scientifically sound studies and had consulted with interested parties in the UK who supported Shell, and that all its actions were according to international regulations, Shell's communications did not *explicitly* address the perception that sea disposal was wrong in principle.

The company's communications were ineffectual because they were faulty, consultants argue. They contend that what the company stated did not make any difference because it did not address the fact that a large number of individuals and groups found the sea disposal method to be wrong in principle. Consultants claim that this is why people protested, not because they did not fully appreciate the procedures Shell had taken, i.e. what Shell's communications emphasised.

However, the type of statements Shell made might have been an attempt to deal with that very issue. Shell's communications did not explicitly state this but, nevertheless, may have addressed the perception that sea disposal was wrong by pointing to the legal and scientific case. But consultants allege that, although Shell reiterated those arguments, people would not have eventually come to accept the company's case as they did not care for this type of argument.

How consultants determine that most people protested because they believed sea disposal to be fundamentally wrong is not clear. It appears that consultants speculate that this was so. Whether everyone opposed to Shell's plan was opposed on that basis is presumed and inconclusive. Nevertheless, consultants draw attention to an important point: the format of Greenpeace's communications and the types of claims made might have been more successful than Shell's for reasons other than what Shell said in its press releases. This could explain the difficulty Shell had in gaining support for its case, and the following chapter discusses this.

June 17

1.   Greenpeace issued a press release stating that the Brent Spar contained 5500 tonnes of oil. Greenpeace based its claims on samples taken by activists during the May occupation of Brent Spar. An independent analysis of these samples by the University of Exeter had revealed that Shell's estimate of the oil remaining in Brent Spar was wrong, Greenpeace stated.

2.   Shell immediately countered Greenpeace's statement in a press release stating that the accusations were totally false, and also criticising Greenpeace:

> Shell ... totally refutes allegations from Greenpeace that over 5000 tonnes of oil remains in the storage tanks of the Brent Spar.
> The contents of the storage tanks on the Spar were flushed out into a tanker in 1991 when the facility was decommissioned, leaving only seawater.
> Samples ... were taken from the storage tanks ... and the results included in the submissions to the Government. These results have also been made public and have been widely reported.
> Shell UK believes that this is yet another example of how Greenpeace are wilfully misleading the public with false and unsubstantiated information (Shell UK News Release, June 17, 1995).

3. In a further press release Shell again criticised Greenpeace and expressed faith in their customers and appealed to them not to base their judgements on Greenpeace's allegations. Once again, Shell repeated the legality of its actions, and that its decision on the disposal method was based on sound scientific investigation as well as consideration for the environment. And Shell also took an offensive stance against Greenpeace:

> It would appear that the so called day of action at Shell service stations called for by Greenpeace has barely occurred. It appears that demonstrators arrived at only a handful of service stations. This has been yet another attempt by Greenpeace to alarm people with inaccurate and misleading information. We believe our customers are capable of balancing the inaccurate and alarmist claims of Greenpeace against the facts, which are that disposal of the Brent Spar in the deep Atlantic poses negligible threat to the marine environment, and is the best all-round solution ... Disposal onshore would have no environmental benefit while safety and occupational health risks would be six times greater. This solution has been painstakingly analysed by independent experts and approved by the UK Government in accordance with all its international obligations. Shell is sympathetic to concerns which misleading allegations may have raised amongst customers and will reply and explain fully to any customer who contacts us (Shell UK News Release, June 17, 1995–6.00 pm).

Shell at this stage can be seen to be trying to contain the crisis. It clearly did not want to see the same type and scale of protests taking place in the UK as were occurring in Germany. The company also appeared willing to communicate directly with its customers; a commendable strategy, according to consultants. It was one that was designed to be a preventative measure against boycotts.

June 18

1.   Greenpeace placed a tender offer in several European newspapers for bids on the dismantling of the Spar. Within this advertisement for tender, the financial gains to be had for onshore industries in banning the sea disposal method are explicitly stated:

> Greenpeace is inviting commercially competitive tenders for onshore dismantling of Brent Spar in order to expose [Shell's] costs.

Greenpeace believes that once these costs are made public, Shell's justification for off-shore disposal will collapse.

Once the sea-disposal route is closed, installations will be dismantled on land. Some 400 other off-shore installations will become available for dismantling over the next few decades.

The advantages to the on-shore industries of this possibility are obvious.[30]

2.   Greenpeace cited another study commissioned by Shell (the HeereMac study) as evidence that onshore disposal would involve lower costs.

3.   Shell rejected this in a press release, claiming that once again the study was taken out of context and distorted by Greenpeace.

The Greenpeace strategy of using scientific studies commissioned by Shell and reinterpreting such findings is one which Shell came up against throughout this period, and this was an effective Greenpeace tactic because it burdened Shell. Every time Greenpeace reported such a study, Shell had publicly to explain why the company had rejected it. Not only was this time-consuming, but it also complicated the issue because of the complex scientific nature of the studies. Shell had to explain the science and its decision, whereas Greenpeace questioned it without having to explain it to the extent required of Shell.

Both parties had scientific backing for the claims and the claims they both made about the environmental risks of the disposal were conducted in and through science. Despite Greenpeace's claim that its campaign was not just about scientific risk analysis, but about the *principle* of sea disposal, scientific arguments were used to 'disprove' Shell's case.

The scientific discourse that Shell and Greenpeace employed, partly because of its necessity in demonstrating environmental impact, created problems for Shell. The way in which science and scientists arrive at the calculation of risks as a matter of probability, within which scientific uncertainty is a condition of the exercise, was a factor that made Shell's argument problematic by making it questionable. The (in-built) uncertainty allowed Greenpeace to cast doubt on scientific findings that the deep sea disposal method was the best environmental option.

Greenpeace's attack on the scientific basis of the disposal method chosen by Shell, through scientific arguments of its own, was an attack on the fundamentals of Shell's case. Moreover, the claims and counter-claims regarding the scientific validity of Shell's plan complicated that plan by creating confusion and distrust about whether it was as appropriate as Shell claimed.

The observations of Beck (1992; 2000) and Giddens (1996; 2000) regarding risk construction are helpful in understanding the situation Shell encountered, in which its arguments were open to criticism despite being scientific. Their analysis of the construction of risks centrally considers the use of scientific discourse, which they view as being necessitated by the condition that risks are scientifically calculated. They argue that the use of a discourse, with its inherent uncertainties, leaves risk construction particularly open and malleable. A condition of that, they observe, is that the understanding of risks is ultimately dependent on factors other than the scientific arguments about them. That observation explains how Greenpeace was able to counteract and create problems for Shell's case (that the sea disposal would not damage the marine ecology) despite the company's appeal to science to justify its action. The wider implications of this will be discussed in the following chapter but the immediate effect was Shell had difficulty in persuading people of the merits of its case, and consequently in managing the crisis.

4.   Shell cancelled its planned 25th anniversary celebration of the Shell Better Britain Campaign, a corporate social and environmental responsibility initiative. The campaign's principal activity was to support conservation projects carried out by volunteer groups in the UK by providing grants, information and advice. In a second press release issued on the day, Shell explained the reasons for the cancellation:

> The decision to postpone was taken by Shell UK, not because of any reluctance by our environmental partners to attend, but because an alarmist and inaccurate campaign by Greenpeace ... has led to an emotional and confused climate in which, for the present, it would not have been appropriate or considerate to the Campaign's many partners to be invited to celebrate the very real environmental achievements of the Shell Better Britain Campaign over 25 years (Shell UK News Release June 18, 1995–6 p.m.).

The press release went on once again to repeat that the disposal plan was based on scientific studies which demonstrated that it was the best environmental option.

5.   In a third press release Shell responded to UK opposition politicians' criticisms. The politicians had supported Greenpeace's campaign and called for boycotts of Shell. Shell's growing disbelief and exasperation about the situation is evident in its criticism of this new development:

It is disappointing that some opposition spokesmen, including Mr Dobson, are not prepared to acknowledge and defend the established framework of policy, regulation and standards which is the essential basis for business enterprise, investment and employment.

Dr Chris Fay, Chairman and Chief Executive of Shell UK, said: 'It concerns us that some politicians appear to be suggesting that we should not take account of safety and occupational health risks in reaching a disposal decision.'

The deepwater disposal plan ... which the Government has authorised, complies fully with established international regulatory principles and standards and is the most responsible course available to us (Shell UK News Release June 18, 1995–6 p.m.).

In Germany, there were new media reports of Shell service station firebombings in the German towns of Buxtehude and Brandenburg (Winter and Schweinsberg 1996). UK press and television reports also focused on the intensifying character of the situation. In the UK, protests and boycotts of Shell were on a smaller scale than elsewhere. Protests and boycotts were taking place in continental Europe but were most acute in Germany, where protesters threatened to damage 200 Shell service stations. Fifty were subsequently damaged, two firebombed and one raked with bullets.

June 19

1.   The Brent Spar, which had been on the move towards its disposal site for the preceding nine days, was, on this day, approximately 100 km from the chosen site in the Atlantic.

2.   John Major defended Shell's position and announced that the disposal would take place according to schedule on the evening of the 22nd.

3.   Greenpeace maintained its stance and its activists remained on the Spar. A Greenpeace spokesman asserted that 'If Shell wants to sink the platform with two Greenpeace members on board, they can do it. We will not leave the platform.' The impression this conveyed was damaging to Shell because it suggested that the environmental risks of Shell's planned operation were as damaging as Greenpeace claimed – worth dying for. Also, a negative image of the corporation may have been conveyed as it proceeded with the operation despite the presence of activists willing to sacrifice themselves.

Shell UK referred to the Greenpeace strategy as highly irresponsible and initiated confidential plans with the UK government to remove the Greenpeace members from the Spar. Neither party backed down.

June 20

1.   Two more Greenpeace activists were lowered by helicopter on to the Spar.

2.   Shell again used water cannon to repel Greenpeace's protest efforts.

3.   Greenpeace stated that the Spar contained 4500 litres of Glyoxal, a highly toxic chemical substance, which legally had to be disposed of on land. Greenpeace called for an immediate halt.

4.   Shell UK, with the help of the UK government, had arranged for two chartered helicopters at a naval base on the Isle of Lewis to carry an anti-terrorist unit from the Royal Navy's Special Boat Service. Their assignment was forcibly to remove the activists on the Spar. An RAF plane circled the area and sent reconnaissance reports back to the air base. The unit of twelve men were on standby to storm the Spar. (This plan was not public knowledge at this time, but immediately after Shell gave up its planned disposal UK press disclosed it.)

5.   The Royal Dutch/Shell meeting of the Committee of Managing Directors (CMD) took place in the Hague. They discussed possible strategies for dealing with the situation they faced. As I have said, whilst Shell had publicly expressed that it would proceed with the original plan, internally there was much dissent as to whether this was the best method, given the amount of protest encountered. The CMD meeting on this date decided the matter. Upon its completion, Chris Fay returned to the UK and proceeded directly to see the Energy Minister, Tim Eggar, at the Department of Trade and Industry, to inform the British Government that the Royal Dutch/Shell Group had formally decided to terminate its scheduled plan for deep sea disposal of the Brent Spar.

While the CMD meeting was taking place in the Hague, the British PM, John Major, who had been assured by Shell that it would proceed with its plan, defended the disposal in the House of Commons. Shell's new decision thus caused much embarrassment to the UK government, who had believed all along that Shell remained firmly committed to the sea disposal plan.

A Shell press release issued on the day explained the reasons for the decision to abort the original plan and outlined the future actions that needed to be taken. Chris Fay also publicised the views stated in the press release at a press conference and in television interviews throughout the day. The press release explained:

> Shell UK Limited still believes that deep water disposal of the Brent Spar is the best practicable environmental option, which was supported by independent studies. Shell UK ... [and] ... the UK authorities ... have handled every aspect of the approval process in accordance with established national and international policies and standards. As the disposal involved the Atlantic deep water, other governments have taken an interest and voiced strong objections. Notwithstanding the efforts to convince these governments of the validity of the approach, most of them remain strongly against deep water disposal. The European companies of the Royal Dutch/Shell Group find themselves in an untenable position and feel that it is not possible to continue without wider support from the governments participating in the Oslo-Paris Convention. Shell UK has decided to abandon deepwater disposal and ... [to consider] again the options for disposal. The Spar is still under tow ... and is now moving slowly towards Norwegian territorial waters [where it will be anchored] ... The next stage in the process will involve conducting further studies ... and will take many months. Any decision ... will depend on the outcome of these studies, further consultation with the UK government and extensive discussions with other external bodies. The resulting disposal plan will then have to be licensed by the UK government (Shell UK News Release, June 20, 1995).

Shell's new terminology for describing its plan as one that was now 'untenable' is an interesting one. As can be seen from the above statements, Shell still firmly believed that the sea disposal method was the right, and environmentally sound course. Thus they still found it defensible, despite no longer feeling that it could be retained because of external circumstances. It is perhaps this central dilemma that has made this case of great interest to many people. How can companies proceed when confronted with situations such as this? What factors contributed to what was a careful scientific plan being made questionable and finally untenable? The consultants claim they have the answers. The following chapter will consider their solutions.

Conclusions

This chapter demonstrates that events grew into a crisis and that problematic issues arose, gained momentum and became severe.

My study shows that, although Shell had made considerable efforts to safeguard the smooth operation of their planned action, had ensured that it was agreeable to potential critics and had gained the acceptance of what the company believed to have been its key publics, the company still faced a situation where its planned action became controversial and ignited criticism of the company.

Greenpeace contributed considerably to creating this crisis for Shell; it was after their campaign that the company met with opposition. Greenpeace's version of the planned sea disposal created problems for Shell by not just questioning Shell's intentions and methods but also by gaining support for their interpretation. The opposition to Shell indicated that Greenpeace was more successful than Shell at communicating their case.

Shell was faced with challenging and unexpected circumstances. My examination reveals many of the conditions that consultants identify as characteristics of crisis situations: an escalating situation, a loss of control and unexpected developments. However, it also indicates that problems were not set from the beginning; they surfaced. I believe the emergent nature of events is, as revealed by this case, one of the most defining aspects of crises.

Shell had not anticipated opposition from certain groups, or that its key publics would change from those the company had consulted (whose approval was necessary and obtained) to Greenpeace and critical publics in Europe (particularly Germany), all of whom disapproved. There was an emergence of publics who were previously insignificant to the disposal but subsequently became very significant. Opposition too emerged, as can be witnessed in the dissension of European governments who had previously accepted the company's position. These were new circumstances and they raised a whole new set of problems for Shell. It is not clear how the company could have forecast these developments, suggesting that it is the very unforeseen and emergent nature of crises that make them difficult to control.

3
Media Coverage and an Analysis of the Consultants' Interpretation of the Case

This chapter considers the consultants' criticisms of how Shell handled the crisis and, in doing so, assesses their proposals for efficient crisis management.[1]

A large part of this chapter looks at how press and television covered the Brent Spar story and, given the centrality of media representations to crisis management, this analysis is important and allows a consideration of the consultants' thinking. Further, this examination shows that the consultants' account of news coverage of the crisis was, in part, a construction manufactured by them to support their own interpretation of this crisis and their own work.

The adequacy of fit between the consultants' claims and the situation under study will also be appraised in this chapter. The assessment of those arguments in the light of the Brent Spar crisis, which they also cite, allows examination of this expert knowledge system – crisis management.

Press and television coverage of the Brent Spar story

The differing claims of media bias that Shell, Greenpeace and consultants make are described and assessed below. The analysis is informed by what media studies observe about bias and by the literature on the construction of news. An outline of the objectives and methods of this study of media coverage, which pertain to all the phases of the crisis under consideration, will also be presented here. This chapter, however, only deals with how the media covered the period already discussed, while chapter four looks at the aftermath of the crisis.

Claims made about media coverage

These claims relate to all phases of the crisis.

Shell's claims[2]

While the company initially maintained that there was a clear media bias favouring the views of Greenpeace, Shell presented a more sophisticated case after the immediate crisis was over.[3] At first Shell argued:

> This is the problem: there is a lot of misinformation. Am I supposed to react every day to misinformation the media takes in and spend all my time arguing against that misinformation when the media does not want to take in the whole story? (Chris Fay, Chairman of Shell UK, *Newsnight*, BBC2: June 20, 1995)

Shell later argued that it was not the case that the media had completely failed to cover the company's views but that the extensive use of Greenpeace footage by television news overrode the accurate portrayal of the situation in both television and press coverage. Therefore, Shell credited the use of Greenpeace's footage by the media as giving rise to a bias against the company's case.

The company made much of Greenpeace's production of video footage:

> Greenpeace have revealed that during their campaign they spent almost £350,000 on recording and transmitting television pictures alone – over a quarter of the £1.4 million total budget. On the Spar the activists installed a complete video-editing suite as used in television studios. Backed by a media base in Frankfurt, the Greenpeace communications machine used satellite transmission and sophisticated advanced computer and telecom techniques [to] transmit pictures ... .[4]

Why was it that this footage was so damaging? John Wybrew, Director of Public Affairs at Shell UK, said:

> Our task was to explain the reasons. The problem was that the arguments in favour of deep sea disposal were more complex and rational; it was difficult to stand up to Greenpeace's graphic pictures and their images, such as the David and Goliath imagery. The German media were hysterically opposed to [Shell]. The UK media was better balanced but there still was an emotional leaning towards Greenpeace and its case based on pictures (in interview: November 18, 1999).

Basically, Shell's argument was that the footage (that Greenpeace provided and television studios used) prevented accurate media portrayal of the dispute by symbolising it.

As the next chapter shows, by advancing a specific rendition of what had taken place, Shell sought to curtail damage to its reputation. An argument that contributed to that objective was what Shell said about the media coverage: it might have created a more volatile situation than needed to be the case.

In addition to offering a specific account of how the media were biased, Shell also argued that its view that television coverage was biased was justified by the television executives' own admission that this was the case. Two months after the crisis, at the 1995 National Television Festival at Edinburgh, television executives said that they should not have used Greenpeace footage because this had compromised their objectivity.[5] It is interesting that the case Shell subsequently made about media bias rests on this admission.[6]

A year after the crisis, on May 20, 1996, at a conference on the media at Cardiff University, Chris Fay, Chairman of Shell UK, advanced a further explanation for the media bias. He declared that the media's 'search for simple truths may obscure the uncertainty of reality'.[7] He went on to argue that there was a need to create a better way of reporting the complexity of environmental issues which 'were not always achieved by the media in reporting on the Brent Spar'. He also maintained that Greenpeace intended to influence and were effective in influencing media coverage because its arguments were simple, whereas Shell's were complex.

The situation here is very similar to an observation Tumber (1995) made when he wrote that, paradoxically, the accusations of corporations – that the media overplay conflict, and oversimplify issues, and do not give enough information to the public – are similar to the ones levelled by the more liberal and radical critics of the media. But it was also the case that the argument Shell made about inaccurate media coverage was conducive to the reinvention of the crisis in terms favourable to the company.

In Shell's view, media coverage had greatly contributed to the crisis:

From April 30, when Greenpeace activists and a group of mostly European journalists illegally boarded the Spar in a Greenpeace International operation, the pressure group waged an expensive, all-out publicity campaign. They used powerful modern global communications technology to speed images and messages – many of them inaccurate and exaggerated – around the world.[8]

The company claims that there was a media bias against its case. We shall see whether this was so.

Greenpeace's claims[9]

Greenpeace's view of media coverage is different from that of Shell. Greenpeace does not say much about how the media covered the immediate crisis but focus on how the media covered the aftermath.[10]

When it won the campaign against the decision of Shell and the UK government, Greenpeace argues, there was a government backlash against Greenpeace that was reflected and conducted through the media. Rose maintains that, immediately after the planned sea disposal was terminated, Greenpeace was unfairly criticised for the way in which the organisation had conducted the campaign. He also claims that the UK government engineered this:

> After the Spar turnaround it was rumoured that ministers rang around television bosses and gave them a roasting for 'their part' in the Greenpeace campaign. One well informed source (who like others will not be named) says that both senior executives of the *BBC* and *ITN* (including *Channel 4*) were called up by ministers and tackled over the use of Greenpeace footage ... Whatever actually happened, the *BBC* in particular certainly behaved as if it had something to atone for and a major debate erupted within television over the use of Video News Releases (1998: 155–6).

Attacks from the government came at a difficult time for television as it dealt with decreased budgets and technological advances, Rose argues. In so claiming, he gives an account of how the governmental criticism might have impelled media criticism of Greenpeace. The government criticism meant that television executives not only had to admit publicly to using Greenpeace's footage but also had to argue that they had been 'co-opted into misleading the public and governments' (1998: 156), Rose contends. Greenpeace, therefore, explains how television executives had come to make the statement that their coverage had been biased. The coverage was not in fact biased, Rose claims, but the (forced) admissions that it was, intended to damage Greenpeace and its past campaign.

Rose contests the television executives' statement by arguing that it is no simple matter to ascertain whether the use of Greenpeace footage resulted in a biased or deceptive coverage, and that this argument was inherently flawed:

This [allegation that television had used Greenpeace footage] was of course partly true, and if you assumed that there had been deception, then it appeared to be evidence for, or proof of that (1998: 156).

Greenpeace further declares that the organisation's well-intentioned admission of a mistake in calculating the amount of oil and its apology for having made this error was widely interpreted in the media as amounting to an apology for the whole campaign – a view Rose vehemently disputes. The case Greenpeace puts forward is that the government and the media used its admission of a mistake, along with the television executives' declaration, to promote the view that the organisation's methods were always, and fundamentally, deceitful:

In August [television executives claimed they had been manipulated by Greenpeace] and September [Greenpeace apologised for its inaccurate oil estimate] as most of Greenpeace's exhausted campaigners were on holiday or engaged in the struggle with the French military over nuclear testing in the Pacific, events conspired to create the perfect opportunity for the organization's critics to bash Greenpeace over the Spar campaign (Rose 1998: 142).

Greenpeace also claims to have suffered a loss of credibility with the media, which was a direct consequence of the Brent Spar campaign:

... some people in the media now [after the Brent Spar campaign] see it as their role to attack everything that is said in favour of an environmental campaign; where possible to ignore protests or actions on the grounds that they are 'for publicity'; and to compensate for past gullibility by simple prejudice against Greenpeace ... (Rose 1998: 164).

Despite winning the Brent Spar campaign, Rose argues, Greenpeace subsequently faced criticism and damage to its reputation, and 'the ramifications of the debacle over the *BBC* and *ITN*'s coverage have lasted to this day' (1998: 162).

Consultants' claims

The media played a major part in the crisis for Shell, consultants maintain. They argue that the media did not convey Shell's case and suggest two explanations for that.

The first is that the media are biased:

> It is inevitable that because of our increasing scepticism and lack of trust in big things, i.e. corporations and institutions, sections of the media may be biased in favour of campaign groups ... There is ... a tendency by the media to call for and critically scrutinize a company's arguments and supporting data to a much greater degree than that of a pressure group (Regester and Larkin 1997: 72–3).

This claim by consultants unintentionally raises a question about their advice: what can companies do in the face of media 'bias' which prevents and excludes their perspectives? This problem is also compounded because consultants do not suggest what companies can do given this 'bias', beyond stating that it is imperative that companies communicate in a format favoured by the media.

Opinion research supports the claim that some groups are more trusted than others, and a survey conducted by MORI, *Survey On The Views Of Oil And Energy Journalists* (1998), demonstrates that at the time of the crisis Shell was perceived by these journalists to be a closed and often difficult organisation from which to obtain information.[11] Although consultants cite diminished trust in Shell and a greater trust in Greenpeace as reasons for why the latter's case was successful, it will be seen later in this chapter whether the media failed to convey Shell's case as consultants allege.

The consultants' second explanation for what they see as the failure of Shell's communications was that Greenpeace knew how to gain media attention and for this reason gained media coverage; Greenpeace's communications appealed to the media. They claim that the format of Greenpeace's campaign prevented Shell from presenting its case to the media, who were more interested in the performance put on by Greenpeace and in covering the sensational allegations made by that organisation:

> Shell seemed unable to counteract the powerful visual icons offered by a very media aware single issue pressure group (Regester and Larkin 1997: 72);
>
> ... the concept of a 'David and Goliath' combat provides mouth-watering potential for sensational editorial (ibid.).

In contrast to Greenpeace, Shell communicated in a format that did not particularly interest the media:

Shell had difficulty explaining detailed scientific analysis succinctly, meaningfully and swiftly. By the time that some allegations were refuted more were made. In contrast, Greenpeace recognised the power of such symbolic visual images and it was the images of Greenpeace members aboard the Brent Spar being attacked by plumes of water fired from nearby vessels, which made instant news and more interesting broadcast viewing than scientific experts 'dryly' assessing the merits of the proposed decommissioning plan [Shell's chosen format for communicating its views] (Regester and Larkin 1997: 71).

What the consultants and Shell suggest, in a sense, is similar to media studies' observation of how sources influence news by appealing to news values. In a study of news access, Cottle (2000) argues that the way in which groups such as Greenpeace appeal to the media construction of news stories may allow them to frame news. Cottle's classification of the nature of published/broadcast voices in news as along two dimensions: private (addressing an individual's own circumstances, familial world and relationships)/public (addressing the world of public affairs and collective concerns), and experiential (emotionally charged or based on experience)/analytic (advancing a rationally engaged form of argument or perspective), calls attention to the fact that:

> ... environmental pressure groups also appear to deploy 'experiential/ public', as well as 'analytic/public', forms of address when accessed by the news media (Cottle 2000: 38).

He concludes:

> Perhaps this tells us something about the green agenda and its deliberate framing within, and appeal to a more personalised, localised and 'human scale' of political action (from Schumacher's earlier 'small is beautiful' to Greenpeace's more recent, 'think global, act local'). In other words, the evolving green agenda may well benefit from an 'elective affinity' with the news media's own evolving and professionally inscribed epistemological appeals (2000: 38).

By engaging processes in the media construction of news stories, sources can exert an influence. Consultants suggest that this is what Greenpeace succeeded in doing, whereas Shell did not do so.

According to the consultants, Greenpeace's views gained representation and favourable coverage whereas Shell's did not; there was an unambiguous media bias. Yet, was it the case that the media, who were entirely one-sided towards the views of Greenpeace, did not cover Shell's side of the story? Is Regester and Larkin's argument (and that of other consultants) that Shell's case was not represented by the media and was overridden by Greenpeace's case accurate?

On the claims of media bias

It is difficult to believe in the idea of a monolithic media response, which makes one wary of the charge of media bias variously made by Shell, Greenpeace and consultants. As described later in the chapter, the media are varied and structured according to different imperatives, governing principles and political leanings. That circumstance, if nothing else, makes uniform coverage doubtful. Also, the charges of 'media bias' might be motivated as that claim expedites and assists the advancement of other claims made by the three parties. For both Shell and Greenpeace, the claim that media accounts were biased can allow those accounts to be dismissed and in that way deal with unfavourable reporting. By alluding to media bias consultants can further their own account of what is now necessary in contemporary society.

Charges of media bias are quite serious matters for media practitioners who are keen to prove their objectivity and the factuality of their news reporting to their audiences. Objectivity is a canon of journalism and is the key professional ethic. However, whether objectivity can be practically achieved is a notion the sociology of the media has challenged (McNair 1999).

Gaye Tuchman (1972) suggests that the media are dependent on establishing objectivity in order to pursue their professional goals, and she observes that journalists routinely employ a particular format – the representation of opposing views – to suggest that coverage is impartial and objective.[12] Tuchman calls this process a 'strategic ritual' (1972: 661) used to achieve a self-serving goal for journalism as that profession seeks to establish credibility. Schiller (1981) notes that journalists habitually utilise that format to escape 'charges of bias or distortion, or other criticisms' (1981: 3). Therefore, even if news reports are partial to a particular view, efforts are made to suggest objective coverage because objectivity is necessary to create authority and legitimacy in the view of the audience.

The notion of objectivity is quite a recent phenomenon, Schudson (1978) argues, because journalism was openly partisan in the nineteenth century. The origin of 'objectivity' is imprecise, but it emerged as a professional standard in journalism. Schiller (1981) argues that by the end of the nineteenth century, propelled by the (positivistic) belief in an objective 'knowable' universe, journalists assumed the existence of a world 'out there' which could be accurately appropriated and made known through journalism. Journalism assumed that the objective world could be objectively reported. That idea was subsequently challenged as positivist ideas declined. Furthermore, Schudson (1978) reasons that certain developments in the 1920s and 1930s, such as the emergence of fascist dictatorships, propaganda and the new industry of public relations, also cast doubt on the idea of objective accounts. The notion that neutrality was attainable became questionable. These developments meant that objectivity as an attainable journalistic condition became replaced with the idea that objectivity was a journalistic ideal (Schudson 1978).

The criticisms of objectivity broadly fall into two categories (McNair 1999). The first claims that there is a possibility of objective journalism but that this is not being realised as journalism is consistently biased. This claim adheres to the view that journalism deliberately shapes content and presentation of the news so that certain interests and ideologies are advanced, and is therefore biased.

The second critique of objectivity is that there can be no objectivity. Objectivity cannot exist. It is impossible to be objective as there is a plurality of viewpoints and more than one account may be valid. According to this perspective, journalism is not, nor will ever be, a neutral, value-free representation of reality. This view is central to the sociology of the media, which views news and journalism as social constructions:

> ... news is never a mere recording or reporting of the world 'out there', but a synthetic, value laden account which carries within it the dominant assumptions of the ideas of the society within which it is produced (McNair 1999: 37).

News values are seen as varying across cultures and also across media. News reporting will be influenced by and will thus vary according to the news values held.

Unlike the first critique of objectivity – which sees objectivity as attainable – the above perspective that objectivity is impossible sees 'bias' as taking place in a different way:

... journalism, regardless of the integrity of individual journalists and editors, is always a selective, partial account of a reality which can never be known in its entirety by anyone (McNair 1999: 38).

However, as McNair also states, despite the above view, the assumption of objectivity remains powerful and prevalent among journalists. While it is acknowledged that attaining objectivity might be difficult, even impossible, it is still upheld as an ideal.

Given all this, it is difficult to sustain the notion of a media bias as proposed by the three main parties whose claims of media bias are being investigated here. Media bias, in the sense that particular interests are being actively and deliberately advanced, is problematic. What might have happened instead is that certain newspapers/television news could have reported the situation with Brent Spar according to their individual outlooks, values, organisational structure and culture. We shall see whether this occurred.

In analysing the claims of bias, I shall talk about 'framing' narratives and how accounts lean towards this or that position because, for reasons explained below, that approach could lead to a better understanding of how the media covered the story of Brent Spar.

On the making of news

This analysis of the media coverage will be informed by the literature on news-making, and so a brief consideration of this is presented here.[13]

Studies of the making of news differ in their description of the factors influencing news content; some emphasise the constraints on the news-making process while some point to other factors, such as the economic and the political. It is possible to take them all as adding to the understanding of the processes involved in the construction of news.

Those who own newspapers and broadcasting services, Milliband (1972) proposes, influence the journalism produced in such a manner as to serve their interests. He believes that not only do proprietors exert an influence on news content, but also that they attempt to ensure that their values and ideas are routinely reproduced and, in so doing, safeguard their prosperity and survival. Thus, a dominant class ensures that their ideology is diffused and pervasive in society (through what is said, written and shown by the media) and thus ensures its, and hence also their, dominance. Hartley (1982) also views economic and political factors as exercising an influence on news content. He argues that news poses as impartial, and must be seen as such, because it is through this condition that the dominant ideology is produced. For

Hartley, news acts, alongside other agencies, in making the dominant ideology appear natural and creating consent for hegemony. The views listed above are exemplars of a perspective that draws on the outlooks of Marx and Engels. For Hartley and for Milliband the economic base (ownership and competition for advertising revenue) determines the form of the cultural and ideological superstructure of which journalism is a part (McNair 1999). Evidence exists to suggest that ownership and control of the news media are concentrated in the hands of a few corporations and individuals: 'four corporations control about 90% of the British press; a handful control the commercial broadcasting organisations' (McNair 1999: 52). And there is also evidence to indicate that some owners seek to influence news content in a way favourable to them. Therefore, it is indisputable that the owners of the media have power, yet it is uncertain whether they always exercise that power.

A different account of the factors influential on news making, which is in some opposition to the above account, argues that accenting the political and economic side of news production says less about the output than if one were to look at the routine constraints on the news production process. From this perspective, the constraints of time and space influence what journalists produce (Rock 1973). Other examples of 'constraints' are audience expectations, demands of deadlines, resources etc. According to this outlook, an examination of the different constraints on the various medium comprising 'the media', and on individual news outlets, would explain the news content. Hence, the organisational structure influences news making.

Many scholars also argue that, in order to understand media content, one must look at the format and how the format structures content (Ericson 1987; Snow and Altheide 1991). They propose that content is secondary to format and that differences in format produce variations in content (Snow 1995). McLuhan (1964) argues that technological differences among the media influence the way in which a message would be interpreted, expressed in his famous adage 'the medium is the message'. Snow (1995) contests that view, arguing that content variations from one medium to the next are not the result of the technological character of the medium but of format or how technology is used to present content. Thus, he proposes that 'the format is the message' (1995: 83). The argument is that each medium utilises a particular format which leads to differences in how knowledge is collected and transmitted, which in turn has consequences for the knowledge structure of society (Ericson 1995).

In addition to the organisational structure, this perspective also sees the professional culture of journalism as exercising an influence on news. As discussed above, journalists must be seen as being objective and in order to achieve this there are a number of conventions that are used in constructing news stories. Tuchman's (1972) account of the routines involved in news construction is useful. It can be outlined as follows:

- Journalists must present both sides, or all sides (that are seen as credible), to the story;
- they must present supporting evidence;
- sources that are (once again, seen as) authoritative and credible must be quoted;
- opinions must be presented as someone else's and (in broadcasting) the newsreader will not give opinions directly as that would break with the conventions of objectivity;
- 'facts' are separated from 'opinion' and 'news' from 'editorial comment'.

As noted by Tuchman's description of journalistic conventions serving a 'strategic ritual', they are observed for the purposes of signifying to the audience that objectivity is being upheld and, therefore, the news report can be trusted.

That journalists are influenced by their culture and environment is something McNair (1999) sees as to be expected. But a key benefit in seeing the influence of organisational structure and professional culture on news is in explaining the existence of set formats in how news is presented by newspapers and television (this was evident in my data and is discussed later), and how that may influence understandings. Furthermore, as Rock (1973) suggests, the rituals involved in the creation of news stories explain why news is characteristically event driven and less about processes.

However, this account of how news is created was criticised for presenting an overly deterministic account of news construction, where constraints and overriding culture decide news content.

A further perspective, termed 'culturalist' (McNair 1999; Curran 1989), emerged, attempting to synthesise and develop the observations of both the above standpoints. This position views 'news' as a product of the interaction between news organisations and their (competing) sources, and other social institutions. Hence, news is not just a product of economic and political factors or professional practices and customs.

Hall et al. (1978) draw attention to how sources may influence news content. They suggest that the powerful exert a greater degree of influence over the shaping of news as a result of a preference given to them by the media as a source of information. Thus, the powerful have better access to the media, which in turn sustains their power. The powerful were thus conceived as 'primary definers' and the media as 'secondary definers', a result of their circulation of those definitions.

Later models of news-making, drawing on but also criticising the work of Hall et al., emphasise the role of sources and their definitional (social) power. Schlesinger (1991) argues against Hall et al.'s conception of a structural 'bias' towards the powerful, arguing that the notion of primary definition, as they developed it, was too close to the idea of a dominant ideology. He contests the idea of primary definition on the basis that there is often no single definition of an issue or an event's meaning. Schlesinger (1991) also suggests that the structure of access to the media (the route by which primary definitions come forth) is not fixed and varies. Different social actors compete, negotiate and contest to encourage the reproduction of their outlook by the media, Schlesinger (1991) maintains. According to him, there is a struggle for access and primary definition is the result of a complex process.

The value of this approach is in the proposition that various attempts, from a variety of sources, with the possibility of varying degrees of success, endeavour to influence media representations. Further, this viewpoint also emphasises the active role played by the media in the news construction process, as journalists are seen as holding certain values and making certain assumptions. Ericson et al. (1989) argue that news is a product of communicative relations between journalists and their sources, and that the interests of both parties appear in the news. In stating these conditions, this approach to the study of the making of news emphasises the complexity and dynamism involved in that process. Although Schlesinger and others who hold this perspective concede that access to the media is inequitable, they avoid being overly deterministic by emphasising competition between sources and their competing ideological positions. McNair (1999) observes that their account also explains why hegemonic worldviews break down and are transformed.

Moreover, this approach is particularly valuable within the context of this study, as it accounts for the existence of activities such as public relations and crisis management that seek to mould news. It gives attention to 'the various categories of source professional now active in the public arena – public relations professionals of various types, who are paid to shape the news agenda and to persuade journalists that certain definitions of events (certain 'spin' on things) are preferable to others' (McNair 1999: 64). Schlesinger, Tumber and Murdock identify investment in media and public relations by a given actor as being 'extremely important' (1995: 99) in determining source advantage. They also add that there has been a developing process of news source sophistication.

My approach to the study of how the story of the disposal of Brent Spar was reported is informed by the above discussion of the literature on news reporting and also by my description of the academic observations on the making of news (covered in chapter one). The position employed in this study is to assume that 'the media' are not simply interchangeable social actors but corporations with strong political and narrative cultures and traditions. And, following Schlesinger (1991), it will be assumed that the way in which the different newspapers and television reports reported the crisis was the result of a complex process wherein different claim-makers sought to shape news content in a way that furthered their own objectives. It will also be assumed that claim-makers and their claims can achieve legitimacy and credibility through media coverage, or coverage might undermine them (Allan et al. 2000). Holding to that notion accounts for how media coverage of the crisis might have affected or influenced the crisis.

In order to investigate whether the media reports favoured a particular interpretation of the story, Tuchman's (1972) observation of framing will be heeded and the types of frames employed and the prominence of different frames in the various news reports will be analysed. How claims and claim-makers were framed will be examined. Whether the media themselves engaged in definitional work will also be explored. Finding that they did, how that took place will be described. Also, an analysis of how claims were inflected, elaborated and interpreted by the newspaper and television reports will identify what kind of ideological work the different media engaged in.

As we have seen in the case of the Brent Spar, there were contending groups/claim-makers who attempted to win support for their views by offering their own 'frames'. As described, it will be held that the news media also took part in this process by accepting or rejecting the frames offered or by offering their own interpretations of the story. It will be assumed that this has consequences for the arguments of the claim-makers. The analysis of the news reports according to their coverage of the claims made and frames employed facilitate an understanding of how the media represented the crisis over the Brent Spar.[14]

Objectives and methods of analysing media coverage of the crisis and its aftermath

This analysis of media coverage is, for reasons of economy and practicality, restricted to UK press and television coverage of the news story of the Brent Spar in the year 1995.

Press coverage is examined through a selection of three newspapers: the *Daily Mirror*, the *Guardian* and the *Daily Telegraph*. Television coverage is analysed through an examination of *BBC*, *ITV* and *Channel 4* news programmes that covered the story of the Brent Spar.

The examination is separated into two distinct periods, i.e. the immediate crisis and its aftermath (see chapter four), because my objective is to test various factors that require an examination of both time periods.

The objectives of investigating press and television coverage of the immediate crisis period[15] are to consider the consultants' claim that there was a media bias towards Greenpeace's perspective, and to test their argument that Greenpeace's case gained representation and favourable coverage whereas Shell's case did not. That examination also addresses Shell's claims about media coverage as there is much overlap between what Shell and consultants have said about this matter.

Media coverage after Shell changed its course is also examined (in chapter four) because my argument is that Shell later managed the crisis by promoting an advantageous account of the crisis situation it had faced. The main objective of that analysis is to discover whether the types of arguments that Shell subsequently made – its crisis management – were being represented in the press and television and whether these received favourable coverage.

Content analysis was chosen as the method of this study of media coverage because it was the most suited for the practical task of assessing and summarising the messages of television and press news content. The analysis of the texts of both press and television news is guided by the news framing approach.[16] Some, such as Neuendorf (2002), would argue that this study is better described as a text analysis rather than a content analysis because it is an exclusive study of limited concerns. The term 'content analysis' is used loosely, as attention is clearly not given to every possible 'content' but to specific areas, as explained below. The type of content analysis conducted here is also descriptive because my aim is to comment on and add to the already existing findings/claims of consultants.

Using the news framing approach used by Miller et al. (1998) and Hansen (2000), the news reports were investigated in relation to certain constructed categories (described below) that relate to how the press and television framed the story of Brent Spar. In examining the claims of media bias the concept and methodological tool of frame analysis is useful for the reasons already stated. The decision to analyse the frames employed in television and press reporting of the crisis was also a response to the fact that there is a notable difference in whether a case gains representation and whether it gains favourable representation.

The coding scheme used for *both* press and television coverage was: (a) how the news reports framed Shell and Greenpeace; (b) the risks of and scientific opinion of Shell's plan; and (c) the protests against that plan. These categories of frames were developed before observation and selected because these areas were conceived as the main themes of the story as well as the key issues that can reveal media representation of the situation and the parties involved.

Although the formats of the presentation of press and television coverage (in both periods) differ, the analytical approach to examining television and press news reports according to how main parties and issues were framed is the same.

The contexts of the newspapers and television news

A consideration of the contexts is helpful in understanding the content of news, and here some background information is provided about the different media (press and television) and the different newspapers and television news on which my study focuses.

The three newspapers inspected are two broadsheets and a tabloid (*Guardian*, *Daily Telegraph* and *Daily Mirror*) each of which have their individual traditions, readerships and political leanings. For practical reasons, these three were chosen as representative of the traditional styles and formats of the British national press.

Stephen Koss (1973), a historian of the British press, argues that the press have always been partisan. However, he maintains that the post-war period brought greater press independence from political parties and government. Koss sees newspapers as having become less partisan because of changes in ownership. The new proprietors were motivated not by politics but by commercial incentives, Koss argues. Consequently, their publications were guided by purely financial concerns.

Others disagree with this view. McNair (1999) argues that the British press have always been, and have always been expected to be, partisan.

Changes in ownership, he claims, did not have any effect on this. Curran and Seaton (1991) contest the view that proprietors are only interested in profit-making and argue that some proprietors are active interventionists in news coverage, seeking not only to improve their economic standing but also to toe certain political and ideological lines. Proprietors, they claim, were not simply market-led pragmatists but also partisan and interventionist. They argue that Koss and other media historians overstate the extent to which political partisanship declined during the post-war period. National newspapers became markedly more partisan from 1974 onwards, Curran and Seaton observe, arguing that newspapers consistently supported certain political parties and views.

Editors and journalists would defend the maintenance of particular viewpoints on the basis that they have a duty to appeal to and reflect the views of their readers. Dependency on securing a distinct readership sustains that practice. Therefore, newspapers have their own traditions, established political leanings and market differences (these, within the three papers examined, are demarcated below). This is acknowledged and is the norm.

Founded in 1903, the *Daily Mirror* became radically left leaning during World War II. Churchill even called for its ban in a cabinet meeting, but instead achieved the opposite effect when that call provoked a press rally to defend the paper (Curran and Seaton 1991). However, Curran and Seaton argue that one of the immediate consequences of Churchill's attack on the paper was that it became less radical. This stance was to continue, but for a different reason. The paper took this position, Curran and Seaton observe, as a response to a decline of radicalism in the wider society and as its readership became more socially and politically heterogeneous. Therefore, it was a response to the market and to changes in public opinion. Although the paper's radicalism was muted in the post-war period, it continued to operate in a popular left-of-centre tradition. When Robert Maxwell took over ownership from Reed International, which had run the paper during the 1970s and 1980s, in a bid to maximise sales he de-radicalised the paper, and its campaigning (of which it had a long history) declined. However, Curran and Seaton argue that the *Mirror* remained committed to the Labour party, as it had always been, but showed that commitment by 'opposing the Conservative Party rather than positive advocacy of a socialist alternative' (1991: 111).

A consortium of banks and other financial institutions owned the paper at the time of the Brent Spar crisis in 1995 and, although it had lost an interventionist proprietor (Maxwell), the paper maintained its long-standing tradition of a political leaning towards the left.[17] Out of the three papers examined, the *Mirror* had the highest circulation figure at 3,266,000.[18] In 1995, the *Mirror* had the second highest circulation figures of the daily tabloids.[19] The paper was at the commercial tabloid end of the British press and had a populist, macho, working-class appeal typical of tabloids (Tunstall 1996).

That the paper followed a 'popular' rather than a 'quality' format has certain consequences for how news is presented. The 'popular' format is simple in structure and strongly opinionated and contains particular characteristics: brief items on simple themes, extensive use of iconic elements such as pictures, and emotive presentation of issues in simple vocabulary or what Ericson describes as 'colloquial expressions and parochial interests' (1995: 18).

The *Daily Telegraph*, in contrast to the *Mirror*, took a right-leaning political position. Founded in 1855, it has tended to support the Conservative Party. Conrad Black, a right-wing Canadian businessman, acquired the *Telegraph* in 1985. Curran and Seaton suggest that he exercised a more direct control on the paper after establishing a base in England in 1989. In 1995 the paper was owned by Black's Hollinger Group and had the highest circulation figures amongst what is termed the quality press. In that year the *Telegraph* was the only quality/high-brow paper to have a circulation figure (1,066,000) at the million mark.

The *Guardian*, the *Telegraph* and the *Times* are seen as the big three 'quality' newspapers. Of the three, the *Guardian* had the lowest circulation figure: 400,000 in 1995. The paper was founded in Manchester in 1821 as the *Manchester Guardian*. It was renamed in 1959 and relocated to London in 1976. The paper takes a self-defined left-leaning position: 'in the increasingly polarised climate of the late 70s and early 80s, the *Guardian's* position as the voice of the left was unchallenged … the coverage of industrial disputes including the 1983 Miners' strike defined the paper's position' (*History of the Guardian*, www.Guardianunlimited.com). McNair (1999) suggests that the paper remains 'independent' in so far as it is not owned by the large publishing organisations such as Rupert Murdoch's News International, but by shareholders organised in such a way as to guarantee the editorial integrity of the paper. The paper has a tradition of being politically left-leaning but also of often taking an independent and liberal stance.

In addition to the differentiation of these newspapers according to their varying political character and ownership, there are further characteristics that arise from whether they are broadsheets/quality or tabloids/popular. Tabloids are more popular and appeal less to a generalised readership than do the quality press:

> ... quality newspapers were protected from the economic pressure to build large circulation figures because over two-thirds of their revenue came from advertising secured by reaching small, elite audiences. Advertising thus discouraged quality papers from adopting popular editorial strategies by making it financially disadvantageous for them to dilute the class composition of their readership (Curran and Seaton 1991: 58).

Tabloids, therefore, depend far more on circulation figures than do the broadsheets, and also, because they are far more commercially oriented, tend to appeal to the lowest common denominator. Consequently, tabloids tend to be more populist and their coverage contains more entertainment news rather than a concentration on 'big' issues such as the economy.

The format differences arising from market differences (popular and quality), exercise an influence on how news is presented and reality constructed. Ericson (1995) argues that, in contrast to the tertiary (emotive) understanding presented in 'popular' formats, 'quality' formats employ primary (factual, 'what happened') and secondary (explanatory) understanding presented in an 'objective' tone. In contrast to the simple structure, vocabulary and parochial understandings of 'popular' newspaper formats, 'quality' newspapers have greater complexity in structure and vocabulary, and have longer news items and continuing stories on complex matters affecting business and political elites.

We shall see whether the newspapers' contexts, such as their individual outlooks, traditions and narrative conventions, influenced the way in which they covered the story of Brent Spar. However, it is imperative to note that, as earlier argued, objectivity is a journalistic ideal and, although newspapers often take a particular line, which they see as both reflecting and appealing to certain groups and (ideological/ political) perspectives, they still strive to present news in an 'objective' manner. But the fact of the matter is that the British press are expected to be somewhat partisan, which is quite unlike what is expected of the television broadcasters. Moreover, television news is also characteristically different from press reports in format, time and space constraints, and objectives.

The British Broadcasting Corporation (*BBC*), established in 1926, was to operate under the provisions of a Royal Charter that constituted the *BBC* as a 'public service' funded by public taxation. From the outset the *BBC* interpreted its public service role to mean that it should be a major provider of information, devoting a large proportion of its resources to news and current affairs broadcasting (McNair 1999). The *BBC* had a monopoly of televised news until 1955, when Independent Television (*ITV*) was launched.

The way in which the *BBC* was set up was to have an impact on the demands and the construction of television news. The *BBC* was supposed to be independent of market forces and of manipulation by politicians and political parties, McNair (1999) argues. It had a remit to be free from influence. However, he observes, relations between government and the broadcasters were never without difficulties and, in some respects, those rifts provided opportunities for the *BBC* to demonstrate their much vaunted independence to their audience. Efforts to show objectivity, as mentioned earlier, are routinely and strategically undertaken by journalists in order to prove their credibility and legitimacy to their audiences. The notion of impartiality was built into the creation of the *BBC* and was also extended to *ITN* news.

ITV, unlike the *BBC*, was a commercial network created by several companies. *ITV* produced its own news and current affairs programmes through Independent Television News (*ITN*), which was jointly owned by all the *ITV* companies. However, *ITN* was run on a non-profit-making basis and in 1981, when *Channel 4* came on the air, *ITN* won the contract to provide that channel's news. At the time of the Brent Spar crisis, the same provider (*ITN*) provided news to *Channel 4* and *ITV*.

Although *ITV* companies could operate on a fully commercial basis, deriving their income from the sale of advertising space, *ITN* 'was subject to the same constraints in coverage as the *BBC*'s news and current affairs service' (McNair 1999: 78). This meant that news had to be impartial. It also meant that both the *BBC* and *ITN* operated under the public service broadcasting remit, which meant they were protected from abuse by commercial or political interests.

The *BBC* was state 'owned', funded by public taxation and had its political independence from government constitutionally guaranteed. *ITV* was a commercially backed broadcaster which was allowed to make profits for its shareholders but was tightly regulated to prevent biases arising in its journalism. The public service principles laid down for the *BBC* in the 1920s extended to commercial broadcasting. Owners, advertisers and other interests were not meant to interfere with or put pressure on *ITN*'s editorial decision-making process.

The different factors governing both gave rise to individual characteristics and traditions, McNair argues. He claims that politicians' attitudes to *ITV* were different from their view of the *BBC*. Although the *BBC* was independent, politicians frequently quibbled with the broadcaster, whereas because *ITV* was not publicly funded they appeared to think that *ITV* was less easily to be censured on political grounds. Consequently, McNair argues, *ITV* news developed a strong investigative journalistic tradition. In contrast, *BBC News* sought to give an impartial account of events: 'For the *BBC*, unlike the newspapers with their openly declared biases, there was to be no taking sides' (McNair 1999: 78).

Television news was also characteristically different from newspaper accounts in several ways. For one thing, there was less time in television news and it was therefore typically 'thin' in content. 'Many more "bits" of information can be contained on the front page of a broadsheet newspaper than can be broadcast in a twenty minute television news bulletin' (McNair 1999: 20). But, of course, the pictorial is a powerful source of information. However, the requirement for television news to be structured in time means that there are few items per newscast and that they are brief (Ericson 1995). Newspapers, structured in space, have scope for longer items in larger numbers. Brevity in broadcast news, Ericson (1995) argues, indicates that television news is much more limited in discursive potential than newspapers.

Ericson (1995) also observes that, unlike newspapers, which are directed at their own readership (a more limited audience), television news is directed at a mass audience and this has several consequences. One is that television news appeals to 'the lowest-common-denominator mass audience' (Ericson 1995: 20). As television competition is for a share of the total audience, Ericson (1995) argues that the popular formula of drama and entertainment is adopted. However, Ericson (1995) also proposes that research has repeatedly shown that, unlike the differences and variations in newspaper coverage, television news production and products are quite similar. Hence, he concludes that the 'quality' and 'popular' news products and the organisational differences associated with them may be more applicable to radio, and especially to newspapers, than to television news, which is more homogenous.

That television news is thin in content is an observation that could initially be made by viewing the news reports on the Brent Spar and comparing them with the press reports. That TV news follows a set format across the different channels and that there are greater differences in format within the press was also readily observable. As will be demonstrated, the governing principle of impartiality in television news also gives rise to a set format in the way television news is presented, which is different from how press coverage took place. Further, attention will be paid to the visual relaying of televised news because the use of Greenpeace footage was seen to have symbolised the dispute.

While much is made of differences in format both across and within media, Ericson and others point out that media formats also influence each other. Ericson (1995) cites Postman's (1985) comment that we are led to 'amuse ourselves to death' as indicating that the entertainment format, prevalent in television, is dominating other media and exercises the biggest influence on other formats. He also notes that this tendency is particularly evident in newspapers adopting 'the peculiar conception of objectivity fostered in broadcast news, where an allegation is quoted from one source, a counterpoint is made by a spokesperson for the organisation subject to the allegation and truth is held to reside somewhere in between' (1995: 39). Ericson believes that this (television's) approach has increased the expectation of impartiality in all media. Hence, even though newspapers are traditionally partisan, an approach suggesting impartiality and objectivity may be taken up. This study shows many instances where, even in the most partial accounts, an objective tone was employed.

While this investigation is concerned with examining how the press and television news represented the Brent Spar crisis, what this instance might reveal about the more central properties of media representations and how they may influence crisis management will also be considered. To that end, and for the consideration of news reports on the Brent Spar, a brief account of the contexts of both television and the press and the different traditions and narrative styles under which they operate have been provided. An understanding of the influences on the construction of news will facilitate a comprehension of how individual newspapers and broadcast news covered the situation over the Brent Spar.

Press coverage

The text data examined in this analysis consist of all the articles containing the words 'Brent Spar' in the three newspapers in the year 1995.[20]

The *Daily Mirror* search revealed a total of 33 articles. The coverage began on May 1 and ended (earlier than the other two papers) on July 28. The *Guardian* had 113 articles and their coverage began on May 6, and continued until the end of the year, as did the coverage of the *Daily Telegraph* which had 106 articles.

Both the *Daily Mirror* and the *Guardian* started their coverage of the story in May following Greenpeace's 'occupation' of the Brent Spar, whereas the *Daily Telegraph* began their coverage on February 17, when Shell announced its plan for the sea disposal of the Brent Spar.

Framing Shell

During the immediate crisis, the *Daily Mirror* repeatedly framed Shell as being a 'stubborn' and 'greedy' company which was trying to 'dump' its waste on the cheap:[21]

> WE SHELL NOT BE MOVED (June 20);
>
> ... stubborn refusal to heed pleas (June 20);
>
> [Shell] raked in millions and won't pay to clean up (May 1).

The *Mirror*'s first article on the subject was headlined: 'MURDER AT SEA' (May 1). Another article had the headline: 'GREED THAT'S POISONING OUR SEAS' (June 20). The *Mirror* portrayed Shell as 'a fantastically rich company which has made millions from the North Sea. It should not be trying to dump rigs on the cheap' (June 20). On the whole, the *Mirror* saw Shell as an irresponsible company solely concerned with profit and as following an environmentally-damaging course of action.

In many ways, the *Mirror's* representation of Shell conformed to its political traditions and to the narrative conventions of a popular/ tabloid news reporting. For example, the depiction that Shell was 'controlled' by the 'management in Holland' indicates the narrative conventions typical of tabloids. From the first article on the subject, it was quite clear that the paper opposed Shell's plan and it showed this partiality by invoking the negative stereotype of 'big business' as stubborn and greedy.

The *Daily Telegraph* took a very different view that reflected its political leanings. It framed Shell as a company that had good reasons for proposing a plan the paper thought was 'reasonable' (June 20). Despite supporting the company's case, the *Telegraph* observed that Shell needed to gain public approval:

Shell has a powerful economic and ecological case for dumping, but a company with a brand image needs to win the public relations battle too (June 17).

The *Telegraph* also emphasised the care the company had taken in arriving at their decision. The argument was that '[Shell] is not free to discard the Brent Spar however and wherever it pleases' (June 20) but had to follow a series of international agreements and conventions. Nevertheless, public approval was something the paper thought was important for Shell to attain:

Shell was caught off guard when Greenpeace first occupied the Brent Spar, perhaps because the case for bringing the thing ashore, as Greenpeace demanded, was such a poor one. Shell is now hitting back with fact sheets, briefings and press releases. It can only hope that an informed debate eventually beats dramatic television pictures when it comes to winning public approval (June 20).

In the above quotations, which are typical of how the *Telegraph* framed Shell and the disposal plan, it is obvious that the *Telegraph* agreed with Shell's plan and supported the company. And despite claiming that Shell did not have public approval, the *Telegraph* framed this as a dilemma faced by many businesses and, in doing so, placed this issue in a wider context and took the spotlight away from Shell:

However much it may think it has right on its side, Shell needs to sell to its consumers, and those who may vaguely believe that Greenpeace is right – some of them merely on the basis that big business must be wrong – can cause the company inconvenience at best or lasting commercial damage at worst. Shell is by no means the first business to be put through this particular mincer (June 20).

While this argument, that any business might encounter the difficulties faced by Shell, may have been a consequence of 'quality' newspapers taking a more abstract view of events, one of the effects of this was to represent Shell as not being responsible for the situation, and as a victim of circumstances. The *Telegraph*'s uncritical view of Shell's plan is also evident in instances where the *Telegraph* directly copied Shell's news releases and, thereby, reproduced Shell's claims:

The Brent Spar contains about 100 tons of sludge, the bulk of it sand. About 10% of it is heavy oil residue, like bitumen on roads... (June 21).

This instance (one amongst many), where the *Telegraph* employed the same similes (like bitumen) that Shell used in its news releases, indicates how much 'news' derives from press releases, the influence of sources on news content and also the paper's empathy with Shell. Clearly, the preferred source for the *Telegraph* was Shell.

It is significant that at the time of the above article, which listed the contents of the Spar, Greenpeace had announced that there was 5500 tonnes[22] of oil contained in the Spar, a figure that was contested by Shell but was as yet not proven to be false. Yet, in the *Telegraph*'s article listing the contents of the Spar there was *no* mention of Greenpeace's contention. Greenpeace's allegation was ignored and excluded while Shell's case was reproduced.

The *Guardian* began its coverage of the immediate crisis by stating that Shell 'is lying low' while its 'lawyers pounce' and quoted Jon Castle, Greenpeace captain, as saying that Shell 'has a big PR image and likes to pretend it cares about the environment when it is lying through its teeth' (May 6).

Like the *Telegraph*, the *Guardian* also highlighted the necessity of gaining public approval but, whereas the *Telegraph* explicitly supported Shell's plan, the *Guardian* was more sceptical:

Their [Shell UK and UK government's] case is watertight, they believe. The law is on their side; they have chosen what they call the 'best environmental option' and considered everything from health to future risk. They brand their opponents 'liars' and 'hysterical'. The trouble is that consumers don't think like multi-billion dollar corporations; business as usual is not enough for the nineties. Shell and the British government are seen throughout Europe to be out of touch when it comes to corporate and governmental accountability (June 17).

The *Guardian* also reported that the Royal Dutch/Shell Group might be willing to call off the plan and, unlike the *Telegraph*, the *Guardian* reported on the discord within the corporation.

Like the *Telegraph*, the *Guardian* framed Shell as a company, like many other companies, which could be adversely affected by bad publicity. Both the broadsheets took a wider view of the situation (and, thus, placed the situation in a broader context) which was in sharp contrast to that of the *Mirror*, which represented the situation in quite simplistic terms: all blame could be assigned to the greedy multinational that stubbornly maintained a malevolent course of action. In a typically 'popular' manner, the *Mirror* represented the situation very simply.

The *Guardian* did not support Shell's plans and the paper consistently emphasised that companies had to behave in a responsible manner; by so arguing the implication was that Shell was not behaving in such a way. The paper took the view that Shell had paid insufficient attention to what the public would consider an acceptable way to dispose of obsolete oil installations. As I have said, the *Guardian* was politically left-leaning and its characterisation of Shell as behaving irresponsibly might have been a consequence of that. Also, this framing of Shell was quite similar to the *Mirror's*, although the latter's characterisation of Shell was far more critical.

The way in which the three newspapers framed Shell was also influenced by and illustrated within their frame of the main opponent to the company's plan: Greenpeace.

Framing Greenpeace

Throughout their coverage, the *Mirror* characterised Greenpeace as being disinterested defenders of public interest. Greenpeace members were seen as 'daring' (May 1), 'brave' (June 20) and 'ready to risk their lives' (June 20) and those who boarded the Spar were described as 'commandos' (May 1) and 'Greenpeace fighters' who, on the Spar faced a 'bitter protest of terrible physical hardship' (June 20). In a manner reflecting its tradition for campaigning, the *Mirror* bolstered Greenpeace's campaign as it promoted and reproduced Greenpeace's view of the situation.

In response to Greenpeace's occupation of the Spar, both the *Mirror* and the *Guardian* covered Greenpeace's claims. The *Telegraph* did not, and took a different route in reporting the news. It described an encounter that gave the information that Greenpeace had occupied the Spar in protest but did not illustrate *why* Greenpeace had launched the protest. Thus, while it reported the news of Greenpeace's occupation, it did so in a way that was not advantageous to Greenpeace. It is worthwhile to quote this vignette in full as it indicates the approach the paper would subsequently take in covering the crisis:

A Greenpeace stunt fell flat at a drinks party held by John Gummer, Environment Secretary. A portable telephone was handed to Gummer by an activist at the do with a smirking 'it's for you'. On the line was Greenpeace's Chris Rose, talking from the disused oil rig Brent Spar which Greenpeace is occupying ... Rose clearly asked Gummer what he was going to do about the Department of Trade's plans to dump old rigs ... Gummer went, spectacularly, on the offensive. Rose was told sharply that rigs were NOT the minister's top priority for next month's North Sea Conference. 'I wish campaigners would get around to the fish stocks of the world', barked Gummer ... 'The most difficult thing about the environment was to retain a sense of priorities'. And with that the Secretary of State hit the 'off' button and with a look of a man who had just squashed a mosquito, handed back the mobile (May 12).

This article is illustrative of the Environment Minister's view of Greenpeace but, significantly, it is also quite typical of the angle the *Telegraph* took as subsequent articles argued that Greenpeace's protests were 'distracting' from the 'real' issue of industrial over-fishing: 'This far more serious problem [modern fishing methods] is almost completely ignored by Greenpeace in favour of Brent Spar type stunts' (June 20). Interestingly, this was also what the government minister had said in the above quote. The *Telegraph*'s coverage of the dispute would continue to parallel the UK government's view, which was also a perspective favourable to Shell.

While the protests against Shell's plans grew, the government tried to shift media attention onto what it wanted to portray as bigger environmental problems – and the *Telegraph* did this. For instance, when Greenpeace reoccupied the Spar on June 8, the *Telegraph* gave minimal attention to an event that otherwise gained extensive press and television coverage. On that day the *Telegraph* reported: 'SCIENTISTS SAY NORTH SEA COD IS FACING EXTINCTION' (June 8). Despite this article focusing on the depletion of North Sea cod, it did not however completely ignore Greenpeace's reoccupation of the Spar. A very brief announcement was made in the last three sentences of the article.

Similarly, at the North Sea conference, when European government ministers protested about the Brent Spar, the *Telegraph* chose instead to focus on another aspect: 'BRITAIN WINS FISH STOCK AGREEMENT' (June 10). In that article, the paper made a token mention of the fact that the Danish minister had protested about the Brent Spar, while focusing on a concern the UK government had identified as more worthy of attention. The *Telegraph* represented and reproduced the UK government's view of the situation:

GREENPEACE DISTRACTIONS

Greenpeace's warm welcome to the declaration of the North Sea conference in the Danish port of Esbjerg should serve as a warning that there is much wrong with it ... Greenpeace ... distracted the conference [from discussing fish stocks] with its campaign against the dumping of the Brent Spar, a huge oil platform which will be difficult to dispose of by any means ... The suspicion remains that Greenpeace chose not to campaign about industrial fishing because it might have challenged the prejudices of its angst ridden support-ers in Holland, Germany, and Denmark, who are obsessed with pol-lution. And that could have led to a reduction in donations. One should always remember that a primary objective of a modern pres-sure group is its own perpetuation. That is not always best achieved by making people think about the really important issues (June 12).

By arguing that Greenpeace's protests were mere 'distractions' and by claiming that Greenpeace was somehow not really concerned about the environment but instead concerned only for itself, the *Telegraph* suggested that there was a sinister side to pressure groups:

The damage [resulting from the Braer oil spill] was minimal. Everyone was mightily relieved, although some detected a twinge of regret in the response of some of the more extreme eco-warriors, as the publicity value of such a catastrophe in a beautiful part of the British Isles was so cruelly wrested from them. The prospect of piti-fully damaged furry creatures dying on camera on the one hand, and those rapacious oil companies seemingly answerable to nobody on the other, would have guaranteed public outrage. Such oppor-tunities do not occur often – perhaps because the oil companies and other big businesses which could cause catastrophe try quite hard to avoid them – and so Greenpeace has had to create one. It has chosen the Brent Spar.

The *Telegraph* repeatedly argued that Greenpeace had no real reason to protest against the disposal of Brent Spar and that Greenpeace was merely using the disposal to further other objectives and persistently employed this frame. The first instance in which the *Telegraph* repres-ented Greenpeace's views was on June 20. It did so, however, as a two-part examination of the case for and against deep sea disposal: 'SEABED MUST NOT BECOME RUBBISH TIP – AGAINST'[23] (June 20) and '30 STUDIES IN FAVOUR OF DUMPING – FOR (June 20). Greenpeace's claims simply did not obtain representation in the *Telegraph*, even though attempts had been made to give an appearance of objectivity, as the two articles above indicate. In spite of these articles giving the appearance of objectivity, which is important to journalists in establishing credibility with audiences, they still favoured Shell's case by framing the issue in a manner favourable to Shell.

The *Guardian* described the Greenpeace activists who occupied the Spar as 'eco-guerrillas' and as 'pirates', but this frame was not as firmly retained as the frames utilised in a rhetorical way by the other two papers. The *Guardian* seemed impressed with the way in which Greenpeace conducted its campaign, frequently describing it as 'efficient' and 'immaculately planned', but the paper stopped short of overtly supporting or opposing Greenpeace.

Although the *Guardian* argued, like the *Mirror*, that Shell should not proceed as planned, unlike the *Mirror* the *Guardian* distanced itself from Greenpeace, the principal group also taking that stance. In doing so, the *Guardian* maintained greater distance between itself and the conflict, which was quite unlike the stance taken by the *Mirror* and the *Telegraph*. This served the paper's desire to portray itself as unaffiliated and impartial – an outlook that corresponded with the traditions of the paper.

Framing risks and scientific opinion

The *Mirror* framed Shell's disposal plan as posing unquestionable risks to the marine environment. The Spar was described as a 'toxic time bomb' and the paper urged Shell to 'spare the environment another killing blow'. According to the *Mirror*, Shell's plan constituted an 'environmental hazard' (June 20) and the first of its kind as it insisted that there were 'hundreds of other Brent Spars' (June 20).

The *Mirror's* discussion of the risks of sea disposal was limited to stating that it definitely constituted a risk to the marine ecology and, in a manner typical of tabloids, its discussion of the scientific arguments of the case was very restricted. The differing scientific views were not explained; instead the paper stated that Shell's scientific findings also supported Greenpeace's scientists, who provided evidence that dumping would damage the marine environment. This was backed up with the statement that Shell's scientists also showed that the Spar contained 'tons of toxic sludge', 'tons of waste oils' and 'tons of radio-active scale'. Hence, the *Mirror* framed Greenpeace's science as being firm and, in doing so, supported Greenpeace's case. The *Mirror* also reported Greenpeace's measurement of the amount of oil contained in the Spar without questioning this amount: 'it contains an estimated 5000 tonnes of oil' (June 20).

Despite sustaining Greenpeace's claims about risks, the *Mirror* did, on the day of Shell's change of plan though before this took place, acknowledge that there was scientific opposition to Greenpeace's argument. However, that observation was deployed to argue for the termination of Shell's plan:

Some scientists support Shell's actions as the best way to get rid of Brent Spar. But with so much *opposition* and so much *uncertainty*, the sinking should not go ahead ... (June 20).

Even though differing scientific opinion was now represented, it was done so in a self-serving manner, as the paper's position was to halt Shell's plan. That representation also shored up Greenpeace's case.

Once again in stark contrast to the *Mirror*, the *Telegraph* backed Shell's case in its discussion of risks and scientific opinion. The *Telegraph* focused on the risks of onshore disposal and did not give much attention to the risks of sea disposal, i.e. the risk of Shell's plan was not discussed whereas the risks of what Greenpeace proposed (onshore disposal) was emphasised.

The *Telegraph* promoted the view that 'scientists' supported Shell's plan and often suggested that expert opinion was on Shell's side:

Do oil rigs dumped at sea damage the environment? ...The answer, according to marine scientists, is that the deep sea is a perfectly reasonable place to get rid of the oil industry's largest structures (May 31).

The risks of deep sea disposal were minimal and 'immaterial', the *Telegraph* also claimed:

Whether it [the Brent Spar] has a few tonnes of sludge in it as Shell maintain, or several hundred tonnes as Greenpeace allege, is irrelevant. In the vast volume of the sea, its effects will be immaterial, and the heavy metal trace elements will be detectable only thanks to the extreme sensitivity of modern measuring methods (June 20).

Dr Tony Rice, one of the scientists who supported Shell, was often quoted by the *Telegraph* at the expense of other scientific opinion:

> Dr Tony Rice, an independent deep-sea biologist ... said that the most likely impact was the death of a number of worms on the sea bed ... (June 20).

The *Telegraph* promoted the view that Greenpeace was exaggerating the risks, arguing:

> Perhaps Greenpeace can be forgiven its fanaticism but Mr Kohl should surely know better. He is guilty of gross exaggeration in telling Mr Major that dumping Brent Spar in deep water raises serious ecological questions (June 17)

And:

> The large metal storage buoy will contain radioactive muds, but these were naturally occurring and have only been concentrated by drilling activity. There may also be traces of oil, but Dr Rice says the effects should be local and limited to within a few hundred metres ... (May 31).

The *Telegraph* insisted that 'there is scant evidence that dumping the Brent Spar would cause more environmental problems than are caused by building a quarter mile of road' (June 12) and viewed the situation as:

> ... a storm in an Atlantic tea cup. Greenpeace have made a mistake and they cannot admit it ... for this structure, at this moment in time, this is the best environmental option (June 20).

The *Mirror* and the *Telegraph* advanced opposing views of risks and scientific views because they both supported one of the two main parties involved in the dispute. The *Guardian* took a completely different view of the situation from that of the other two newspapers, arguing that what to do with the Spar was not really a scientific argument:

> ... just like last year's Anglo-German furore over BSE ... the battle lines are more cultural than scientific (June 17).

For the *Guardian,* the real issue was not the scientific arguments but how Shell and the UK government responded to public sentiments. The paper was also careful to prefix claims made by Greenpeace about the contents of the Spar that could pose risks to the marine environment with a 'Greenpeace claims'. However, in its first article on the subject, the *Guardian* appeared to support Greenpeace's argument that the planned disposal would set a precedent:

> Greenpeace sees this week's action as the start … that could ultimately determine the fate of 60 major ageing installations in the central and northern North Sea … they all contain tons of hazardous and radioactive wastes specifically outlawed by two conventions on marine dumping (May 6).

Later articles reported Shell's argument that the UK government's policy was to consider disposal on a case by case approach. But the first report on this policy is on May 30, whereas the first article about the Brent Spar (May 6), and subsequent ones, had suggested that this form of disposal was applicable to the other oil installations in the North Sea. In doing so, the *Guardian* reproduced Greenpeace's claim and downplayed Shell's denial that the Spar would set a precedent. Thus, once again we see another instance where the conventions of demonstrating objectivity were employed (attaching a 'Greenpeace claims' to statements which the paper also reproduced and promoted), whereas the paper's coverage in fact leant more towards one side of the dispute rather than the other.

Framing protests

The three papers framed protests in quite distinctive ways. The *Mirror* saw the protests against Shell's plan as a remarkable expression of democracy at work:

> … campaigners, men and women, from Britain and several other countries were in control [as they erected the] 'Save the North Sea' flag [on the Brent Spar which] 'flew triumphantly' (May 1).

According to the *Mirror* there was a 'huge groundswell of protest' and 'voluntary boycotts' as opposition grew to Shell's plan (June 20).

The *Telegraph,* in contrast to the *Mirror's* framing of civil protest as an expression of democracy, saw it as an expression of civil disobedience and the rise of a public willingness to be unlawful:

PROTESTERS TAKE LAW INTO OWN HANDS. CIVIL DISOBEDIENCE: Campaigns have targeted poll tax, animal exports and new motorways. More and more demonstrators are willing to act illegally to further their various causes ... Protest groups agitating for every conceivable cause ... have used civil disobedience to promote their views (June 5).

The nature of protests and protesters in England and on the Continent was described differently by the three papers. After the firebombing of Shell garages in Germany, the *Mirror* differentiated between two types of protests and protesters, arguing that the 'Green terrorists' in Germany, where 'Wild West scenes' took place, were in contrast to protests in England and to Greenpeace protesters. A Shell station worker in Germany is quoted as having said that 'the whole country has gone mad' (June 20). The paper's framing of the different types of protest in England and in Germany helped Greenpeace because other newspapers had criticised Greenpeace for spurring on the violent protest in Germany – an allegation that Greenpeace denied.

The *Guardian* also reported a variance in the type of protest taking place in England and in continental Europe:

On the Continent, the Brent Spar now has been front page news for weeks, here consumer protest is building slowly (June 17).

The *Guardian* also published a letter on the different public attitudes in England and on the Continent ('LETTER: ONE NATION FACING CATASTROPHE WITH QUIETUDE – AND A PINT IN ITS HAND'), which argued that there was 'an apathy and lack of foresight by the majority of the British public when confronted by even the most major potential catastrophe' (June 19). That view succinctly illustrated the paper's position on this matter.

Like the other two papers, the *Telegraph* also reported on the different types of protest in England and on the Continent but, unlike the other two papers, the *Telegraph* had a specific gripe against German protesters:

ANTI-BRITISH MOOD RISES IN GERMANY

There were signs yesterday that German criticism of the plan ... was becoming another excuse for the release of anti-British feelings (June 21).

The impression that Germans were anti-British was furthered by subsequent articles in the *Telegraph* which strongly criticised that population. While the other two papers interpreted continental opposition to Shell's plan as being a consequence of their sentiments towards the environment and values regarding corporate responsibility and so forth, the *Telegraph* saw it as a consequence of an 'anti-British' predilection. That representation reflected and promoted the paper's view of the protests as baseless.

Observations on the press coverage

Strong organising perspectives clearly existed in the case of the *Mirror,* which supported Greenpeace's claims, and the *Telegraph,* which supported Shell's plans. The *Guardian* appeared more aware of an apparent need to be objective, even though it also promoted the view that Shell should relinquish a poorly supported plan. My analysis shows that the *Telegraph* also attempted to appear objective. That might have been a result of the two being 'quality' broadsheets, which are expected to be partisan, yet more impartial than the tabloids. The one paper that was not so concerned with the posture most clearly adopted by the *Guardian* was the *Mirror* but, as I have argued, this might have been a consequence of its overtly stated partisanship, its tradition of campaigning and its 'popular' format.

My analysis shows that all the news reports were value laden.

A key finding of this study – one that Hansen (2000) also found in his examination of newspaper coverage – is that newspapers covered the crisis in very different ways and employed quite distinct frames of the main parties and issues involved. This discovery contests the view that 'the media' covered the crisis in a uniform manner. My observations do not support the consultants' and Shell's claim that there was a media bias against the company.

The three newspapers had their individual views about the situation, and two of the three examined supported – though in varying degrees and under different positions – Greenpeace's call for an abandonment of the sea disposal and the one supported Shell's plan. The different politics, narrative cultures and traditions of the three newspapers was described earlier. My analysis shows that these factors exercised an influence in how news was constructed and reported because the way in which the newspapers represented the main parties and issues conformed to their individual contexts.

Observing the situation whereby news reports leant towards this or that position was facilitated by an examination of how issues and entities were framed. This analysis shows that certain newspapers reflected and emphasised the views of some claim-makers over others and, in doing so, presented those views as legitimate. That the different papers sought to legitimate different claims was demonstrated.

If we compare these findings with what Schlesinger (1991) maintains about how different groups (sources) compete to gain representation of their outlook, and that the media accept or reject the 'frames' offered by sources or invent their own frames, my findings provide examples of the three possibilities. When, for instance, we look at how the papers treated Shell's claims, it is evident that the *Telegraph* accepted much of what Shell claimed and (re)produced reports that appear to be influenced by how the government wanted to frame the issue.[24] The *Mirror* rejected Shell's claims and instead accepted those offered by Greenpeace. And the *Guardian* offered its own interpretations/frames (that the real issue was not scientific argument but cultural expectations).

This study also demonstrates that the newspapers engaged in their own definitional work. Even when the *Mirror* and the *Telegraph* supported the two main parties involved, (Greenpeace and Shell respectively), their coverage was not merely a case of reproducing their views but also furnishing them through the advancement of supporting arguments. Thus, for example, the *Telegraph* saw the protests against Shell as civil disobedience and the *Mirror* argued, towards the end, that because there was so much scientific uncertainty (which the paper had not previously mentioned), Shell's plans should be abandoned. And with regard to the invention of their own frames and definitions, the *Telegraph's* view of Greenpeace as posing a threat to democracy and indicating the rise of civil disobedience reveals this as these interpretations were the paper's own. These frames were not provided by a primary source but were invented by the paper. Therefore, in addition to the reproduction and legitimisation of claims, the press also engage in offering their own interpretations of the situation and offer their own definitions that support that outlook.

My findings not only dispute the contention that there was a media bias but also do not support the assertion that Shell's case was not represented. The *Guardian* and even the *Mirror,* although deeply opposed to Shell's plan, represented Shell's claims. The strongest contention of the consultants' claim is evident in the *Telegraph*'s coverage of the crisis. With the exception of one article that came towards the end of the crisis, the *Telegraph* did not cover any of Greenpeace's claims.

The paper excluded opposing views and not only represented but also reproduced, promoted and endorsed Shell's position.

The finding that representation of claims took place even though news reports favoured a particular interpretation conforms to Tuchman's (1978) and Schiller's (1981) observations regarding the journalistic conventions employed to suggest that accounts are factual and impartial and, therefore, credible.

In addition to the finding that the individual papers' subscription to specific partisan perspectives is reflected in what they produced – by how they framed issues and groups – my study also reveals that these frames were consistent from the beginning. Hansen (2000) also found that condition and his study corroborates mine. Certain frames were preferred and prominent from the outset, and it was also the case that these were sustained in each newspaper as events developed. Thus, I found that the coverage of the crisis within each paper did not vary as the initial frames employed remained and did not change. One could draw from this situation the conclusion that news construction is a process driven and greatly influenced by the wider context (such as the political leanings, organising structure, traditions and the outlooks) of the individual newspapers. This has consequences for the capacity to influence or control the way claims are framed by individual newspapers, an observation that Hansen also makes in arguing that there are 'limits to claims-maker influence' (2000: 71). Therefore, while journalists can secure legitimacy towards a certain claim/viewpoint, ensuring that that legitimacy is obtained is rather uncertain. This has repercussions for what consultants advocate because measures to influence news coverage – through crisis management – might be quite constrained and, hence, achieving the intended effect might be far from straightforward.

Television coverage

Television coverage of this story began much later than the press coverage and ended earlier. The time constraints and greater competition for TV news time seemed to influence the coverage. In comparison with TV news, press coverage also seemed more in-depth and less event-led. None of this contradicts what media studies isolate as typical characteristics: television news is less in-depth than press reports, and is dominated by a popular format because of its 'visuals', simplifying features and a concentration on the dramatic (Ericson et al. 1989).

Coverage in the year 1995 began on May 22, and the last television news item on the subject was on September 5.[25] There were in total 18 *BBC News* programmes (ten during the immediate crisis), five *Channel 4 News* programmes (two during the immediate crisis) and five *ITV News* reports (two during the immediate crisis).

Television news, across the three channels, followed a very set and typical format identifiable as the formal features of news in this medium. It would begin with the news presenter announcing the item to the accompaniment of a still photo. The report would then proceed to a 'voice over' and or a video of a correspondent who would have 'the report', i.e. a more in-depth account following on the introduction by the presenter in the studio. Typically, the Brent Spar coverage would begin with the studio presenter, who would have behind him a still photo of the Brent Spar, sometimes accompanied by the Shell and Greenpeace logos with a caption such as 'Dispute' or 'Brent Spar'. The reporter would be introduced and would take over relaying the news, which would be accompanied with video material that coincided with what was said. For example, when reporting about firebombed Shell garages in Germany, the video would show those garages. That conformed to the observations of media research that using visuals helps to establish factuality and objectivity as they authenticate what is reported (Fiske 1987) (Graddol and Boyd-Barret 1994).

The visual relaying of news is one part of the two-part (visual and verbal) equation involved in televised news; it 'binds messages to context' (Ericson 1995: 6) and is particularly important not only because it is a significant component of how the story is told in this medium but also because consultants, Shell and television executives draw attention to this aspect, arguing that it contributed to the creation of bias. In order to investigate their claim that the inclusion of Greenpeace video in television news created bias, I generally paid attention to the visual communication of news and gave specific attention to the Greenpeace video. I was also attentive to whether any sort of labelling of footage existed because television executives suggested that bias was created not just by the use of the Greenpeace footage but also because they had not labelled the source of the material. At the 1995 Television conference at Edinburgh, where *BBC* and *ITN* executives admitted to biased coverage, they argued that in the future any external video material ought to be labelled on its first frame. The suggestion was that this was not done and that the broadcast of Greenpeace material, especially without a label, created bias.

The news reports during the crisis did typically contain a visual scene that consultants, Shell and television executives describe as a source of bias. I will term this the 'Spar scene' (see page 249). It showed the Brent Spar with nearby ships hosing the areas surrounding the Spar with water, a Greenpeace ship and some Greenpeace dinghies navigating around the structure. When Greenpeace reoccupied the Spar by landing two activists on the installation by helicopter, television news also carried a video of this. This, like the Spar scene video, was produced by Greenpeace. As is evident through their description of it, the contentious Greenpeace video, the use of which Shell and television executives claim gave rise to biased television coverage, was not the 'helicopter' one but rather the Spar scene video.

The contentious video, like most other visuals in television news, was used in conjunction with a verbal report and, in my view, what was said in that report can influence interpretations of that video. Therefore, particular attention was paid to *how* this video was used, that is, what was said while it was shown. It is not unreasonable to suppose that the verbal account could guide the impressions drawn from the video, given that videos are used in television news typically to illustrate and exemplify the report.

This investigation will not assess how everyone 'decoded' this video, which is not possible. Media research suggests that people decipher visuals very differently (Liebes and Katz 1990) and this presents a problem with the claim that the visuals created a distinct, uniform view of the situation. The claim of bias will be investigated by looking for what could be drawn from the video. Bearing in mind the argument that news accounts are 'metaphorical reconstructions' (Fiske and Hartley 1978; Ericson et al. 1989), it is interesting that the use of Greenpeace video was singled out for criticism. Why were the visuals blamed for the allegedly biased coverage? Why not just blame the simplifying features of television news, for instance? Could it be that blaming Greenpeace was advantageous for those who did so? For example, the television executives were not disinterested commentators and they did have to make a defence against Shell's accusations of biased news reporting, which they could do by holding Greenpeace responsible and, in that way, dodging the critical spotlight. And, as I subsequently argue, it was in Shell's interest to claim that there had been a media bias.

Yet, the claim of media bias appears convincing, given media researchers' observation that television news scenes are imagistic and symbolic (Carey 1989; Dayan and Katz 1992; Liebes and Curran 1998). Further, in the context of the researchers' observation that television news is guided and determined by what can be shown, the Greenpeace provision of footage appears quite significant. So the case might have been credible – that is necessary for it to be taken seriously – but credibility, by itself, does not mean that that is in fact what happened.

The greater imperative for television news to be impartial and the conventions reporters use to suggest impartiality were observable in the television coverage of the Spar story and, hence, my analysis points to problems with the case that consultants, Shell and television executives put forth.

BBC

That there was an overriding concern with appearing objective and impartial was suggested by a formulaic approach to presenting the news: reporters withheld judgement, abstained from supporting a particular argument and spokespersons for both sides of the argument were shown making their statements. Representation of the two standpoints is a part of the ritual of impartiality practised by the media, where one viewpoint balances another. Most of the *BBC News* programmes delineated both sides of the dispute, as did *BBC* current affairs programmes.

A good example of this concern to appear objective, and the employment of the traditional format of one viewpoint balancing the other, was the *Breakfast with Frost* programme on June 18. There both sides of the dispute were covered as Chris Rose (CR), Greenpeace Campaigns Director, and Tim Eggar (TE), Trade and Industry Minister, responded to the central issue of the environmental risks of the planned action:

DF:[26] Is it actually dangerous or not, in your opinion?

CR: We believe it is, yes. There's a lot more toxic chemicals and oil [aboard the Spar] than the government was led to believe by Shell. There's 5000 tonnes of oil on it and Shell said there's about 40 tonnes. We [obtained the estimate] from a sampling that happened when we went on the Brent Spar the first time ...

TE: Chris talks about trace contaminants in the Brent Spar. Leaving this morning I picked up this [shows a small medicine bottle]. It weighs 100 grams. There's about 200 grams – two of these [holds up bottle] in weight of trace contaminants on the Brent Spar. So Greenpeace is grossly exaggerating the problem, completely misconstruing the independent studies that have been carried out – the *independent experts* [his emphasis] who have looked at this very much support the government and Shell's approach.

CR: Well I think that's just wrong. I've got here a sworn affidavit from a worker [hands the document to Frost and then to Eggar who ignores it] who says that he was asked to seal in 3500 gallon barrels of chemicals that aren't on the inventory – they are entombed in concrete – they are going to go down with the Brent Spar and we think that there is a lot more chemicals in there that you [looks at Eggar] don't know about.

An incident on this programme also illustrated the presenter's concern to appear impartial and thus conform to the governing principle of television news to be objective. David Frost, the presenter, ended the discussion thus:

OK [interrupts the debate between Eggar and Rose] we are going to leave it there. Thank you both for a very, very lively debate. You have dramatised the different issues very well. Ultimately everyone wants their own way ... we leave it to you [addresses camera]. The verdict, as they say on television, is yours (*BBC* 2: *Breakfast with Frost*, June 18).

Frost parodied that television convention, yet also conformed to it.

Quite dominant in the *BBC* coverage was the formulaic approach to news reporting, where both sides of the dispute are represented, but there were four exceptions.

The *On the Record* programme (June 18) was one such exception in having spokespersons only for Greenpeace's case. In that programme Frank Dobson, Shadow Environment Secretary, and the Liberal Democrat Matthew Taylor were both very critical of Shell and both supported a boycott of the company. Dobson said:

... we believe that it's wrong of Shell to propose to just dump their spare equipment, their clapped out equipment ... here you have got a multi-million pound multinational company being allowed the cheapest option: dumping at sea.

The two ministers saw Shell very much in the same way as characterised by Greenpeace and *On the Record* did not present a different depiction of Shell from that put forward by the ministers.

Even though this programme represented a partial view of the situation, an incident took place that revealed the programme makers' and the presenter's very self-conscious aspiration to be objective. The presenter, John Humphreys, had asked Frank Dobson whether he was calling for a boycott of Shell, but Dobson had been evasive. When he finally received the answer: 'Yes I think they should', the presenter expressed his approval but was immediately concerned that his reaction might be mistaken for agreement with the minister's position, and thus construed as bias. So, he explained and drew attention to that not being the case:

> Right. Good. I didn't mean 'good I agree with you' but thank you for answering my question.

The *BBC* wished to appear objective even in a programme that presented views critical of Shell.

The presenter also brought up, for the very first time on the *BBC*, the legality of Greenpeace's protest activities, which meant that the report did not entirely lean towards Greenpeace's position. These factors once again show that demonstrating impartiality was considered important.

The second *BBC News* report on Brent Spar, *BBC* 9 O'Clock News, June 12, was also an exception to the dominant mode of *BBC*'s coverage. The report suggested that the Spar contained toxic substances that would damage the marine environment and that its disposal would set a precedent for the disposal of other installations and, in doing so, echoed Greenpeace's claims. These issues were presented as fact rather than being fiercely contested. Moreover, the traditional ploys employed to suggest impartiality (in this case, the attribution of that view to Greenpeace and stating that Shell claimed otherwise) were also absent. The report inclined towards Greenpeace's position and ended with the observation that 'more rigs are likely to be dumped at sea', which once again reinforced Greenpeace's position.

The third exception was the *BBC* 9 O'Clock News, June18, which excluded claims that Greenpeace had earlier made on *Breakfast with Frost*, yet repeated counter arguments to Greenpeace made on that same programme. These were Eggar's criticism of Greenpeace for 'not representing the facts' and his admonishment that: 'you [referring to Greenpeace] are completely misconstruing the independent studies, and misrepresenting the situation of Brent Spar, and as an organisation you're behaving highly irresponsibly' (*BBC* 9 O'Clock News, June 18). However, the news item did not cover what Chris Rose of Greenpeace, had said to Eggar on the earlier programme: Greenpeace's disclosure that their measurement of the oil remaining on board the Spar far exceeded Shell's estimate and that Greenpeace had a sworn affidavit from a Shell worker who claimed to have followed orders and sealed toxic waste into the structure of Brent Spar for a secret disposal of these toxic substances. These two claims did not gain coverage in *any* of the *BBC* news programmes and it appears that this was not just for the reason that the news is supposed to deal with fresh events rather than recycle the old, because Eggar's criticism of Greenpeace (previously broadcast material that also was advantageous to Shell) was subsequently repeated.

Greenpeace's claims about the high level of oil and the toxic substances supposedly hidden in the Spar did not gain coverage by the *BBC* despite receiving press coverage, and the central nature of these claims to Shell's disposal plan and their exclusion is all the more unusual given that television favours the sensational and the dramatic. That may point to a deliberate exclusion of those claims rather than an accidental one.

Although one side of the dispute was more favourably framed, the programme included the rival view. Again, this was to suggest that the report was objective, but the manner in which this was implied (a representation of a critical view of Shell counterbalanced with a view supporting Shell) suggested impartiality but also leant towards Shell's position.

I have said that most of the *BBC* news programmes presented both sides of the dispute, but that position was entirely eschewed on June 19 when the *BBC* explicitly ratified and legitimised Shell's case. The *BBC* science correspondent argued in this programme that Shell's case was the more scientifically sound and better argument, which also had support from scientists. In describing what the Spar contained, the report ignored Greenpeace's oil estimate and its claim about hidden toxic waste and concurred with Shell's account:

It's now full of sea water but at the bottom of its tanks 100 tonnes of sludge. According to Shell 90% of it is sand, the rest is a heavy oil like bitumen. The sludge also contains some heavy metals.

Much news may simply be a recycling of press releases, but the reporter's use of the same comparison that Shell used in its news releases to describe radioactivity emanating from the Spar as 'it's … no more than occurs naturally in the granite houses in Aberdeen', indicates that the preferred source was Shell.[27] And Greenpeace's claims regarding risks to the marine environment were, implicitly, discredited.

The report gave some concession to Greenpeace's argument but its presentation suggested that it was overridden by the scientific opinion on the subject, which was depicted as supporting Shell's case. Moreover, Greenpeace's claim that new findings regarding the contents of the Spar increased the environmental risks of Shell's plan was once again excluded. Further, the science correspondent also furnished Shell's claim that the environmental impact would be small and harmless:

> Compared with the millions of tonnes of shipping sunk in the Second World War the impact of Brent Spar will be small. Many experts admit it will cause damage to the local environment and kill organisms but they are not worried (*BBC* 9 O'Clock News: June 19).

Partiality was evident in the way that certain claims were ignored but, typically, most *BBC* news programmes represented both sides of the issue. And, even where reports leant towards one side or, in some cases, represented one side of the dispute, the fact that there was a different side to the argument was noted. I have suggested that such inclusions of opposing views may have been attempts to demonstrate objectivity while a particular viewpoint was in fact advanced.

ITV

The *ITV*'s news coverage of the crisis was limited to two news programmes, both on the same day: June 16 (*Lunchtime News* and *News at Ten*).

The *ITV* coverage began at a time when the issue had already developed to a heightened stage and the news appeared very much to be event-led. The two events that gained attention and coverage, the fire-bombing incident in Germany and Greenpeace's activities in re-boarding the Spar, were both dramatic and appealed to the popular format. '[T]he pattern for *ITV* more closely approximates to the pattern displayed by the tabloid dailies', note Schlesinger, Tumber and Murdock (1995: 113), and that might explain why the coverage was event-led and centred on the sensational. The decision to cover these events and examine the story at a time when opposition had intensified was influential on the coverage because the central theme in both *ITV* news programmes were the protests against Shell – they both began and ended with that.

ITV Lunchtime News led with the picketing of Shell's petrol stations:

> Petrol stations owned by Shell are being picketed today because of the company's controversial operation to dump the redundant Brent Spar oil rig in the Atlantic.

And that report ended with the announcement of more protest:

> The campaign to stop the Brent Spar will come closer to home tomorrow when Greenpeace mounts a mass picket of Shell's stations across Britain.

ITV News at Ten also began its coverage with the announcement of opposition to Shell's plan:

> Germany's Chancellor Helmut Kohl is under intense pressure from environmentalists to oppose the plan (*ITV News at Ten*, June 16).

And the news report ended with the repetition of Greenpeace's plan to picket Shell's stations the following day.

Although there were instances in both programmes where conflicting views on a matter were represented – through the standard manner of signifying objectivity – balance was mostly achieved not so much within each individual news programme but when the two were taken together, because the two programmes (on the same day) each represented the two positions. The first news programme drew attention to Greenpeace's perspective and the second concentrated on Shell's.

The first programme initially gave equitable coverage to both Shell and Greenpeace's claims regarding the risks of Shell's plan in the typical manner which I have described:

> Shell says the decommissioned hulk will cause minimal environmental damage when it is dumped in 2000 metres of water. But Greenpeace claim it is a toxic firebomb (*ITV Lunchtime News*, June 16).

However, the report then included a clip reproducing Greenpeace's view while excluding Shell's. Chris Rose from Greenpeace was shown claiming:

> The Brent Spar has long-life industrial toxic chemicals on board. There is about, we believe, 130 times more oil than Shell has claimed, about 5000 tonnes. That will be oil pollution, there's [aboard the Spar] heavy metals pollution, PCBs which cause long-term changes in mammals... .

The only representation of Shell's position in this news report was in the inclusion of John Major's statement that:

As far as I am aware the disposal of the Brent Spar is in accordance with international law.

Despite minimal representation of Shell's views in this programme, the next (*News at Ten*, June 16) focused on Shell's views. It included a clip of Chris Fay, Chairman of Shell UK, responding to Greenpeace's action in airlifting two activists on board the Spar and arguing that Greenpeace's action was probably 'outside the international rules of flying', and that this type of protest 'is indeed evident of the types of things they have tried to do'. The reporter had earlier claimed that Shell had stated that the action was 'irresponsible' and, in keeping with television news conventions, the quote from Chris Fay was used to illustrate that view.

Unlike the first news report, this one did highlight that Greenpeace's claims about the disposal was 'far from universally accepted' and included a clip of Dr Tony Rice, who was a key scientist supporting Shell and frequently quoted in the media:

> Oh, I think they [Greenpeace] are honest in *believing* [his emphasis] that the impact will be greater in the deep sea. We are saying that *they are wrong* and they are simply giving the wrong impression to the public (*News at Ten*, June 16).

In spite of giving a greater representation to a particular position in each of the two reports, *ITV* also presented the news in a way that suggested impartial coverage. The news reports simply outlined both views and refrained from analysing them. Although the other channels also did this, *ITV* did it to a far greater degree. This lack of analysis, suggesting a mere recording and announcement of developments, worked towards indicating objectivity, and this route was perhaps taken in order to create that impression. *ITV*'s focus on events (such as the firebombing and pickets), rather than the arguments for and against sea disposal, also functioned towards signifying that the news coverage was impartial.

Channel 4

Channel 4 News began coverage of the issue more or less at the same time as *ITV*, that is, on June 15 and 16. Although the dispute between Shell and Greenpeace was reported, *Channel 4 News* did not consider the story to be a major one. The first report on the matter maintained that the dispute was a distraction from the bigger issue of the situation in Bosnia. That programme reported Kohl's decision to raise the issue of the disposal of the Spar with Major at the G7 summit:

> Chancellor Kohl has come in here [the G7 summit] saying that he has something of a bone to pick with Mr. Major, insisting that the British government should not allow the Shell oil company to sink that oil platform, the Brent Spar out in the North Sea and that he will be making an issue of it with the Prime Minister (*Channel 4 News*, June 15).

The report depicted Kohl's decision to bring this up with Major as giving undue attention to a not very big issue, arguing that other matters should concern the G7:

> So much talk but a sense already of how little will be achieved here [at the G7 summit] if world leaders choose to side-step the number one issue: Bosnia.

In sharp contrast to *BBC* and *ITV* news, *Channel 4 News* on June 15 said nothing about Greenpeace's claims or its actions and nothing was shown about its campaign and direct action taken against Shell. And it is only from a video of Kohl stating that 'people in Europe and especially in Germany are unhappy with Shell's decision' that one gets a sense that Shell faced opposition. This lack of interest in the specifics of the altercation was a consequence of the report's view that it was not an important story. The second news report also took that stance.

That programme placed the wrangle over the Spar in a wider context, as the situation was represented as a challenge faced by the oil industry in its operations in the North Sea. The main theme of that report was outlined as follows:

> We examine the legacy of twenty years of North Sea oil ... Has North Sea oil been the godsend we thought it would be? (*Channel 4 News*, June 16)

And, after some discussion on the protests against Shell in Germany, the report once again returned to a broader context:

> The row [over the Brent Spar] is just the latest in a series of controversies generated by the exploitation of North Sea oil ... Our [report] assesses now who's gained, who's lost from the exploitation of Britain's black gold.

The main topic was the history of North Sea oil:

Ironically today should have been a day of celebration for the oil industry. It is almost twenty years to the day that the first North Sea oil came ashore.

Following an examination of that history – which did not include any material on or pertaining to the quarrel between Shell and Greenpeace – the news report concluded:

For environmentalists, politicians and technicians alike, North Sea oil has always thrown up fresh challenges. For the [oil] industry the future looks as bright as it ever has. But only if it meets the environmental challenges of the nineties with the inventiveness it has always shown.

In this way the dispute over the Spar was represented as a minor issue (a 'challenge') and linked with what was characterised as the bigger story: the history of the oil industry's involvement in the harvesting of North Sea oil. It is quite possible that *Channel 4* had archive material on the North Sea that it could use, but the decision to cover the conflict between Shell and Greenpeace in a very minimal way meant that, relative to *BBC* and *ITV* news, very little attention was given to the specifics of the row.

The traditional format of *Channel 4 News* (a longer examination of fewer stories rather than several headline stories and almost an hour as opposed to *BBC* and *ITV*'s 25 minute news slots) allowed for an in-depth examination, yet an extended consideration of the claims Shell and Greenpeace made was not undertaken. This reflected *Channel 4*'s lack of interest in the matter.

Despite not examining the particulars of the situation, the report did represent the two main contenders in specific ways. Both Shell and Greenpeace were depicted as steadfast and resolute in their efforts to achieve their conflicting goals. Shell was portrayed as the aggressor:

Greenpeace helicopter comes under attack by Shell as the company tries to dump an oil platform.

Although little was said about the situation, *Channel 4* deployed certain standard conventions. For example, the June 16 report stated: '[Shell's plan is] endorsed by Britain's offshore industry' and then, in order to establish that, quoted Dr Harold Hughes of the UK Offshore Operators Association defending Shell's stance. And a clip of a Greenpeace spokesman, Chris Rose, maintaining the contrary view, followed that statement.

After an examination of the visual coverage of the crisis, I will consider what my observation of the deployment of certain standard narratives in television news means for how this crisis was covered, and will discuss what that means for the claims made about television coverage.

The visual coverage of the crisis

That television news used Greenpeace footage was clearly discernible because the source of some videos was labelled as Greenpeace. In view of that labelling, it is odd that television executives claimed otherwise and this circumstance suggests that there may have been other reasons for that claim.

A particular Greenpeace video that consultants, Shell and television executives isolate as creating bias: the 'Spar scene',[28] was frequently shown. Essentially, they maintain that it portrayed Shell as the malevolent, thoughtless aggressor and Greenpeace as the benevolent, courageous victim. Whether 'the public' interpreted the material in such a way is speculative, yet largely assumed in that argument.

The argument that the broadcasting of this material resulted in biased television coverage is simplistic. In order to examine the issue of whether the visual coverage of the crisis and, in particular, this video created the symbolic imagery they claim, I focused on *how* the videos were used, paying particular attention to the accompanying verbal reports, because those narratives, I believe, play a role in the portrayal and the understanding of the situation shown by the visuals. Having taken that approach, my observations call into question what the consultants, Shell and television executives maintain with regard to the visual coverage of the crisis in general and the use of Greenpeace footage in particular.

With regard to the labelling of the controversial footage, my findings from investigating *BBC*, *ITV* and *Channel 4* news are that the Spar scene video was sometimes shown unlabelled by all three channels, but was either labelled when it was subsequently shown or had been labelled at previous times. Greenpeace footage, other than that video, was also often labelled. The suggestion that Greenpeace material was not labelled is not true.

The claim that a lack of labelling led to bias is further problematic because, although television executives made much of the labelling of the footage, I wondered whether it made much of a difference. They assumed that it did or they might have felt they had to state that it did, but it is not certain whether audiences notice the labelling of the source of a video and, even if they do, it is not certain whether they make the appropriate adjustments to their judgements. For instance, Ericson et al. (1989) argues that the television viewer, unlike the newspaper reader, has no chance for retrieval unless news is recorded, which is not how television news is normally consumed. And research suggests that, even if it is held still and motionless (on 'pause') and not watched in the 'normal' manner, different reactions to television news can be obtained (Ericson et al. 1989).

Whether the Spar scene conveyed the symbolism and imagery that consultants, Shell and television executives claim was not, I felt, as uncomplicated and tangible as they suggest. Furthermore, my examination of the verbal reports that went along with the video on the *BBC* and *ITV* programmes did not support consultants', Shell's and television executives' claims about the promoted impressions of Greenpeace and Shell.

The *BBC* used the video in combination with a description of what was taking place. That description stated the reason *why* Shell was using the water hoses and, in doing so, gave an account of the situation that did *not* support the wicked Goliath fighting the well-meaning David imagery, cited by consultants, Shell and television executives as creating a biased view:

> The water cannon deters sabotage dinghies launched by a Greenpeace vessel *Altair*, itself engaged in a game of cat and mouse with a patrol boat (*BBC* 9 O'Clock news, June 12);

> Protected by water cannon at a support vessel the Brent Spar rig is continuing its slow progress towards its proposed graveyard in the Atlantic (*BBC* 9 O'Clock news, June 18).

The verbal report accompanying the visual portrayed the situation as one where Shell 'protected' the Spar and 'deterred' 'sabotage' attempts by Greenpeace. Therefore, the view that the dominant Shell attacked the powerless Greenpeace was not promoted, in contrast to what consultants, Shell and television executives uphold.

The *BBC*'s use of the visuals as a description of Greenpeace's protests, rather than just Shell's actions, also contradicts what they claim. Contrary to what has been said regarding the depiction of Shell and Greenpeace, the descriptions that accompanied the contentious video characterised Greenpeace rather than Shell as the more potent, aggressive and powerful party in the conflict:

> After a weekend of conflict at sea, Greenpeace is now trying for another opportunity to try and block the sinking of the Brent Spar and, with more rigs likely to be dumped at sea, these scenes seem certain to be repeated (*BBC* 9 O'Clock news, June 12);

> A Greenpeace ship continues to shadow the rig as it tows towards its disposal site (*BBC* 9 O'Clock news, June 15);

> A Greenpeace vessel is monitoring every move. And with two of its activists on board the storage tank it is determined to stop Shell from sinking its redundant rig (*BBC* 9 O'Clock news, June 18).

The verbal reports did not depict Greenpeace and Shell in the manner claimed. Shell, rather than Greenpeace, was presented as under siege.

ITV also used Greenpeace footage, which was apparent because the source of some videos was labelled as Greenpeace. The Greenpeace video of their helicopter attempting to land on the Spar's heli-deck while avoiding the water hoses was used, along with the Spar scene video, as in *BBC* news programmes. In total disparity with the suggestion that television news did not divulge the source of video footage, the *ITV* reporter *explicitly* drew attention to the clip of the helicopter being a Greenpeace video:

> This Greenpeace video shows the latest clashes ... The vessels towing the rig out to sea surrounded it with a curtain of water. Greenpeace couldn't get through the water jets so they decided to go over it instead (*ITV News at Ten*, June 16).

Once again, that account does not portray Shell and Greenpeace in the manner claimed. Instead, Greenpeace was depicted as determined and Shell as surrounding the installation with a 'curtain of water', which is not a critical description of the company or its action in deterring Greenpeace from boarding the Spar.

The report continued with comment on Greenpeace's action, which included views on this from both sides:

The operation was not without risk. The Greenpeace helicopter flew through jets of water. Courageous, say the campaigners. Irresponsible, say Shell (*ITV News at Ten*, June 16).

This was followed by a video of the Chairman of Shell, Chris Fay, criticising Greenpeace's manoeuvre. Here, the use of Greenpeace footage permitted Shell to argue in a manner that was critical of Greenpeace and, hence, worked in the company's favour. That is far from the claim that the use of Greenpeace footage compromised Shell's position and argument.

In contrast to *BBC's* and *ITV's* reports, the verbal reports given by *Channel 4 News* promoted a similar view of Greenpeace and Shell to that which consultants, Shell and television executives claim. Shell was quite clearly depicted as the aggressor in the description that Greenpeace's helicopter 'comes under attack'. The last time the two Greenpeace videos were shown (the helicopter and Spar scene were used and labelled), *Channel 4 News* had the following verbal account:

In the North Atlantic today it looked like a battle scene ... A Greenpeace helicopter was pounded by water jets as it approached. Even so, two protesters managed to get on the rig. Shell says sinking the oil rig one and a half miles under sea is the safest option (June 16).

The above account portrayed Greenpeace and Shell in a similar manner to that which consultants, Shell and television executives claim. That there was a 'battle' and that Greenpeace were being 'attacked' and 'pounded' does frame the main parties in specific ways. For example, whereas *ITV* had depicted Greenpeace as going over the water jets, *Channel 4* portrayed Shell's water hoses as attacking the helicopter. However, as previously observed, *Channel 4 News's* reports of the situation did represent the views of both sides of the dispute, as is also evident in the above quotation which included the representation of Shell's views.

Despite not entirely invalidating what has been claimed about the visual coverage of the crisis and the use of Greenpeace footage, my observations point to certain problems with that argument, not just because the source of the video was often identified but also, more importantly, because the verbal reports that went with the video did not always guide perceptions in the way consultants, Shell and television executives claim. That finding has consequences for the claims about how television news scenes symbolised the dispute between Shell and Greenpeace. Even if we consider the possibility that the visuals supported the imagery claimed by consultants, Shell and television executives, the finding that *BBC*, *ITV* and *Channel 4* news reports did not support that depiction, coupled with the finding that the *BBC* and *ITV's* verbal adjuncts to the visuals also did not support that imagery, is significant to the accusation that television coverage was biased and to the question of whether that was how television news represented the crisis.

Observations on the television coverage

My examination of television coverage of the crisis, as with the press coverage, does not support the consultants' and Shell's claim that there was a bias and that the company's case did not gain representation. What we have principally learned from the examination of television coverage of the crisis is that television news was quite concerned to be impartial and also to demonstrate it. That the television news was more impartial than the press coverage is also discernible.

Earlier, I stated that both the *BBC* and *ITN*, the news provider for *Channel 4* and *ITV*, operated under the public service broadcasting remit and had a governing principle to be impartial. Impartiality is not only expected from television news but is also a valued goal. I have demonstrated that *BBC*, *ITV* and *Channel 4* news coverage employed certain conventions to suggest impartiality. Thus, we have seen how that principle exercised its influence on the way in which the crisis was reported, because the format of most news reports covered the conflicting views of the situation and all were concerned to appear objective.

I found that *ITV* and *Channel 4* news coverage did not appear to lean towards any party involved in the dispute. Most *BBC News* programmes, as with *ITV* and *Channel 4*, were also characteristically impartial. Nevertheless, there were instances where coverage leant towards one side of the dispute. Quite significantly, towards the later stages of the immediate crisis, *BBC News* favoured Shell's case. That observation of a leaning towards Shell's views is in stark contrast to the nature of bias as held by Shell and consultants, who accuse television coverage of a bias towards the views of Greenpeace. My investigation shows that this was not the case.

Determining the validity of consultants' and Shell's claims regarding bias in television coverage is complicated, but not entirely hampered, by what they have said about the role played by the exhibition of a Greenpeace video. I have suggested that, as it is widely acknowledged that television news scenes can be imagistic and symbolic that claim could be made, yet it is by no means certain that it is valid. However, it seems that it is not necessary to prove that something actually was the case but credibly to argue that it could have been.

I will later elaborate on how my observations on television and press coverage are consequential to crisis management.

On the consultants' interpretation of this case

This section compares the case with the consultants' recommendations and the specific arguments they make about this case.

The previous chapter demonstrated that events were not only unforeseen but also had an openness and emergent quality that made prediction difficult. Almost everything was open to interpretation, changeable, and constituted by the situation as it unfolded. My analysis of this case draws on that line of reasoning, which bears on the consultants' argument that Shell could have better managed the issue to prevent crisis, and that the crisis itself could have been better handled. Could Shell's difficulties in managing the crisis be explained in terms of the difficulties involved in predicting the future? And are consultants' criticisms a case of hindsight being twenty-twenty? If so, what does that reveal about the criticisms they make and about their recommendations?

The outline of the consultants' recommendations I use below and in the next chapter (rationales 1 to 5) is one that is compiled from an examination of the consultants' account of crisis management described in chapter one.

Rationale 1: Prevent crises through issues management. Coordinated and centrally controlled responses have to be made and managed at an early stage as contentious issues arise. The organisation facing a crisis must present itself as united.

Situation: Despite accepting that the Royal Dutch/Shell Group was entirely taken by surprise when they faced a crisis over the Brent Spar, consultants argue that the company should have foreseen opposition but did not. They claim that, because the company did not recognise potential problems, it did not effectively manage troublesome issues, which ultimately resulted in the full blown crisis. Moreover, consultants propose that Shell's earlier response to the situation damagingly revealed that the corporation was divided over the issue of how best to dispose of the Spar. My examination of this case lends some justification to these claims, but there are problems with them.

Firstly, Shell had not encountered any criticism when its sea disposal plan was publicly announced two months before Greenpeace's protest activities. Thus, before Greenpeace's occupation of the Spar and before opposition, Shell was unaware that its plan could become controversial. As I demonstrated, the first sign of protest that Shell encountered was when Greenpeace occupied the Brent Spar. Shell was oblivious to the existence of an 'issue' that required management. On the face of it, this seems to justify consultants' criticisms, but the fact that Shell was unaware and therefore unprepared poses problems for the maxim of addressing issues at an early stage. How does an organisation go about managing issues of which it is not aware? Furthermore, before Greenpeace's protests there were no indications that the sea disposal plan would become contentious.

The lack of early preparation by Shell, according to consultants, was a central reason for the crisis situation. Nevertheless, there is a dilemma that exists within this. The company may have imagined that, once the Greenpeace supporters had been removed from the Brent Spar, the disposal would proceed smoothly. Moreover, the company may also have supposed that the protests would blow away once the public and critical politicians came to see the efforts Shell had taken in arriving at its decision, which it repeatedly outlined in its news releases. Of course this did not happen, but it is often no simple matter to determine the outcome certain courses of action would have until after the event. Macnaghten and Urry argue: '... many interventions ... generate unexpected and unpredictable reactions which can escalate the issue and the problem far away from what is apparently intended' (1998: 249).

Consultants maintain that key personnel should have a visible presence, pay attention to potentially problematic issues and get involved in handling the crisis because without such 'focus at the absolute top of the organisation reputations and performance are quickly threatened' (Regester and Larkin 1997: 69–70). They argue that 'the chief executive did not make these decisions at an early stage' (Regester and Larkin 1997: 70). This claim is justified as Cor Herkstroter, Royal Dutch CEO, decided only at a later stage of the crisis, on June 15, i.e. a week before the scheduled date for the disposal, to take charge of the situation personally. Consultants attribute to this aspect a determining causality, and Regester and Larkin correctly argue that this is one significant reason why Shell found it difficult to handle the crisis.

There should have been a coordinated communications effort at an early stage, consultants argue:

> ... faced with managing an issue, a company must never appear divided. Perceptions matter. The perception was that Shell did not speak with one voice ... it is imperative that ... there is always a single, consistently communicated position on an issue, with authorized spokespeople assigned to represent that position (Regester and Larkin 1997: 73–4).

That Shell did not communicate a single consistent view of the situation at an early stage is demonstrated in my examination of the case. Even when Greenpeace occupied the Spar, Shell UK did not communicate this development to the other European companies. But neglecting to inform other companies was a result of the structure and the culture of the corporation; Shell UK and its subsidiary, Shell Expro, were the only companies in the corporation which were meant to make decisions concerning the Spar. That oversight, however, showed disregard for the fact that what was said about 'Shell', in a worldwide debate of the Brent Spar issue, affected the image of the whole corporation. Responses to control that circumstance could not be coordinated and managed at an early stage because senior management did not have knowledge of the situation and, therefore, could not make strategic communication decisions and protect the image of the corporation.

Furthermore, it was not until nearly a month after the first Greenpeace occupation of the Spar that the public relations operation for handling the situation with Brent Spar was moved from Aberdeen to London (on May 23), even though Peter Duncan was in daily communication about the volatile situation in Germany with Chris Fay, who was based in London. A lack of coordinated communications meant that a series of contradictory public announcements were made which complicated the situation.

In hindsight we can see that the absence of an earlier coordinated response had damaging consequences, but for the corporation that was not apparent at the time. While such a strategy makes sense, it was nevertheless difficult to put into practice given that the corporation was structured in a decentralised way and different approaches to business and different operative cultures were very much a part of the culture of the organisation. Consultants criticise 'Shell' for having taken this or that action but, in reality, 'Shell' was not one entity with uniform views, as the conflicting attitudes of Shell Germany and Shell UK quite distinctly showed. Contradictory communications also emerged because the corporation was in actual fact divided over the issue – they were not just a result of a mistake but expressions of differences of opinion within the Royal Dutch/Shell Group of companies. Given such fragmentation, it is difficult to envisage that one view of the situation *could* have been disseminated at an *early* stage, though a uniform view of the situation *did* emanate from the organisation at a later date, as my analysis shows.

Perhaps this state of affairs was inevitable, for how are decentred organisations to portray themselves as a single unit with uniform views when the fact of the matter is that each component is differentiated from the others? And even though an organisation might accept that such a posture is necessary in an abnormal situation, recognising that an abnormal situation has arisen which warrants that response is not always feasible. That indicates problems with the consultants' advocacy of early management. In retrospect it is quite easy for the consultants to pinpoint the stage at which Shell should have centrally controlled its communications. For the corporation, operating at the time, this was not so clear.

While what I have stated above does not refute the consultants' argument that the company followed a misguided course, it does show the problems involved in identifying which courses of action would be beneficial and which damaging as events are taking place.

The consultants' argument about the necessity of early management of contentious issues appears sensible but as can be seen though Shell's experience, knowing what will become contentious is inherently uncertain. And, when contention arises, what actions need to be taken in such circumstances are also unclear.

Rationale 2: Understand and respond to public emotions and perceptions of the issue. Consultants maintain that negative perceptions demand a response, even if the company feels that the issue is not very serious or that the perceptions are wrong.

Situation: Regester and Larkin take the conventional view amongst consultants that in this instance a crisis arose because Shell had not assessed and responded to perceptions of sea disposal at an early stage.

168 The Principles and Practice of Crisis Management

Shell is depicted as having completely failed to understand and respond to perceptions.

Having examined the circumstances, I would claim that it was not quite this simple. Shell did not *entirely* fail to respond to perceptions and there are difficulties in ascertaining whose perceptions are important and must be addressed.

Firstly, the initial circumstances assured Shell that there was no problem. All the regulatory and legal procedures had been followed. Under the UK government's guidelines for the disposal of an offshore installation Shell was required to carry out consultations with various interested groups. For the company at the time, those groups, together with the governmental organisations, were its key audiences. All the company's key publics, at this time, had accepted the position of the company and no opposition or protest followed the public announcement of its plan. Given this situation, it is incorrect to state that *at this stage*, Shell had not addressed perceptions of the issue because there was no indication that there were negative perceptions of the plan.

Although Shell had consulted and gained the acceptance of those who were key audiences (at the time), consultants argue that the problem was that Shell had not consulted *widely* enough. However, determining how widely to consult is not straightforward. Deciding who your key publics are is a complex venture, as they not only differ according to a company's disparate activities but they may also change as events develop.

The circumstances of this case confirm that certain publics become key as events develop. The general public in the UK and elsewhere became significant to Shell as public protest emerged and as Greenpeace addressed that public in its campaign. And the same can be said of the German public. The fact that the German public, along with the general public elsewhere, later protested and thus subsequently evolved into key publics, points to problems with the consultants' argument. Clearly those publics emerged as key ones as events developed. Predicting that is not necessarily feasible. Consequently, this case illustrates how the relevance of certain groups may change according to circumstances. Whether it is possible to prevision and predict this process is not as simple as consultants suggest. There are some very real practical difficulties with the proposal that perceptions have to be assessed and addressed. A relevant observation of symbolic interactionism is that 'significant others'/key publics emerge and are constituted by the situation as it develops (Rock 1979). They are not necessarily there initially and thus cannot always be discerned at the outset.

Consultants argue that an organisation such as Shell, which operates on an international level, should have been familiar with a variety of diverse publics in various markets especially with the dominant views on environmental matters, an issue on which the oil industry is particularly susceptible to criticism. But as Herbert Blumer argues in his writings on public opinion, public opinion crystallises around issues as they emerge; it is not static (Shibutani 1970; Blumer 1986). Hence, had Shell conducted a poll to ascertain public opinion on sea disposal, and proceeded with its plan on that basis, the company might still have faced the same situation because public opinion fluctuates. The situation is even more complex when groups such as Greenpeace seek to influence public opinion, as happened in this case.

Consultants argue that in contrast to Shell, Greenpeace's campaign addressed different audiences in different ways, and in doing so incorporated and appealed to their diverse views. Winter and Schweinsberg (1996) certainly argue that this was so. That Greenpeace's campaigns in the UK and in Germany had different focuses shows that Greenpeace assessed and responded to the different perceptions of these distinct audiences. Mary Douglas (Douglas and Wildavsky 1982) observes a situation very much borne out by the Brent Spar case, that is, that perceptions of risks are cultural; different cultures have dissimilar ideas about what constitutes dangers. Accordingly, there were different responses to Shell's plan in Germany and in the UK.

The consultants ask the loaded question that if Greenpeace had recognised that the German population is more susceptible to environmental issues, why had Shell been slow to appreciate this? But it is not as uncomplicated as they suggest.

Shell did not predict that the disposal of the Brent Spar would become a worldwide issue, or even one that would be considered questionable, and there are very real problems in foreseeing that. As demonstrated by this, it is often unclear at an early stage who would become 'key' publics, and when that is apparent and manifest, responding to those perceptions might also be compromised due to such responses being overdue. Consultants recognise that when Shell encountered opposition it was too late to review, assess and respond to the German public but they do not allow for the fact that key publics emerge as events develop.

With regard to the consultants' contention that Shell's communications failed to respond to perceptions, after examination of Shell's news releases it does not seem as if the company completely failed to address perceptions of the situation, despite outwardly failing to respond to one crucial perception. Greenpeace's opposition to the disposal of the Brent Spar was very much based on the claims that:

(a) it would set a precedent;
(b) sea disposal would endanger the marine environment and land disposal would be environmentally less damaging;
(c) sea disposal was wrong in principle.

Shell's news releases denied (a), stating that the options for disposal available to the other oil installations would be considered on a case by case approach, and responded to (b), by presenting its scientific studies that demonstrated that this would not be the case but seemingly ignored (c). While Shell's communications did address the sea disposal method and argued that this method was preferable in the instance of the Spar, they did not explicitly address the perception that sea disposal was wrong in principle.

Consultants claim that Shell did not address the perceived seriousness of the sea disposal method as it continued to believe that there was no real reason for the opposition. Shell reiterated in its communications that all its actions had been lawful and considerate of the environment. The consultants assert that this type of statement ignored the basis of much of the opposition, which was based on a perception that it was not all right to throw industrial waste into the sea. My analysis of Shell's press releases show that Shell failed, to an extent, to see that people might believe that sea disposal was undesirable, unacceptable, and even immoral. But, as mentioned in the previous chapter, Shell may have intended to address that view by presenting its scientific and legal case. Perhaps Shell was responding to the moral dimensions of the opposition by proposing that scientific methods (such as environmental impact studies of disposal at sea) were better responses to the problem of disposal than moral ones. The company's argument, however, was not a moral one, nor would it necessarily address moral responses to the chosen disposal method.

Shell may have failed to take account of the following. The disposal was seen as polluting, and pollution, as Douglas argues, critically hinges on moral and cultural questions of boundaries, purity and transgression. Her book, *Purity and Danger* (2001), argues that what a particular culture considers unclean and unacceptable is determined by what that culture endeavours to achieve, i.e. 'the ideal social order' (2001: 73), as she calls it. Following from that, considering the sea disposal of the Spar as unacceptable and wrong is determined by what a particular society finds acceptable and right. Thus, it is a moral issue. Douglas's analysis of pollution helps in understanding the opposition against Shell as she showed that people respond to pollution concerns on a symbolic and moral basis. Protests against Shell prohibited the company from carrying out an act that contravened the ideal social order. The protests were attempts to create, maintain and sustain a particular culture – a culture that did not look favourably on sea disposal. The claim that Shell's planned action was dangerous also related to that endeavour because Douglas shows that evoking danger attempts to prohibit actions that might imperil the ideal social order. Therefore, Shell's argument that the sea disposal was not dangerous, made with reference to scientific findings, could not address what was really at issue.

As we have seen, Shell certainly proffered and reiterated its case, which was based on rational scientific arguments about the limited risks the Brent Spar would pose to the deep sea, and the greater risk to safety and the environment posed by land disposal. But this argument was ignorant of the symbolic and moral power of notions of pollution and danger to the environment which were elements driving the opposition to Shell's plan. What Shell's communications did not do explicitly was counter the perception that sea disposal was fundamentally wrong. In following this course, Shell failed to address a crucial perception that Greenpeace's campaign relied on and made use of. But it was not at all the case that Shell wholly failed to address perceptions, as the consultants maintain.

The consultants view what happened in this case as illustrative of what they claim typically happens in most cases involving risks. They uphold a particular construction: people often respond to risks in an emotional and irrational manner, attitudes to risks are driven by perceptual elements that may be based on irrational assessments of risk, and crises and issues are frequently triggered and fuelled by public fear and anxiety (Regester and Larkin 1997; Seymour and Moore 2000; Bland 1997). These irrational elements, consultants argue, decide perceptions of company reputations and corporate responsibility.

Some sociologists who have made similar observations support this view. In their studies of a growing concern with risk, Beck (1992; 2000) and Giddens (1996; 2000) view responses to risks as often being not entirely rational. They would argue that the limits of rationality are revealed very starkly in situations such as the disposal of Brent Spar, where rational responses to risks, such as the scientific, were overridden by other concerns that were equally, if not more, powerful and relevant. Similarly, in *Contested Natures* (1998) Macnaghten and Urry argue that 'nature is a hugely significant concept in western culture' (1998: 253), there is no single nature, only natures, 'each is contested … no one nature is more obviously natural than any other' (1998: 250) and that 'how people value nature is often highly ambiguous and contradictory; that values only appear to inhere in nature in particular and context-specific way ... [v]alues are not free-floating but intertwined with senses of insecurity , globalisation, anxiety, individualisation, mounting mistrust with politics and scientific expertise, the enhanced role of the media, and so on' (1998: 250–1).

Although consultants prefer to see things along the lines of rationality and irrationality, and use the contrasts of emotional versus rational in interpreting this case, the circumstances of this case are better understood through studies which highlight the symbolic and moral power of pollution and the contested nature of 'nature'. Mary Douglas's observations also express some of the issues consultants wish to emphasise and are not entirely unlike what they wanted to propose, i.e. she suggested that what is seen as dangerous and polluting is determined by factors other than what might actually be the case. However, one must also bear in mind that the consultants' evocation of the notions of emotional versus rational implies that one approach is better than the other. And arguing that Greenpeace appealed to emotion whereas Shell was more rational (an argument that consultants and Shell retrospectively make), belittles Greenpeace's claims. As I later elaborate, the retrospective use of that argument by Shell is beneficial to the company as that view disparages the opponent and justifies its own approach.

Consultants also state that the success of claims about risks is also determined by trust, suggesting that this is why Greenpeace's claims were believed. Through reference to this case, Furedi (1998) argues similarly, claiming that who the public trusts determines what interpretations of the situation are likely to be believed. Even so, the consultants do not see this as an unassailable problem, arguing that what is essential in communicating about risks is to respond to perceptions of risks, but clearly, and even in their view, there are other issues involved. Furedi's and consultants' observations about trust make communicating about risks a difficult enterprise, especially for corporations, who are often not trusted (*Survey On Public Attitudes To Big Business*, MORI: 1998). That responses to risks are by no means limited to scientific findings and arguments (a circumstance the consultants also identify) also shows the difficulties involved in influencing perceptions of risks.

I have argued that there are problems with assessing perceptions, but if Shell had found the existence of the perception that sea disposal was wrong prior to the crisis, the company would have faced three choices: ignore it, discount sea disposal altogether, or raise this issue and convince a wide audience of the merits of sea disposal. Consultants advocate the latter approach, arguing that because Shell did not convince the public about the merits of its proposed plan at an early stage it lost a lot of money and risked its reputation as an environmentally concerned company. But there are problems with that argument. Consultants downplay the fact that the existence of views against sea disposal, especially strong views couched in morality and expressed symbolically, would mean that reversing such a perception would not be a simple matter and might in any event have made sea disposal problematic. Furthermore, by raising the issue, the company might have inadvertently precipitated the very same crisis it wanted to avoid. That aspect, as I have previously said, is most often disregarded in the consultants' proposal to manage issues at an early stage.

Rationale 3: Cultivate knowledge of all relevant audiences, especially that of opponents and their agendas and 'how they are likely to behave' (Regester and Larkin 1997: 72). And communicate with such key publics in order to gain their acceptance.

Situation: As discussed above, Shell had trouble isolating, verifying and handling the views of all its relevant audiences and there are tenacious difficulties involved in doing so. An audience/group that became important for Shell was Greenpeace. According to consultants, Shell's lack of intelligence about Greenpeace's planned campaign seriously compromised the company's ability to respond successfully to the crisis when Greenpeace cast doubt on the disposal plan. Regester and Larkin argue:

> Shell appeared to have no knowledge of the planned campaign by Greenpeace and was [when Greenpeace occupied the Spar] seemingly taken by surprise ... [Shell should have had an early warning system which] involves gathering information on *all* relevant audiences, however peripheral in the beginning (1997: 72).

Greenpeace is a perennial 'other' for Shell, and oil companies in general, as the organisation had an ongoing position against oil exploration and production. Central to the environmental group was an imperative to pressure big oil companies to invest in non-polluting renewable energy sources, such as solar power, instead of fossil fuels. There had been earlier Greenpeace campaigns against Shell and other oil companies.[29] Moreover, as Greenpeace divulges, they had, on previous occasions, used a similar strategy to that used in the case of Brent Spar of contesting disposal of the by-products of industries to stop the main activities of such industries:

> Greenpeace had fought a successful campaign to limit the produc-
> tion of nuclear materials and the spread of nuclear energy by closing
> off options for nuclear waste disposal ... There were obvious, though
> incomplete, parallels with the Spar ... A similar 'back-end' strategy,
> in which the industry was made to take away all its wastes and pay
> to deal with it, would force the oil industry to internalise costs cur-
> rently externalised at the expense of the environment and the tax-
> payer and put a brake on oil expansion into the oceans.[30] This was
> one of many rationales for campaigning against the dumping of the
> Spar ... (Rose 1998: 184).

However, and as Greenpeace admits, much of its activity at this time
had focused on the sea disposal of industrial waste rather than that of
oil installations:

> When the Ospar convention [which regulated the sea disposal and
> land based pollution in the North East Atlantic] was negotiated [in
> 1992], it is true that Greenpeace did not actively campaign to
> prevent the adoption of the rules in Annex III [which allowed the
> sea disposal of obsolete oil installations] ... Greenpeace was focused
> on campaigning for the prevention of the dumping of radioactive
> wastes ... For Greenpeace, as for the rest of the environmental com-
> munity, the dumping of decommissioned offshore installations was
> still perceived as an issue 'for the future' (Rose 1998: 43).

It is conceivable that even if Shell had expected Greenpeace to protest
(the company denies this), the success of that protest might not have
been expected. Also, it was obvious that Shell had not expected the
protest to be conducted from the Spar, as revealed by the company's lack
of preparation for it. Further, although Greenpeace was, for oil companies, an 'other', Shell might not have expected that organisation to emerge
as a significant other in the particular instance of the Spar disposal.
Moreover, as Shell had not initially met with opposition and had countered the potential opposition of quite a number of other groups, the
company was understandably unprepared for the situation that arose.

However, consultants insist that Shell would have known that Greenpeace would not find the plan acceptable if they had paid sufficient
attention to this public:

> In the case of issues relating to health, safety and environmental
> protection it is essential that organizations pay particular attention
> to special interest groups. Building a profile of the working methods

and organization of such groups through examining the characteristics, style and approach to campaigning, membership recruitment, funding, promotional activities and current agenda setting, will provide valuable intelligence for planning purposes (Regester and Larkin 1997: 72).

It was not, however, the case that Greenpeace's campaign plans were publicly accessible. The Director of Public Affairs at Shell UK, states:

Personally, I was quite friendly with Greenpeace and knew Peter Melchett, Director of Greenpeace UK, quite well but Greenpeace kept its plans well hidden (in interview: November 18, 2000).

After the crisis, Shell did engage voluntarily in consultations with various interested parties, including Greenpeace. By that time, circumstances had made Greenpeace a key public and made it easy for Shell to recognise that.

In the crisis management activities that followed the crisis, Shell stated that:

We accept that we could have consulted more widely and earlier in the original Spar disposal process – but this does not refer just to Greenpeace. We aim to communicate openly and listen to people's concerns and to take part in an industry-wide effort to do this (*Brent Spar – The Way Forward, Your Questions Answered*, Shell UK: October 1995: 4).

In making that statement, Shell agreed with the consultants' allegation that the company should have been better prepared and should have communicated with all its audiences. But, as I subsequently elaborate, what Shell said later was part of the company's crisis management and statements such as the above were made in order to represent Shell as a company willing to listen and accommodate its critics. The fact that what Shell said matched consultants' proposals might have more to do with the company constructing rhetorical realities than with denoting that these proposals are feasible.

However, consultants do capitalise on statements like the above to justify their stance:

[Shell] later looked back on its Brent Spar experience in an insightful and refreshingly frank [manner]. The lessons Shell learned are applicable to all companies facing an issue with the potential to become a crisis. Managers at Shell concluded that: the company should have consulted a wide range of stakeholder groups; it failed to appreciate the need for ... dialogue; it should have considered people's emotional reactions ...; it should have realised that the general public would be interested ...; it needed to adjust its messages for different cultures ...; it needed to educate its key audiences, particularly the media, before the crisis occurred (Seymour and Moore 2000: 16).

Whilst Shell certainly made statements to that effect (see chapter four), it is telling that the consultants draw attention, and attach the greatest significance, to those statements that agree with their own outlook.

In concluding their examination of the Brent Spar crisis Regester and Larkin quote Shell:

> Ruminating on the consequence ... Shell UK's director of public affairs wrote: 'Businesses will now ... have to come to grips with ... symbolic gestures' (1997: 75).

And that is a point that consultants also underscore.

However, the fact of the matter is that no one can know who the 'all' are before the event. Identifying who key publics are, and when 'others' would become 'significant others' and in what circumstances, is a persistent problem and will always be a liability for businesses, especially those as large as the Royal Dutch/Shell Group of companies with numerous audiences, in various and often disparate countries.

Rationale 4: Present and communicate the case clearly, quickly, repeatedly and succinctly for the message to be effectively conveyed via the media.

Situation: Consultants argue that Shell failed in communicating its case to the media, and hence also to a wider audience, because the company communicated scientific and technical details too complex to be conveyed by the mass media:

> Reliance solely on the availability of scientific or technical data without communicating clear messages that distil key findings in a manner that responds to potential public concern about a particular risk is simply not enough to prevent or win the debate ... clear message points repeated over time help to make sense of complex

issues ... the avoidance of complex language and statistics is essential ... instead the use of analogies to emphasize the low degree of potential risk to the environment, coupled with basic facts, message points and illustrations are effective mechanisms for making a clear and compelling case. This type of approach ... is about focussing on a few points, and constantly and consistently communicating those points to secure understanding and ultimately, support ... (Regester and Larkin 1997: 71).

Consultants claim that their experience led them to this maxim, but it also reflects their notion of what is the best way to influence media coverage and is based on a logic of public relations familiar to them.

My analysis of Shell's news releases shows that Shell's communications at the time of the crisis did in fact follow the very course Regester and Larkin (1997) later claimed the company should have taken but did not. Their critique of this case recommends that Shell follow this course: repeat messages, present analogies, 'demonstrate the remoteness and depth of the disposal location', 'the potential for marine life to colonise the structure over time', and 'the health and safety benefits of offshore disposal' (Regester and Larkin 1997: 71). That Shell did follow those suggestions is demonstrated below.

Shell continually repeated its message that deep sea disposal was the best environmental option:

> ... deepsea [sic] disposal of the Spar has been independently assessed as the best option from an environmental point of view, and in terms of several other considerations including health, safety and economic efficiency (Shell UK news release: May 16).

> The careful weighing of all the environmental, safety, public health and economic considerations shows that the deep-water sinking of the Spar is the best solution (Shell UK news release: May 23).

> The environment, safety, health and economic considerations have been responsibly balanced ... the responsible balance for the Brent Spar ... is carefully managed deepwater [sic] disposal (Shell UK news release: May 31).

> Aberdeen University have concluded that deepwater [sic] disposal is the best practicable option from an environmental point of view and that deepwater [sic] disposal is up to six times safer (Shell UK news release: June 15).

... deepwater [sic] disposal is the best practicable environmental option (Shell UK news release: June 18).

This message was repeated throughout the crisis situation and even on June 20, after deciding against the plan:

Shell UK Limited still believes that deep water disposal of the Brent Spar is the best practicable environmental option which was supported by independent studies (Shell UK news release: June 20).

Additionally, conforming to Regester and Larkin's recommendation and contrary to their criticism, Shell presented analogies:

The irreducible sources of possible contamination [left on board the Spar] represent such low levels of radioactivity ... the level of radioactivity ... will be no more than would emanate from a group of granite buildings in Aberdeen (Shell UK news release: May 16).

The consultants' criticism that Shell did not refer to the remoteness and depth of the disposal location can also be disproved because that was frequently cited and implicit in Shell's repeated description of its plan as 'deep water disposal':

... deepwater [sic] disposal [will take place] at a location some 150 miles out in the Atlantic where the water depth is more than 6000 feet (Shell UK news release: May 16).

... the designated disposal site, more than 150 miles off the west of Scotland, is in the deep Atlantic at a location where the water is more than 1.2 miles deep. The environmental impact of disposal at such a location will be negligible (Shell UK news release: June 15).

Furthermore, although the consultants claim the company did not do so, Shell often emphasised the benefits of sea disposal by making the very arguments consultants recommend, and criticise the company for not making (that marine life will colonise the structure and that there are health and safety benefits of offshore disposal):

... in the United States the government has since the mid eighties encouraged oil companies to use many structures as artificial reefs in place in the Gulf of Mexico, on which marine life has proliferated specifically to the benefit of fishermen (Shell UK news release: May 16) (Shell UK news release: May 31).

Numerous studies have shown that on balance there would be no environmental benefit in onshore disposal ... while safety and occupational health risks would be higher (Shell UK news release: May 31) (Shell UK news release: June 15).

... numerous independent studies over 3 years which have conclusively demonstrated that in the unusual case of the Brent Spar, deepwater [sic] disposal in water 1.5 miles deep, some 150 miles from land in the Atlantic ocean is not only the most responsible environmental solution but incurs six times less risk to the health and safety of those involved (Shell UK news release: June 18).

With reference to Regester and Larkin's specific criticism of Shell's communications, I have demonstrated that Shell did indeed undertake the type of recommendations they make. For one thing, they are wrong in arguing that Shell acted contrary to their recommendations when in fact the opposite was true. As I have said, the conception of communicating in this manner follows from a logic of public relations which is familiar both to consultants and to those conducting public and media relations within Shell. My demonstration that Shell did follow a course also recommended by consultants is significant in that Shell can be shown to have acted in a manner consultants advise, yet gained no benefit from doing so; the promised results did not emerge. Here is a clear case where Shell followed the communication tactics consultants suggest yet, according to their claim that the media did not convey Shell's messages, the advice the consultants give was adopted to no avail.

Rationale 5: Communicate and cooperate with the media and understand how the media function.

Situation: In addition to arguing that the media did not represent Shell's case, consultants also claim that Shell did not appreciate that an issue confined to a single nation could rapidly grow into a worldwide issue as a direct consequence of technological advances within the mass media:

Issues that involve an international industry and regulatory environment rarely stay local. Transmission of information and opinion through a host of newly available electronic media cannot be geographically constrained. Similarly, changing political systems and agendas demand constant review and assessment no matter how removed from equivalent national institutions. Shell in London acknowledged that it was astonished by the depth of German feeling on environmental issues relating to oceans. Why? An international organisation should be tuned into policy-making in all the markets in which it operates, particularly those that could be affected by a potential change or development like the Brent Spar (Regester and Larkin 1997: 74).

Thus they claim that, while the disposal was the legal responsibility of Shell UK, it did not necessarily mean that the issue was confined to the UK (which was Shell's view) as events in continental Europe did influence Shell's planned action.

The circumstances of this case have implications for the globalisation views which propose that a new world society is being created, connected by advanced electronic media and transnational economic and cultural forces (Giddens 1991; Castells 1997). According to such globalisation perspectives, a shared economy and culture brings about a greater connection, and political, economic and cultural concerns are lifted above national boundaries and national culture (Giddens 1999). Castells (1997) argues that one of the primary indicators and driving forces of globalisation is new technologically advanced media that allow rapid transmission of information and ideas. Yet here was an instance where a corporation operating on a global level did not quite behave in a global manner. Disparate responses from the UK and Germany also contest the view that transnational cultural forces operated. This situation is intriguing for it reveals that globalisation cannot always be demonstrated to be the case.

However, one could argue, as consultants would, that the failure of Shell to behave in a global manner and the resulting damage demonstrate the new requirements on corporations in the current globalised world. For example, the state of affairs brought on by Shell's failure to recognise and react to the circumstance that opposition expressed in one part of the world could have an impact on another part of the world could be viewed as supporting 'the social science of globalisation' (Urry 2003: x). And it is the case that some conditions of this situation support the globalisation perspectives. The fact that the action of a company based in the UK, and acting with the consent of the UK government, could be opposed on a European level demonstrates a greater integration. The growth of knowledge about protests via a technologically sophisticated, advanced and ubiquitous mass media also tends to support the idea of a globalised world. Yet, perhaps it is as Urry argued: '... globalization is never complete. It is disordered, full of paradox and the unexpected' (2003: x); that the situation Shell encountered over Brent Spar demonstrates 'the profound limitations of any linear view of the global' (Urry 2003: x).

With regard to the consultants' and Shell's claims about how the media covered the crisis, my findings do not corroborate their claims that the media were biased and did not represent Shell's arguments. The strongest refutation of those claims arises because I have shown that the media did not cover the crisis in a uniform way. As far as I am aware, consultants do not point to any studies on media coverage to support their claims. Whilst my examination, for practical purposes, was restricted to UK press and television coverage, it still exposes how the consultants' account of news coverage is a specific and advantageous construction that functions in upholding their particular interpretation of this incident and in supporting their account of how to manage such affairs.

Conclusions

Whilst the consultants cite the Brent Spar case to demonstrate the legitimacy and necessity of their approach (crises are better handled and even prevented through the early management of issues), my analysis of this case contests their interpretation of it and develops some observations on their arguments about this case and about crisis management.

Although most of the consultants' arguments about this incident are borne out by circumstances, the criticisms they advance, the mistakes they identify and the courses of action they recommend, are made with the benefit of hindsight. This is significant, and has implications for their claims about this case and for their advice, because what they maintain after the event is not as clear at the time and, by the same token, there may be practical difficulties in applying their recommendations. The case I make here is a general one and does not just relate to the Brent Spar incident, because the point I make about the contingent and emergent character of crises is relevant to other incidents and also criticises the consultants' main case: early action prior to events.[31] My argument is that predicting which issues will develop into a crisis is largely an imprecise exercise, although readily identifiable in retrospect.

In relation to early identification and response to issues, I have argued with reference to this case that it is difficult to identify which issues will become contentious. Being unaware that doubtful issues exist compromises the ability to 'manage' and control issues from an early stage, and many issues are also dependent on opposition in order for them to become contentious. Even where some opposition exists and issues are disputed, it is difficult to ascertain whether that dispute would escalate into a crisis. In short, it is impractical to spot which issues will develop into crises and to confirm the effects of certain courses of actions until after they have taken place.

Also easily observable in hindsight but not at the time, as the Brent Spar case clearly demonstrates, is which publics will become key publics, as they are not initially manifest and surface as the situation develops. Determining at an early stage exactly which audiences require consultation, monitoring and attention, and the extent of the threat posed by these groups, is ambiguous, imprecise and tricky. Identifying key publics at an early stage is further complicated when large corporations such as the Royal Dutch/Shell Group have diverse and numerous publics in countries differentiated by political, economic and social conditions as well as different cultural expectations.

I also took issue with the consultants' allegation that Shell did not communicate in a manner endorsed by them (i.e. quickly, clearly and repeating its key messages), and demonstrated that Shell did indeed communicate in that fashion. It is odd that consultants maintain a claim so easily disproved. Conceivably they had to make this claim to support their assertions that the media did not cover Shell's case and that the company failed to manage its crisis because it did not communicate as they suggest.

The circumstances of this case also demonstrate that learning and responding to perceptions is not as simple a matter as is presented by consultants. Contrary to them, I argued that Shell did address perceptions of the problem. What Shell appears to have been defeated by was the highly theatrical quality of Greenpeace's protest (what Macnaghten and Urry (1998) describe as 'carnivalesque'), which was a different kind of communicative form from that used by the company (the press release), and Greenpeace's moral case against Shell. The consultants suggest something similar by (incorrectly) arguing that Shell's case did not address perceptions.

I also argued that the situation Shell faced is better described not in consultants' language of emotional versus rational – it was not a simple case of 'emotional' arguments superseding 'rational' considerations – but in terms of the moral and symbolic basis of the protest. The consultants' claim about this matter is not entirely dissimilar to that which I proposed, that is, both interpretations see the main reason for the protest as being driven by concerns other than the actual risks to the environment posed by Shell's plan.

The consultants' claim that Shell should have been more aware that the opposition to its plan was not just to do with the actual environmental risks of the disposal is, in retrospect, validated. However, at the time this did not seem an apparent oversight to Shell nor may such matters be so transparent when events are taking place. The consultants point to this case and say it demonstrates the prevailing circumstances of contemporary society but their analysis of this case sidelines the very real difficulties posed by these circumstances.

We can not only witness in this case the conditions the consultants and the risk society perspective observe in contemporary society, but also that the risk thesis shows some problems with the consultants' proposals.

Concerning the first point – the risks of Shell's plan were clearly open to social definition and construction. If they were not, Greenpeace would not have been able to offer a different interpretation of the risks of that plan from Shell. And the involvement of Greenpeace points to the 'sub-politics' that both the consultants and risk theorists identify. Technology certainly played a role in Greenpeace's campaign, and technological changes in the media undoubtedly facilitated the coverage given to this case. This case also clearly demonstrates that public acceptance was a very big issue, as consultants and risk theorists argue; Shell subsequently found its plan 'untenable'. The fact that this case reveals certain conditions that risk theorists and consultants observe might add to our appreciation of what the consultants see as now being necessary, but this is a different matter from whether the consultants' proposals are feasible and, therefore, this circumstance should not be taken to qualify the consultants' recommendations.

I believe that the observations that risk theorists and the consultants themselves make point to certain difficulties with the consultants' arguments. Consultants undermine the effects of the processes they identify on crisis management.

Take, for example, the consultants' and the risk theorists' classification of a decreased trust in corporations. Both parties contend that the issue of trust determines how risk is defined, and identify the decreased power of corporations in this matter and the growth of other parties more able to command trust and hence also define risks. Even so, consultants do not see the problem of communicating about risks to be an indomitable one. The consultants' recommendation that controlled communications which address perceptions can influence perceptions, downplays the possibility that corporate communications may have little effect and that controlling perceptions, *however such attempts may be structured*, might be rather more contingent on factors external and hard to direct than the consultants concede.

There is little suggestion on how to counter external circumstances, which threaten the actions advocated. For instance, consultants say that corporations have to engender trust but that is something much broader in scope, time and space than the concern of handling crises. Also, it may simply not be in the power of the corporation to bring about changes in societal dispositions that might be entrenched. How corporations can gain the acquiescence of protesters opposing their activities on moral and symbolic bases is unclear and remains a predicament. Corporate communication efforts, regardless of how they may be ordered, might nonetheless fail due to circumstances that may be beyond the control of the corporation.

The consultants appear to contradict themselves. On the one hand, they identify conditions which they concede are intractable. On the other, their recommended actions assume that these conditions are manageable. I do not believe that consultants would do themselves out of a job if they accepted that contention, but their task of convincing clients of the merits of their case would be made more difficult. It is in the consultants' interests to portray circumstances as not just problematic (so that crisis management appears desirable) but also straightforward and manageable (so that crisis management does not seem pointless).

This can also be witnessed in their claims about the media. Both risk theorists and consultants agree that the media play a central role in risk-defining, and the shared view that the media may be more doubtful of corporate statements, and that complex scientific arguments are not conducive to media coverage, compromises corporate efforts to explain their case. The consultants' claim that communications with the media can ensure better crisis management is not certain, for the reasons that risk theorists and they themselves note – the restricted possibilities for influencing media coverage.

My examination of news reporting suggests that organisations may actually play a very restricted role in the 'presentation of self' (Goffman 1959) and their situation, which has consequences for what consultants promote. The findings that strong organising perspectives were present in the press coverage of the crisis, and that certain frames were set from the start and were consistently repeated, have consequences for the capacity to control media coverage as consultants recommend. Changing existing and preferred frames is not necessarily practicable.

The greater requirement of television news to be impartial creates problems for crisis management because that imperative requires television news to give representation to differing views. Although this may be merely a gesture towards appearing objective, this practice can diminish the particular version that crisis management measures would intend to circulate.

The journalistic convention of reporting views on opposite sides might be little more than an inert posture, as accounts can still favour one interpretation over another, but it has some effect in curtailing the circulation of one perspective; it detracts from its propagation. In doing so, this convention has a pre-emptive function, however mediocre and token. It also has repercussions for crisis management because this approach limits the advancement of a particular angle, as consultants recommend because it seems, particularly in television news, that a contrasting perspective will usually also gain representation.

However, it was also demonstrated that, in spite of the depiction of opposed views, television news sometimes leant more towards one side than the other and that press reports, which were more partisan than television news, also did so. For crisis management, that circumstance too suggests complications, for how does one ensure that a particular outlook is, in such conditions, favourably represented? Both circumstances, where impartiality reigns and where reports promote a particular account over others (examples of both conditions were shown), pose difficulties for crisis management.

What I have found with regard to the central characteristics of the mass media is that their traditional formats, individual traditions, political outlooks, narrative conventions, audiences and governing principles appear to influence how news is covered. These conditions constrain crisis management because such measures intend to direct news, yet their influence is one amongst many. Crisis management measures are further constrained because other sources seeking to influence news are present in the process.

Consultants' recommendation of a tailored approach to managing communications with the media, which is based on an assessment of perceptions, allows for the central properties of mass media representations that I discerned as it recognises that news is value laden and that those different values and individual organisational traditions appear to define how news is constructed. Individualised approaches, made on the basis of how the different media and the varying approaches within each medium view the situation, might be a response to how the distinct and varied media, as my analysis shows, might be influenced.

Yet the very fact that the media are varied, structured according to different imperatives, political leanings, directing codes and formats, and that these factors appear to exert an influence over how news is constructed, impose restrictions on what consultants seek to do. My analysis suggests that directing media coverage is not as assured a matter as consultants often portray. This is not to say that crisis management measures have no value, or that sources cannot influence news (on the contrary, this study of crisis management shows how that is aimed for) but to point to the limitations and constraints on managing news. It is all the more important to distinguish this because the consultants do not point to these factors.

A key finding is that while the Brent Spar case shows merits in the consultants' case, it also reveals its limitations. Both the consultants' axiom regarding the early management of issues and their citation of this case as supporting that view are problematic. The consultants' interpretation of this case as justifying their claims is questionable, and this attests to how consultants further a specific interpretation of past incidents to advance their arguments. Although a commendable approach in theory, I have questioned the consultants' claim that crises are preventable, and that the escalation of a situation into a crisis can be curtailed through the instigation of certain measures, by showing that there are constraints to what can be done and that it is not as simple a matter as consultants maintain.

The fact that in hindsight problematic areas and solutions are easier to identify than in the immediate situation casts doubt both on the legitimacy of the consultants' arguments about this case and also on the adequacy of their advice. What the consultants principally offer is perception management but, I have argued with reference to risk theorists and what they themselves note, the possibilities for influencing perceptions during crises might be more limited than consultants portray. I also drew attention to the contingent properties of crises and how audiences emerge out of the process itself. My analysis of this case shows the difficulties involved in predicting events – circumstances were not static, evident from the outset and unchanging, and the situation developed and evolved in unforeseen ways. I would suggest that crises are often inherently volatile, complex, inextricable situations that may elude and complicate efforts to manage them, and it appears that controlling the development of crises is far more obscure and intricate than how the consultants depict it.

4
Crisis Management After the Crisis

This chapter demonstrates how crisis management goes beyond the handling of the immediate crisis situation, showing how Shell applied crisis management principles at this phase of the crisis and benefited from doing so. That examination allows a consideration of the consultants' case that crisis management after crises is less effective and inferior to their advocated approach.

Shell publicly acknowledged that it took measures to address the remaining problems:

> While the immediate crisis was over, several problems remained. The immediate situation and problem was to explain Shell's position and change of plan. On the day of the decision, Chris Fay devoted the rest of the day to giving TV interviews and attending the *Newsnight* programme ... [An objective of the] 'New Way Forward' [Shell's new communication strategy] was ... to be extremely open. The difference that resulted from the Brent Spar incident was the acceptance [by Shell] that it was no longer good enough to explain a company's action and position but it was also necessary to listen to people outside the organisation. It was a mission to explain and engage in dialogue (John Wybrew, Director of Public Affairs, Shell UK, in interview: November 18, 1999).

I will be arguing that Shell's new communications strategy, or its crisis management, reconstructed the past crisis and that this strategy adhered to consultants' recommendations.

A new communications strategy

All communications were handled internally during the crisis. However, following the decision to abort the original plan, Shell International sought the advice of communications consultants. The appointment of these consultants shows that Shell decided that crisis management was necessary, that the company did engage in crisis management measures after the crisis, and that the management of the crisis continued beyond the end of the immediate crisis.

The *MORI Survey on the Views of Oil and Energy Journalists* (1998) reveals that Shell had put more effort into improving its communications and relations with the media and that these efforts were, at the time, fruitful:

> Shell's dedication to its press relations in recent times is bringing dividends ... Journalists ... praise Shell for making every effort to learn from its mistakes ... many are generally impressed. As one put it: 'they are very good. A few years ago they would have been at the bottom of my list' ... Shell UK's ... PR is praised by the majority of journalists. Eight out of ten rate [it] as good.

Journalists are quoted as having said:

> They [Shell] have totally changed their attitude since Brent Spar;

> After [Brent Spar] it [Shell] is putting more effort into the PR side. It is more willing to communicate ...;

> They [Shell] woke up after Brent Spar and it has produced a greater professionalism in the way they do things ...;

> [Shell has] gone through a transformation since Brent Spar;

> They have dealt with the Brent Spar issue with a lot of care ... and they have put a lot of effort into that. So, that's been impressive. They have gone from having difficulty with that subject to dealing with it.

According to Greenpeace, the start of a greater communications effort by Shell after aborting its plan:

> was the beginning of the spinning of a new history for the Spar campaign. A propaganda war was underway ... The result was a whole new mythology about the Spar campaign (Rose 1998: 132);

This book [a Greenpeace publication on the Brent Spar written by Chris Rose, campaign director] tells the story of what happened afterwards as I see it ... After June 1995, although it continued actively to promote a ban on ocean dumping, Greenpeace moved onto other things, but Shell spent millions on public relations in an ultimately futile attempt to rerun and win the Spar campaign (Rose 1998: 15).

While it is in the interests of Greenpeace to maintain that Shell did this, my examination backs the claim. Immediately after the decision to scrap the original plan, Shell managed perceptions of what happened during the crisis through the creation and instigation of the company's 'New Way Forward' programme. One purpose of that programme was: 'to develop [new] proposals for the disposal or reuse of Brent Spar' (Shell UK news release, October 11, 1995). But central to that programme was the open acknowledgement that the company's reputation was damaged and that it was trying to improve the situation. Moreover, external communication was not just recognised as important but was also used as an explanation for the crisis:

> ... reputation and the public trust and confidence that goes with it depend on ... underlying performance and [the] ability to communicate externally ... the Brent Spar affair has reminded us that this [external communication] is simply not good enough. We have to redouble our efforts to give the public at large a better understanding of what we are doing ... (Heinz Rothermund, Managing Director, Shell Expro, 'Brent Spar').

Shell named 'widespread acceptability' as a new criterion for judging any new proposals for the Spar, and whereas the company had earlier maintained that it had taken this approach in arriving at the original disposal plan, it now appeared to accept the criticism made during the crisis that it had not done so:

> We have acknowledged that we originally set out to dispose of the Spar without explaining what we were doing early enough or widely enough. As the Way Forward develops, we aim to share information with a varied mix of interested parties ... (*Brent Spar – Next Stage in New Way Forward*, Shell UK Ltd., July 3, 1996).

This stance conforms to the consultants' advocacy of a constructive *Mea Culpa* in order to create favourable impressions of the company. Clearly, Shell wanted to rebuild confidence in the company.[1]

Two years after the crisis, in 1997, the British Association of Communicators praised Shell's communications in explaining the situation with the Brent Spar. In accepting an award for the company's CD-ROM on the Brent Spar, Eric Faulds, Decommissioning Manager at Shell Expro, outlined what was involved in the new communication strategy employed following the crisis:

> It [the CD-ROM] is an integral part of a communications initiative which includes our dedicated Brent Spar Website [launched in May 1996], dialogue seminars in the UK and Europe, media briefings, speeches, articles, and helping students and academics with case studies. We believe all this is helping to spread wider understanding of the complex issues surrounding the Brent Spar and decommissioning in general (Shell UK news release May 19, 1997).

The first part of this chapter analyses two 'communication initiatives' the company took, which lucidly illustrate the case Shell made after the crisis:

- An article written by Shell UK Director of Public Affairs, John Wybrew, which was published in the journal of the Institute of Public Relations [Vol. 14, No. 2, July 1995].
- A speech delivered by Dr Chris Fay, Chairman and Chief Executive of Shell UK, to a conference on the media at the University of Wales, May 20, 1996.

An overview of events and arguments

While new disposal options were being considered, the Brent Spar was kept in Norway. Late in June, a scientific study published in the journal *Nature* concluded that Shell's original studies had been scientifically sound and conducted using rigorous scientific standards. In July, Shell UK commissioned the Norwegian certification authority Det Norske Veritas (DNV) to conduct an independent audit of the Spar to verify its contents and re-check Shell UK's previous inventory. Until October, when DNV submitted the results, Shell did not have any independent way of refuting Greenpeace's allegations about the contents of the Spar. However, events proceeded in a highly desirable manner for Shell and the company exploited these opportunities to further its case.

Firstly, on August 26, at the 1995 National Television Festival in Edinburgh, television executives publicly supported Shell's view that the television coverage had been biased. David Lloyd, *Channel 4*'s Senior Commissioning Editor of News and Current Affairs, said:

> On Brent Spar we were 'bounced'...we [news organisations] all took great pains to represent Shell's side of the argument, but by the time the broadcasters tried to intervene with scientific analysis, the story had by then been spun far, far, into Greenpeace's direction.[2]

Richard Sambrook, *BBC* Editor of Newsgathering, concurred:

> I think in some sense over Brent Spar we were 'had'...we need to wake up. It was our own fault, the media's fault. There was never enough distance between ourselves and the participants. Greenpeace had spent approximately £350,000 on TV equipment and feeds, far more than the *BBC* could have afforded.[3]

According to Greenpeace, media claims of manipulation had been forced by the UK government and Shell, but, according to Wybrew, Shell had not influenced or played any part in generating that admission.[4] The very fact that Greenpeace as well as Shell focused on this development showed how central it was to understandings of the past crisis.

While we may not know for certain how the admission had come about, it was good for Shell. On the back of the television executives' declaration, Shell could construct an efficient defence of its original stance and more convincingly claim that the problem was not its lack of concern for the environment but that Greenpeace had unjustly influenced the media against the company's case. In doing so, the company limited the damage encountered during the crisis.

The second crucial event that helped Shell's case was on September 5, when Greenpeace apologised to Shell UK for the inaccuracy of its claim that the Spar contained 5500 tonnes of oil. (This happened prior to DNV's corroboration of Shell's estimate, but Greenpeace's motivation for this declaration might have been the fact that DNV, an independent body, was examining the issue and in meetings with Greenpeace DNV had warned the organisation about its forthcoming announcement.) While admitting a mistake, Greenpeace was anxious not to create the impression that it had been wrong about its other claims. Still, Shell's interpretation of this admission was precisely that. The company suggested that if Greenpeace had made such a mistake, it must have also been mistaken over many of its other previous claims. This was a further argument that helped Shell (re)interpret the crisis.

Greenpeace downplayed their error and depicted this development as not detracting from their campaign:

> Instead of the depths being measured at the top of the storage tanks they were taken from [sic] top of vent pipes that give access to the tanks. As a result of this, the estimate for the amount of oil remaining in the Brent Spar is likely to be in error ... 'Although regrettable, Greenpeace does not consider the misunderstandings in our calculations to be of primary importance. It does not deflect from the strength of our case against sea dumping,' said Sue Mayer, Greenpeace UK Science Director. The Greenpeace position on the Spar has never been based on kilos or tons, but on the principles of dumping (Greenpeace News Release: September 5, 1995).

Nevertheless, Shell and others believed that this figure had helped Greenpeace's campaign, and Greenpeace addressed this belief by arguing that this estimate did not make much difference to the campaign:

> The results were published only five days before Shell reversed its decision to dump the Brent Spar (Greenpeace News Release: September 5, 1995);

> As well as receiving almost no publicity, the wrong oil estimate came too late to affect public boycotts, Chancellor Kohl's lobbying of John Major at the G7, the political decisions at the North Sea Ministers [Conference at Esbjerg] ... or any of the other key parts of the campaign (Rose 1998: 145).

Greenpeace argued that its decision to admit and apologise for a mistake indicated the organisation's integrity, and the apology for the mistake was couched in a narrative that criticised Shell and the UK government:

> Greenpeace relies on the trust of the public. Because of this we were happy to make it known that we had made a minor mistake. Greenpeace only wishes that Shell and the UK government would be as honest and publicly admit their mistakes ... (Greenpeace News Release: September 5, 1995).

Shell was quick to react to Greenpeace's predicament and cast this development as justifying the negative characterisation of Greenpeace Shell had always maintained:

Chris Fay [Chairman of Shell UK] called the gesture 'a step in the right direction' and then said the affair illustrated how easily public pressure groups could use 'mischievous methods' to challenge a decision that had been made on a 'factual and scientific basis' (Winter and Schweinsberg 1996: Section C).

In a news release on the same day Shell suggested that this development proved its case:

> We welcome this development, which provides further confirmation of the care and integrity which has characterised Shell UK's approach to all aspects of the Brent Spar disposal over the last four years.

Shell further implied that Greenpeace's other claims would also be proved wrong by arguing that the DNV inventory would put the matter to rest.

Both Shell and Greenpeace employed the rhetorics of persuasion, as is evident in the above news releases. While Greenpeace acknowledged its error, the organisation presented itself as being honest and virtuous because these were the very conditions that developments had called into question. As demonstrated by what Shell now maintained, this development gave Shell an opportunity to imply that Greenpeace's disclosure affirmed the company's arguments and standpoint, and it also gave a greater leverage than before to Shell's criticisms of Greenpeace.

Greenpeace correctly argued that Shell used these two developments to propagate a particular interpretation of the past. But, in arguing that Shell applied these two developments for that end, Greenpeace, like Shell, sought to offer its own interpretation of history. Greenpeace's publication of a book on the Brent Spar was such an exercise.

Undeniably, these two incidents presented good prospects for Shell but what is significant is not that these events were, in themselves, favourable to Shell, but that Shell gave them a centrality they might not otherwise have had. The company capitalised on these developments. What Shell said demonstrates this, and the fact that Greenpeace too focused on Shell's response to the developments.

Shell's case: Making external aspects problematic

The company principally managed this crisis in its aftermath by employing three distinct arguments that explained/reworked the crisis. (These arguments are noted here as the examination of the article and the speech elaborates on them.)

In general terms, Shell reconstructed history by offering a specific interpretation of how the crisis had come about:

> Greenpeace acted as a catalyst and gave the deepwater disposal of the Spar a symbolic significance out of all proportion to its negligible environmental impact...[5]

This interpretation not only reconstructed history but also reconstructed the other, i.e. Greenpeace, Shell's main opponent during the crisis.

Shell argued that Greenpeace's campaign had given an inaccurate view of what Shell planned to do; had influenced perceptions of the disposal plan – those perceptions did not reflect reality; and that the campaign had also been successful in precipitating negative media coverage of the sea disposal plan. Hence, Greenpeace was blamed for having created opposition to Shell and for misinforming and misdirecting the public and the media. By pointing the finger at external factors (Greenpeace and its campaign and the media coverage of the crisis), and by making these problematic, the blame for the crisis was shifted away from the company. In that way Shell sought vindication.

But, as we have seen, Shell also publicly admitted that its response to the crisis had been misguided:

> In Shell we will need to do more to take into account the views and feelings of external stakeholders.[6]

Shell now maintained that perceptions were at the crux of the protests against its plans and gave perceptions a centrality in explaining the crisis. By claiming that perceptions gave rise to the crisis, Shell simultaneously implied that the realities of the situation would not have been problematic. In this way, the company belittled the opposition to its plan, vindicated that plan, and defended the company's stance. Thus, the third area that Shell made problematic – its own approach – was, in some respects, absolved from blame.

The company advanced its arguments immediately after abandoning its contentious position and thus prior to the two developments I noted earlier, nevertheless, those developments allowed corroboration of the company's outlook.

Although the central, publicly stated aim of Shell's new communications strategy, dubbed 'The New Way Forward', was to find an 'acceptable' solution to the disposal of the Brent Spar through 'openness' and 'dialogue', its hidden, but equally significant, aim was crisis management. The main theme of Shell's crisis management, as will become evident below, was to deflect attention away from the company and on to areas *other than Shell's actions* during the crisis. Furthermore, the explanations the company gave were clever and persuasive.

Brent Spar – A Public Relations Disaster? – An article by the Public Affairs Director of Shell UK

Published soon after the disposal was postponed, this article introduced many of the main arguments that Shell made after the crisis. It was part of the company's crisis management and, although it was published in a specific journal, the case was being made to a wider audience. The article was included in the company's website and in the information packs Shell handed out to 'interested parties', including myself.

The argument was that the situation Shell faced was not just unique to Shell and the disposal of the Brent Spar but could be encountered by any business; the crisis was symptomatic of certain difficult areas for businesses in general. Wybrew identifies Greenpeace's campaign tactics – and by extension also Greenpeace – as a major problem.

He states that the messages Shell had to communicate were complicated, rational, scientific arguments which were:

... not a particularly simple set of messages, but nonetheless a sound case ... However, it is not a case which lends itself to short sound-bites; nor is it visually dramatic. Importantly, it is a case based on sound science, reason, and careful balance. But it found itself under attack from an aggressive 'single issue' Greenpeace campaign which freely exploited dramatic visual stunts, and was adept at packaging misinformation in ready-to-use word-snips. In many ways, this was an unusual clash between the head and the heart – a conflict in which scientific reason and careful judgement were set against the power of emotion, fear, and even myth. Particularly in northern Europe, Greenpeace succeeded in turning the Brent Spar into a symbol – a symbol of man's misuse of the oceans, irrespective of the reality. They aroused powerful emotions ... European government ministers [opposed the plan] not on its rational merits but on its symbolic significance ... (John Wybrew, Institute of Public Relations Journal Vol. 14, No. 2, July 1995 p. 3).

Sociological studies on environmental groups and on the discourse employed by those groups have made similar observations in suggesting that they utilise symbolic means to construct, represent and negotiate environmental issues. In a study of environmental discourse, Harre, Brockmeier and Muhlhausler (1999) argue that 'the stand-off between humankind and nature is a perennial theme of environmental discourse' (1999: 188). Anderson (1997) also argues that the symbolic means employed by environmental groups are also conducive to media coverage. She maintains that environmental groups often formulate environmental issues in simplistic black and white terms, not just because they are then readily accessible and understood but also because such representations 'fit' media values. That might explain how such representations could be perpetuated within the media. Greenpeace would also argue that issues are simplified in order better to communicate them. Nevertheless, the formulation of environmental issues in crude terms might also account for how such representations could naturally produce a mismatch between image and actuality, which offers further support for Wybrew's claim.

Whilst the argument is plausible, it is impossible to determine whether the success of Greenpeace's campaign was for the stated reason that the organisation turned the disposal of the Spar into a symbol. However, whether this claim was validated or not is not as important, within the context of crisis management, as the fact that Shell argues that it was so. The very fact that Shell makes much of the supposed symbolism created by Greenpeace in explaining the crisis is significant in itself, because that explanation of the crisis reinterprets and reformulates the crisis as 'unfairly' encountered by Shell.

My contention is that Wybrew's argument is not just an important insight that has parallels with some academic observations on the area, but also a significant crisis management measure. The very fact that the parallels were there helps the company's case; an appearance of authority is given to claims made. The argument put forward reconstructed history and also reconstructed the other by making problematic Greenpeace's actions. The argument that the type of actions Greenpeace took has certain implications for businesses and even society also reworked what actually happened and took the spotlight away from that specific situation. Wybrew wrote:

> The real debate – and it is a vital one – centres on the role of emotive, single-issue campaigning in the democratic process, and on how, within a democratically established framework of reasoned

discussion, painstaking evaluation, and thoughtful consultation, the best practicable environmental solutions can truly be reached. These are not just issues for industry and its regulators but profound issues for society as a whole. When the Brent Spar is eventually disposed of, they will remain.

Greenpeace would have a different view of this situation. Greenpeace would argue that theirs is a balanced rational assessment of a dangerous situation. In protracted disputes the possibility that the opponent will be dismissed as irrational is there and we can see Shell employed that claim.

What can also be witnessed in this article is that a specific vision of reality, which supports an interpretation of what had happened, is given. This outlook is also promoted by disregarding other views on what had occurred. For instance, excluded from the discussion was Greenpeace's views about that situation. Such narratives are quite clearly conducive to the reconstruction of history and central to such exercises.

By stressing the effectiveness of the campaign techniques used by Greenpeace (an external factor), Wybrew shifted critical attention from Shell to the 'other' and to wider (societal) issues. Thus, the impression conveyed was that the crisis was not brought on by what Shell did and had planned to do, but by unfair and problematic (external) circumstances:

> If there is a more general 'lesson to be learned', it is perhaps that businesses will now have to include in their planning not just the views and rational arguments of all concerned – whether opponents or supporters – but will also somehow have to come to grips with an area of deepseated emotions, subconscious instincts, and symbolic gestures.

And he asked rhetorically: 'Is this simply a matter of "PR"?' The argument was that it was too 'simplistic' to view this incident as a failure of public relations; it happened 'because people don't have a deep understanding of science, responses are often emotional as well as rational. And given that campaigns often appeal to emotions it becomes necessary to do more than to explain rationally' (Wybrew, in interview, November 18, 1999).

Frequently repeated in Shell's communications about the crisis was the phrase 'hearts and minds'. The suggestion repeatedly made was that, while Shell's case had been rational (mind), it had not succeeded because Greenpeace had secured opposition against it by appealing to irrational fears and emotions (heart). The emotional vs. rational argument was beneficial to Shell in reconstructing the past crisis.

Not Black and White but Shades of Green – A speech by the Chairman of Shell UK[7]

The two central aspects within Shell's reworking of what had happened in June (the impact of campaigning tactics and news reporting) were observable in Wybrew's article examined above and are also manifest in Chris Fay's speech.

Although Chris Fay states that his intention is 'to discuss some of the fundamental questions about the role of journalists in reporting environmental issues', his speech is a criticism of that process:

> Journalists seek to cut through complexity to provide the clarity and simplicity their readers and viewers desire. But, with issues as complex as the impact of human activity on the natural environment, the search for simple truths may obscure the uncertainty of reality.

By arguing that the journalistic imperative to simplify matters was to the detriment of accurate portrayals, he makes the news construction process problematic.

Fay contends that there was a need for a 'better understanding of complexity' in three areas that are 'central to environmental progress'. These three he classifies as science, technology and business management.

Regarding the first, Fay argues that environmental decisions should be made with 'due regard to science and scientific methods … [and] decisions must be made on careful scientific analysis of risks'. Communicating risks is a difficult thing to do, he argues:

> [Scientific analysis of risks] is a complex subject which is difficult to communicate. Relative risks are easily misunderstood and give rise to alarmist interpretations … Almost everything we do, consume, or are exposed to has some risks. Modern science has given us the ability to measure minute quantities of substances. But what is important is the extent of our exposure to them. We have to decide which risks require tackling, with what priority, in what way, to

what extent, and at what cost. We can only proceed safely by balancing all the risks – taking into account the extent of our uncertainty and ensuring sound science underpins our choices. And we [cannot try] to avoid all risks. That is simply impossible.

By arguing that scientific developments have allowed for a greater ability to discover risks, Fay describes a situation Beck (1992) and Giddens (1999) identify, that is, the rise of a greater concern with risks as a result of a greater scientific ability to detect and measure risks. By holding that there are risks associated with every activity and by claiming that certain choices have to be made regarding which risks are acceptable and which are not, Fay indicates and justifies how Shell went about deciding on the deep sea disposal method, i.e. that Shell had, on the basis of science, chosen between the risks posed by the different disposal methods. His claim that risks are misunderstood and cause unnecessary alarm depicts the opposition to the company's plan as unjustified.

Fay criticises the media coverage of Shell's disposal plan by contending that the basis of the plan had been misrepresented and misunderstood but, significantly, he does so not by directly claiming this but by describing how such a misrepresentation could arise:

My point is that environmental science is much more complex than the impression we often gain from the media. I can appreciate that describing technical data and detailed risk evaluation is difficult for busy journalists with limited time and space.

Next, with reference to the second issue he raised, technology, Fay argues that the media should rectify public misunderstandings:

The Brent Spar debate revealed a widespread ignorance of the technology of North Sea oil and gas. Media coverage has not fully reflected the industry's impact on this country's economy over a quarter of a century – or the scale of its technological developments … If people are unaware of such engineering issues, or assume that they can easily be solved, it is natural for them to think that companies are only concerned about costs. I make no apologies for taking costs into account in environmental decisions … But there are always many other factors and in the case of Brent Spar, these were decisive.

Once again, the crisis was explained in terms of people not understanding the disposal plan rather than there being problems with the plan itself.

This is also manifest in Fay's third point, where he evokes, what are basically, imputed public perceptions of businesses, and in his argument that the media were in a position to develop a better understanding that could bring perceptions in line with reality:

> Many people see business management in very simple terms. They believe that ... the company's environmental standards are dictated purely by regard for profits. There is no doubt that all companies require profits ... But management is not so simple. Thousands of people – staff, contractors and suppliers – are involved in the company's operations. They must constantly make decisions about their work, balancing many different factors – technical, human safety, environmental, and, of course, commercial ... It is those individual decisions which determine our environmental, and business performance.

In saying that costs were not pursued at the expense of environmental and safety matters, he defends Shell against criticism of its motives in choosing sea disposal. The argument that the public did not understand these matters and that the media did not facilitate such understanding also allows him to 'explain' what happened with the Brent Spar and, in doing so, he offers a specific interpretation of the crisis. Problematic public perceptions as well as media representations provides the platform from which Shell's stance during the crisis is defended.

Fay goes on to censure Greenpeace's tactics, arguing that they made untrue, simplistic allegations that nonetheless gained media attention and coverage:

> They [Greenpeace] knew that activists in rubber boats among the massive ironmongery of the North Sea made good television – David against Goliath ... And, like all good spin doctors, they knew how to manage the debate with a flow of simplistic allegations ... We now know that most of those allegations were unsound.

That last statement exploits Greenpeace's admission of a mistake. Even though only one charge was proven wrong, the argument was that Greenpeace had run the entire campaign on untrue accusations, that it had achieved coverage of its claims by engaging perceptions

(David and Goliath) and by preying on existing misunderstandings of the issues he had earlier made problematic.

He also uses the television executives' admission of a biased coverage in August 1995:

> I know that senior television executives have questioned whether broadcasters surrendered their independence by relying too much on one side for coverage and accepting too uncritically one argument. Certainly it was difficult for the complex details of risk analysis – which take time to explain – to make headway against such compelling visuals, simple arguments and sensational allegations.

The speech ends on the following note:

> The most important [lesson the media could draw from the Brent Spar incident] is that the environment is not a simple issue, with clear rights and wrongs and easy answers. Society needs the help of open-minded journalists in unravelling its complexities if we are to make the right choices for our future.

Thus, the crisis was portrayed primarily as a result of misunderstandings and misrepresentations.

Speeches such as this, and other communication initiatives, were a part of Shell's crisis management strategy as the company attempted to make wider publics receptive to the interpretation it then offered. Still, what Shell maintained after the crisis raises a central issue fundamental to how that crisis could be understood: that the two organisations employed quite disparate communicative styles, one invoking the powerful iconography of pollution, purity and danger, and the other of risk assessment. The very fact that Greenpeace could effectively challenge Shell's risk assessment does reveal something of how effective those types of communications were. And, as I have said, that might also account for the initial success of Greenpeace and Shell's puzzlement at its communication failures.

However, Shell was not alone in applying scientific arguments to support its case as Greenpeace too appealed to science, both rhetorically and substantively. In environmental discourses, recourse to science is often for such ends (Harre, Brockmeier and Mulhausler 1999). Why then did Shell focus on the symbolism created by Greenpeace – important as it is – rather than its employment of scientific arguments? One reason is that that explanation fit the claim that there was differential employment of 'emotional' and 'rational' arguments. I would also suggest that it was because the argument Shell put forward regarding the symbolism and imagery Greenpeace created and used is plausible and hence also better able to persuade that it was so. Shell's argument is conceivable and credible but, vitally, it is also self-serving as it proposed a particular, advantageous translation of the past crisis.

We shall now see whether Shell's case was reflected in the way the media represented the past crisis. That allows for a tentative consideration of the company's crisis management.

Did Shell's case gain support in the media?

The short answer to this question is that I found it did. This analysis of press and television coverage after the crisis is important because, even though one could argue that by that time moral identities and impressions had probably stuck, it is still worthwhile to see whether Shell's later attempts to counter those impressions worked.

While the *Guardian* and the *Telegraph* (but not the *Mirror*) examined the issue throughout the year, *BBC*, *ITV* and *Channel 4* news coverage was quite limited. On June 20, when Shell terminated the disposal operation, the story of the Brent Spar became headline news for two days in the *BBC*, *ITV* and *Channel 4* news programmes. After two days, however, the story was abandoned until September 5, when it once again became headline news as all channels covered Greenpeace's admission of an error with its oil estimate. This conformed to the convention of television news being event-led. During the preceding period, the only television coverage was by the *BBC*, which had two short news reports on June 29 and July 11. After September 5, no more television coverage was given to the story of the Spar in that year – which is the range of this study.

As previously reasoned, the wider contexts and formats of televised and print news affects what is reported and how reporting takes place. Brevity is characteristic of televisions news, which is constrained by time and limited in its discursive potential. Impartiality is also a greater concern for televised news than for the press. A direct consequence of these features of news reporting is the greater opportunity for Shell's arguments to be elaborated on and even endorsed in press reports rather than in television news. This, together with my observation that there was a greater discussion by the press than television, plus the greater quantity of press articles, meant that Shell's arguments after the crisis did gain greater coverage in the press. I found that press accounts were beneficial to the propagation of what Shell maintained after the crisis. Although television news reports are far more bound by the greater imperative to be impartial, I also found that television news reporting was also advantageous to the promotion of Shell's arguments.

Television coverage

BBC

There was a partiality towards Shell's claims in the *BBC*'s coverage during the later stages of the immediate crisis, and its coverage after the crisis also exhibited a leaning towards Shell's views.

However, the *BBC* also criticised Shell for having failed to communicate its case successfully and for bungling its public relations. These arguments reflected those that Shell held afterwards. The view that public relations was pivotal in explaining what had happened directed attention to Greenpeace's campaign:

> ... Greenpeace ... stole the limelight with their dramatic occupation of the Brent Spar. In the wake of their success ... many more businesses will now be reassessing the power of the pressure groups (*Newsnight*, June 20).

The nature of that attention in *BBC* news was a critical framing of Greenpeace.

Greenpeace was represented as having 'dictated the public relations battle' (*BBC* 9 O'Clock News, June 20), as being an organisation very much concerned with gaining publicity and as being willing to disregard the actuality of a situation if it interfered with its ability to obtain publicity for its case:

> Greenpeace's communications centre has live satellite links with its boats at sea. Pictures are headed straight from here to TV stations and newspapers ... International public opinion responded to a series of high profile actions taken in the live sea. It's not new. For 25 years, Greenpeace has courted publicity – here against acid rain [a video of a man jumping from a height, whose parachute opens up to reveal the Greenpeace logo]. There is funding of 100 million pounds a year from 3.8 million members world-wide. [A video of a Greenpeace dinghy close to a large ship at sea when the dinghy capsizes and the people fall in the water was shown accompanied by the next commentary.] But the flare for photogenic stunts has earned Greenpeace a reputation for overlooking scientific fact if it spoils a good story.

By fostering the notion that Greenpeace habitually and deliberately ignores the facts of a case in pursuit of publicity, the *BBC*'s coverage reproduced Shell's negative characterisation of Greenpeace.

My examination of *BBC* coverage also revealed how much news is self-referential i.e. news programmes appeared to be influenced by what was said on preceding programmes. In the instance of the *BBC*'s coverage, this process favoured Shell's interpretation of events. A *Newsnight* interview of Chris Fay on the day of Shell's change of plan, I found, influenced what subsequent *BBC* news programmes said about the past crisis. This is discussed below.

On *Newsnight* Fay said:

> This is the problem. There is a lot of misinformation, let's just get two basic facts. February 16: the UK government writes to the Ospar Convention – all the European governments – [to inform them] of their decision to issue a licence for the deep sea disposal. By April 16, no answer, so you can assume that everyone agrees, at least they don't disagree. They [UK government] then issue a licence. Suddenly two weeks after that, all of a sudden – and maybe for another agenda perhaps – something starts to happen. Now from a PR point of view – can you second guess that?

Fay argued that the totality of an issue rather than a single issue perspective must be employed when arriving at decisions such as the disposal of the Spar, and also made problematic the media's role in covering the dispute:

> ... the media takes in [a lot of] misinformation ... the media does not seem to want to take in the whole story ... I think society has to be persuaded of what is actually the overall picture rather than a single issue.

The presenter argued similarly to Fay:

> Green guerrillas have beaten big business ... No one doubts the surrender to the Green campaigners is the most dramatic example yet of the way single-issue pressure groups can sometimes beat multi-billion businesses ... [it was] a David and Goliath battle.

The arguments Fay made on *Newsnight* influenced the following day's news as *Working Lunch*, a current affairs programme, *BBC*

1 O'Clock News and *BBC* 9 O'Clock News, covered the story very much from Shell's perspective.

Working Lunch reported:

> Under the great heaving weight of the Green lobby Shell have relented ... In years to come it will be a textbook case for business students – the defeat of one of the mightiest, richest companies in the world by an environmental pressure group ... it was the impact that Greenpeace's campaign had on politicians across Europe which forced the U-turn.

This interpretation meant that Greenpeace's campaign gained attention. On this programme it received a critical frame; the programme included an interview with a Greenpeace spokesperson and showed a clip of Fay on *Newsnight* in which he said:

> This is [an issue for] international business; it's not just Shell. What are the rules under which we should act – we have to act legally. It would appear that single-issue groups can act illegally and get their little bite in ... everything had been single-issue ... you have to take a balanced approach.

The studio presenter's questions to the Greenpeace spokesperson were along Shell's suggestions and showed a partiality towards Shell's case. He asked Paul Horsman, the Greenpeace spokesperson:

> This is no victory at all if you are forcing the company to do something that is more unsafe and ecologically unsound.

And the second was similarly critical:

> Now, are there any limits to what kind of illegality you would go to in order to get your point across, illegality you will encourage?

Greenpeace was, of course, given the opportunity to respond but the type of questions asked of the organisation framed it in an unfavourable manner. In this instance, the questions implied that Greenpeace had acted illegally, irrationally and irresponsibly.

Subsequent *BBC* news programmes also focused on Greenpeace's direct action and furthered the criticism of how the campaign had been conducted. The view Fay had publicised on *Newsnight* appeared to become established within *BBC* news reporting, which reproduced what Fay had said. *BBC* 1 O'Clock News on June 21 reported:

> After more than a year of feasibility studies, the plan was submitted in 1993. Then in the beginning of February 16th it was passed on to the European governments and approved by Britain. No governments protested within the 65 days statutory notice period. Only at the eleventh hour, under a barrage of environmental pressure – the German led European protest – which yesterday resulted in Shell's spectacular U-turn.

The programme also included a diagram of the key dates of the crisis and what was listed as 'key dates' were those Fay had earlier identified. The report also duplicated Shell's views.

In keeping with the necessity of appearing impartial, the news programme included an interview with Lord Melchett, Executive Director of Greenpeace UK, but the reporter was generally critical of Greenpeace:

> Lord Melchett, isn't there a problem with the way in which this decision [the abandonment of the sea disposal] was taken? Shell went through this very complicated procedure and in the last minute changed their minds. Should such an important decision be taken like that?

That question was followed by:

> Doesn't it worry you that decisions like this kind should be taken in a cool and collected manner and you have effectively forced this decision in a very heated manner?

And:

> Aren't you worried that while this thing is being dragged around in the North Sea to an uncertain destination, it might break up?

In maintaining that line of questioning, the reporter implied that Greenpeace's solution was problematic, in particular, that it could cause greater environmental damage. That implication was made explicit on the *BBC* 9 O'Clock News on the same day, when the difficulties of onshore disposal were emphasised:

Dismantling the Brent Spar will be difficult ... The Brent Spar would be toppled so ... it would be horizontal, it will then have to go into a dry dock – one may have to be specially built. The sludge at the bottom and oily scale on its sides would have to be removed and treated. Finally, the shell and concrete will be cut and recycled or dumped in landfill sites.

The report also reproduced Shell's standpoint that sea disposal could benefit the marine environment by creating artificial reefs:

Off the coast of Mexico some dumped installations form reefs for fish and some experts suggest something similar could be done here ...

Having covered Shell's claims and having favourably depicted the company, the report proceeded to criticise Greenpeace:

Environmentalists have said that Shell's climbdown was a victory for European public opinion. It was certainly a victory for a Greenpeace campaign including controversial actions or what the organisation calls 'direct action'. Today's headlines declare Shell's climbdown and put Greenpeace where they want to be: front page news. It's a triumph for the environmental group's publicity machine, which made sure that the cameras followed every move at sea.

The argument that Greenpeace's campaign had been motivated by publicity was again promoted. The fact that Greenpeace often openly states how important publicity is for their campaigns facilitates this assertion. A member of Greenpeace, Blair Palese, was shown claiming this very thing and, thus, corroborating the argument:

The first rule for us is – is the story visual? If so, can we tell it with pictures? In the case of Brent Spar, it was just as important to get images of the rig, support ships hosing the activists trying to get on board as it was the action itself.

The rest of the programme was devoted to criticising Greenpeace, representing the organisation as having pursued publicity at the expense of the facts of the case. What the Chairman of Shell had said on *Newsnight* clearly did have an impact on what subsequent *BBC* news programmes reported but a leaning towards Shell's outlook by the *BBC* was also earlier discerned.

The next two *BBC* news programmes were very brief. The July 11 programme said that the Norwegian government had given permission for the Spar to be kept in a fjord. The June 29 programme announced that new scientific evidence demonstrated that the sea disposal of the Spar would not have damaged the marine environment, which reinforced what Shell and previous *BBC* programmes had upheld. The decision to cover this development might have been motivated by that very condition because this development was not covered in any other television news outlet.

How the *BBC* covered Greenpeace's admission of a mistake on September 5, far from Greenpeace's allegation about this matter, was a model of how the formula to suggest impartial coverage is employed. As the *BBC* had previously been rather censorious of Greenpeace, one would expect it to use this opportunity to criticise Greenpeace further, as the organisation claimed the *BBC* had, but this was not so.

The report began as follows:

> Greenpeace tells Shell it's sorry. It got its figures for pollution from Brent Spar oil rig quite wrong ... In an extraordinary admission of error, the Executive Director of Greenpeace has admitted to Shell UK's Chairman, Dr. Chris Fay, their estimates for the pollutants on Brent Spar oil rig were wrong. Shell insists that its approach to the disposal of oil rigs has been vindicated (*BBC* 1 O'Clock News, Sept. 5).

The report also reproduced Greenpeace's explanation of how the mistake had been made, which was beneficial to Greenpeace. The report quoted from Greenpeace's letter to Shell:

> The letter says that Greenpeace made an error in sampling the contents of the Brent Spar. It states: 'the sampling device was still in the pipe leading into the storage tanks rather than in the tank itself'. It goes on: 'I apologise to you and your colleagues'.

The report included Greenpeace's claim that the organisation apologised because 'we wanted to do the decent thing and let people know as quickly as possible'.[8] And the *BBC* covered Greenpeace's argument that the mistake did not detract from the argument that sea disposal was a wrong method of disposal: 'Greenpeace says it's never right to dump waste – an argument it insists is still right despite its mistake.'

The programme was critical of both Greenpeace and Shell. In an interview with Peter Melchett, the Executive Director of Greenpeace, the reporter asked:

Surely the words 'apology' and 'misunderstanding' are a bit inadequate. You said 5500 tonnes of oil. Apparently, there is 10. I mean this is an error on a cosmic scale.

In an interview with Chris Fay the reporter said:

You don't come out of it terribly well, do you, because if you had stuck to your gun, if you had stuck to your figures, you might not have been defeated by the campaign as Greenpeace actually did defeat you.

And:

It's a terrific condemnation of your corporate affairs and your presentation. You had the figures on your side but you did not advance them as you should have done.

This criticism of both sides, together with the representation it gave to both Shell and Greenpeace (they were given the opportunity to advance their case) is, demonstrably, very much a part of the ritual of objectivity, which was evident in how the *BBC* covered this development.

ITV

With the exception of the coverage on September 5,[9] there was one *ITV* programme that covered the aftermath of the crisis: *'News at Ten'*, June 21. That report framed the situation as involving two main issues: the spoiled relations between Shell and the UK government and what Shell planned to do next. Of these two areas, the first received the greater coverage as the political impact of Shell's decision was emphasised over other considerations. This demonstrates how the media can be selective in the way they choose to represent issues and thus emphasise some factors and angles over others. *ITV* reported differently from the *BBC,* drawing on differing issues.

ITV focused on the UK government's response to Shell's decision and reported that the government disapproved of it:

John Major, who defended the principle of dumping rigs at sea yesterday, is understood to be furious at Shell's decision. He said apparently that they behaved like wimps and he and other ministers are angry at the way events unfolded yesterday.

To reinforce the extent to which the UK government supported Shell, *ITV* reported:

Tonight it appears that the government may have been prepared to go to extreme lengths to clear protesters off Brent Spar [as it has been suggested by a Labour MP that] SAS-style troopers had been flown to Stornaway prepared if necessary to storm the rig.

ITV represented Shell's explanation of its decision to halt sea disposal:

Shell say because of international pressure they had no other way but regret the way the decision was reached (*ITV News at Ten*, June 21).

And the company's apology to the UK government was covered. Extracts from Shell's letter to John Major also characterised Shell as having expressed regret about the position in which it had placed the UK government.

What is most striking about *ITV*'s coverage is the near total absence of a commentary on Greenpeace. That calls attention to how much of that was present in the *BBC* reporting. *ITV* said little about the organisation beyond stating that it had declared a victorious end to its campaign: 'the victory they claimed seemed complete'. In focusing on the two areas of what Shell was next going to do and the political implications of its decision, the three arguments Shell made after the crisis were not reflected in *ITV*'s coverage at that time.

In contrast to the previous report (and to *ITV*'s coverage of the immediate crisis period), the two *ITV* programmes covering Greenpeace's announcement of an error on September 5 focused attention on the organisation. Greenpeace was now depicted as having played a key role in creating opposition to Shell's plan:

They [Greenpeace] have had to apologise for getting facts wrong about the Brent Spar oil platform after mobilising a massive international protest against Shell petrol company. They campaigned for Shell to abandon dumping the platform at sea. Then, Greenpeace claimed it contained over 5000 tonnes of oil. Now, they are saying their measurements were inaccurate (*ITV Lunchtime News*, September 5).

Although Greenpeace received more attention and was attributed a central role in the crisis, the organisation was not portrayed negatively and its arguments were reproduced.

ITV Lunchtime News represented Greenpeace's claim that it had apologised only for the oil estimate and not for the whole of its campaign, and *ITV*'s *News at Ten* repeated that several times. These news reports also explained how the error had been made and, in doing so, reinforced Greenpeace's explanation.[10] Thus, Greenpeace's argument that the error did not affect the basis of its campaign was reproduced in *ITV* news and Greenpeace was represented as having made an 'honest mistake'.

Still, *ITV* news presented Greenpeace as having lost credibility as a consequence of that mistake: 'The technical gaffe has done Greenpeace's credibility no good at all' (*ITV News at Ten*, September 5). And in the interview with Peter Melchett, *ITV*, like the *BBC*, asked questions that suggested a critical view of Greenpeace:

> Is an apology enough? You have cost Shell millions of pounds, tarnished their reputation, they have had their petrol stations firebombed and boycotted;

> Let's get to the broader point here. Isn't there a problem that the public have been misled and that the real debate about the scientific issues at stake never took place because of the emotive campaign that you were able to mount?

Despite posing critical questions, as with the *BBC* interview of Greenpeace, it provided an opportunity for the organisation to promote its view of the situation which, as a consequence, was represented by *ITV*.

The new focus on Greenpeace brought another novel aspect to *ITV*'s coverage, namely, a concentration on Greenpeace's campaign method of filming images and providing these to television studios:

> Greenpeace sent their own news films of the occupation of Brent Spar around the world. Today, they were untypically reticent after their embarrassing gaffe (*ITV Lunchtime News*, September 5);

> Pictures that Greenpeace triumphantly sent around the world: the Brent Spar occupied by their activists frustrating Shell's attempts to dump it, and its contents of allegedly toxic chemicals, in the Atlantic. But Greenpeace today had to apologise. Samples they took on board the platform were, they confess, misleading and just plain wrong (*ITV News at Ten*, September 5).

ITV's portrayal of Greenpeace as having provided its film to the media was mentioned but not elaborated on. But it was mentioned in both reports, quite unlike the *BBC*'s coverage, which entirely ignored this aspect. Despite identifying that factor as problematic, *ITV* news did not discuss or analyse it. There was no analysis or examination of the organisational nature or campaigning methods of Greenpeace, as conducted by *BBC News* and *Channel 4 News*. Quite typically, and in comparison with press reports, television news carried very little commentary. But *ITV* news had less commentary than the other television news outlets. A consequence of this was that *ITV*'s coverage was not conducive to mirroring the type of arguments Shell made after the crisis. Still, one such argument was, to some extent, reflected.

In noting that Greenpeace had supplied its own footage to television stations, *ITV* implied that media coverage of the crisis might have been problematic (as Shell upheld). It was only through that implication that *ITV*'s coverage might have helped Shell's case. Additionally, *ITV* only paid attention to that aspect after Greenpeace's admission.

Channel 4

In the aftermath of the crisis, there were three *Channel 4 News* programmes on June 20, 21 and September 5.

As with most television news programmes, *Channel 4 News* reported the views on both sides of the dispute. This was particularly evident in the programme on June 20, which covered Greenpeace's reaction to Shell's new decision and represented Shell's explanations of why that decision had been made. Even though the report conformed to the convention of suggesting impartiality, it did give the story a particular slant:

> It was in the area of public relations that Shell was hardest hit by what it calls 'Greenpeace's campaign of misleading information'... experts say Shell has lost the public relations battle with Greenpeace (June 20).

Subsequent news reports also perpetuated this interpretation.

During the crisis, *Channel 4* had not examined the particulars of the dispute, but it did so after the crisis.

The news on June 21 concentrated on Greenpeace and facilitated the advancement of Shell's claims about Greenpeace, even though the programme took a different view from that of Shell.

The focus on Greenpeace's campaign was reflected in the main question the programme began with and sought to answer: 'How real is the power of the environmental lobby in Britain?' This question was followed by two more that the report also depicted as central: 'How did Shell and Mr Major get it so wrong?' Attention was also given to examining 'new claims that [the Brent Spar] might be more of a pollution threat than first thought'.

The *Channel 4* report on the 'new claims' of the Spar being a greater 'pollution threat' than previously anticipated was the first television news report to discuss Greenpeace's claim that the Spar contained more oil than Shell admitted.[11] *Channel 4 News* intimated with Greenpeace's case by assuming that the Spar definitely did pose the level of pollution threat that Greenpeace had stated. The science correspondent referred to the Spar as a '14000 tonne dustbin', which was a statement Greenpeace also made, and argued that:

> Shell provided [the information about what was inside the Spar] for the environmental impact assessment when they were given a licence to dump the rig at sea. But measurements taken by Greenpeace on board the Spar suggest the assessment may have been seriously flawed. Shell said that the oil storage tanks on the Spar contained little but sea water [and] a total of around 50 tonnes [of oil]. Greenpeace dropped probes into the tanks ... The estimate from Greenpeace laboratories at Exeter University – which is yet to be confirmed – is that there are 5500 tonnes of oil and oil sludge on the Spar, 100 times more than Shell's figures.

Despite noting that it was an unconfirmed estimate, the report sided with Greenpeace's estimate rather than Shell's. This was done by casting doubt on Shell's estimate by suggesting that the Aberdeen scientists (who had arrived at the original estimate) had not taken their own samples:

> The original assessment was drawn up by scientists at Aberdeen University. They took no samples of their own. They relied on Shell to tell them what was in the tank.

In examining the question the programme had begun its report with, *Channel 4 News* gave an account of how Greenpeace operated:

> Greenpeace have through a combination of direct action and acute understanding of the media captured the imagination in a way many established politicians would envy. It has a membership in this country of 300,000, nearly as many as Labour and operates, like the companies it opposes, at a multi-national level. Its tactic, as with Brent Spar, is to try and distil complicated issues into simple choices.

Greenpeace was presented as knowledgeable in how to handle the media to ensure publicity and as successful in 'mobilising public opinion'. This was depicted as a characteristic way in which the organisation functioned. As we have seen, *BBC* also focused on Greenpeace and claimed similarly to the above. Unlike the *BBC*, however, *Channel 4*'s account was not critical of Greenpeace and the account also seemed appreciative of how the campaign was conducted. Greenpeace's 'victory' was attained in a 'classic' way, *Channel 4 News* reported:

> It was achieved by a classic pressure group pincer movement: Shell was squeezed, on the one hand, by direct action on the North Sea and, on the other, a consumer boycott in important markets.

The concentration on Greenpeace and the view that the organisation had conducted an efficient campaign in which its messages were competently conveyed did not entirely mirror the critical claims Shell made about Greenpeace and its campaign, but did reflect the general notion behind what the company claimed. In that way, that account was conducive for the advancement of what Shell alleged.

The report also suggested that, although Shell's case was scientifically sound, the company had failed to communicate it. The report endorsed the view that where Shell and the UK government had gone wrong was in misreading public perceptions, whereas Greenpeace successfully played on 'emotions' and influenced public opinion:

> [It is the case] that you have to battle science against emotion. Here ... Greenpeace effectively played on emotion – dumping the rig in the sea – and effectively defied the science which may have been slightly on the other side ... the government did not get good enough environmental advice, I mean advice that did not look at the emotions of what was being done ... so, in a sense [it is essential] to be a pulse reader and someone who's aware of the scientific implications.

By suggesting this, *Channel 4 News* appeared to contradict the earlier suggestion, on the same programme, that Greenpeace's oil estimate was more credible than Shell's. The above statement also echoed Shell's own acknowledgement that it had failed to communicate its case, respond to public perceptions, and its argument that 'emotion' had won over a 'rational' approach.

The description given by *Channel 4 News* also came close to Shell's account of the media coverage of the crisis. Although *Channel 4 News* did not make media coverage problematic, as Shell did, the observation that Greenpeace efficiently communicated its case through the media, coupled with the suggestion that Shell had a more scientifically sound case, echoed the company's claim that there were problems with media coverage.

Channel 4's report on September 5 once again presented what both Shell and Greenpeace said. However, the programme also accented Greenpeace's argument that the mistake over the oil estimate did not detract from its campaign. The news began with this notion:

> The oil giant Shell has welcomed an apology from Greenpeace. The environmental group has admitted it got its figures wrong in the battle of Brent Spar but insist its campaign against dumping the platform at sea was justified.

And this view was also repeated:

> [Greenpeace] say that it [the error] doesn't really matter. In a letter to Shell admitting the error they say that 'the argument was about whether it was right to dump industrial waste of any sort in the deep ocean'. Not the amount of oil onboard.

Channel 4 News reproduced Greenpeace's view that the mistake made no difference to its campaign.

Channel 4's coverage of this occurrence, in comparison with that of the *ITV* and the *BBC*, was the briefest. *ITV*'s science correspondent Lawrence McGinty, who had also given a similar, albeit, longer account for *ITV*, also prepared *Channel 4*'s news report. So the claims that Greenpeace's credibility was damaged as a result of the error and that Greenpeace had 'sent its own news films about the occupation around the world' were once again made. This reflects the fact that ITN provides both channels' news. However, I have shown that there were differences in how television channels covered the story, yet this instance also calls attention to how ownership and operating structure can affect how reporting takes place.

How could television coverage affect what Shell proposed after the crisis?

My analysis demonstrates that television news routinely represents what disputing parties say, especially when there are clearly delineated opponents such as Shell and Greenpeace. As I explained, this is a news convention used to imply objectivity, but one effect of this is that conflicting claims are often represented.

I have established and illustrated that *BBC*, *ITV* and *Channel 4* identified circumstances that Shell also drew attention to and made problematic. That finding is significant to the advancement of the type of arguments Shell made after the crisis.

Although similar descriptions of conditions were made by Shell and television news, I also found that none of the news outlets reflected and elaborated on those conditions that they did identify. Also, none described Shell as having made problematic those factors which they also focused on.

On the face of it, these findings suggest that Shell was unsuccessful in having its case reproduced by television news but, in fact, television news coverage did help Shell's claims by commenting on factors that Shell also isolated and remarked on. Television news attention to these circumstances publicised them and, hence, assisted the kinds of arguments Shell made after the crisis. For example, even though *Channel 4* was not very critical of Greenpeace's campaign, it promoted the notion that it had been an efficient operation and one that had made use of the media. That account allows Shell to criticise the campaign and to make problematic public understanding of what the company had proposed. In that manner, television news's similar focus on conditions Shell also identified could, however inadvertently, help Shell's case.

Furthermore, the very fact that television news identified similar circumstances to the ones identified by Shell, without attributing this to Shell, gave the company's arguments a greater credibility. Seemingly independent recognition of the factors Shell pointed to helped sustain and confirm Shell's case.

One reasonable explanation for why there was that similarity is that they were simply independent accounts that happened to be analogous. However, it is just as possible that what Shell said after the crisis, and its propagation via the numerous 'communication initiatives', structured news reporting. A most striking instance of this was where what Chris Fay said on *Newsnight* structured subsequent *BBC* news reporting in ensuing programmes. Although it may not be possible to identify the 'real' reason or reasons for why this happened, as I showed, the fact of the matter quite clearly remains that the way in which television news reporting took place was beneficial to the advancement of Shell's case.

Press coverage

Press coverage after the crisis greatly favoured the furtherance of Shell's arguments. They were not just mentioned but also reproduced to a far greater degree than in television news.

My investigation of press and television coverage during and after the crisis showed that the press could be more partisan than television news, and that this condition allowed the case Shell made after the crisis to gain reproduction in the press.

I will first outline the general trends in the way in which the newspapers covered the period after the crisis, and then elaborate on how I see this as affecting Shell's case.

The abrupt end to the *Mirror's* coverage

Unlike the *Guardian* and the *Telegraph*, whose comment on the crisis continued throughout the year, the *Mirror's* coverage of this story came to an end a month after Shell's decision to abort sea disposal. The *Mirror's* decision that the story was over was not conducive to the coverage of Shell's claims made after the crisis.

The *Mirror's* response to Shell's decision to rethink the disposal was to announce, rather audaciously, that the paper had played a central role in bringing about this outcome:

HOW WE DID IT: BRENT SPA [sic] SCANDAL WAS FIRST REVEALED BY DAILY MIRROR WHICH HIGHLIGHTED POTENTIAL DISASTER (June 20).[12]

The *Mirror's* account after the crisis was much more direct and personal than before, as it cast itself in a central role in pressurising Shell ('Mirror quizzed Shell' (June 20)) and having campaigned to gain this result. This is succinctly illustrated by the paper's list of 'key dates in the battle to force Shell to scrap its plans to dump the rig' (June 20):

6pm: Shell announced its U-turn and revealed they will bow to pressure from Greenpeace, the Mirror, and the public.

During the crisis the paper did not explicitly state that it was playing the pivotal role it confidently asserted after the crisis. Having taken that position, it might have been damaging for the paper to cover subsequent developments that favoured Shell's original stance. As I noted in the consideration of media coverage during the crisis, the difficulty in gaining coverage of views opposed to that of a stance adopted by a paper demonstrates the limits to obtaining favourable media coverage (or indeed any coverage) of corporate claims, as the consultants recommend. The *Mirror's* stance after the crisis also demonstrates that difficulty.

That the *Mirror* considered the story over might not have been unusual behaviour for the paper; it might just be that the *Mirror*, as a tabloid, has a limited attention span. But that also indicates a problem with consultants' recommendations, because how then can damaging accounts, subsequently proved wrong, be dealt with? The *Mirror* certainly did not retract its claims, and neither did the *Guardian*.

The *Guardian's* shifting allegiances

During the crisis, the *Guardian* had supported Greenpeace's argument that Shell should change its course. While the *Guardian* had written little about risks and scientific opinion then, after the crisis the paper corroborated Shell's case that the sea disposal would not have harmed the marine environment. *After* the crisis, the *Guardian* argued that Shell had a good, scientific case for the sea disposal of the Spar and that Greenpeace had been wrong to campaign as Shell's case had extensive scientific support:

> ... almost all independent experts contacted by reporters regarded the disposal – the proposed burial at sea – as the best, or least bad, solution for the Brent Spar ... according to a majority of marine experts, the floating tank could be sunk without anything like the environmental damage that would be caused by dismantling the structure and disposing of its pollutants on land. If Greenpeace has evidence to the contrary it should spell it out. Asserting dumping at sea is wrong is not enough (Sept. 7).

While the *Guardian* had noted during the crisis that Shell had scientific support for its plan, after the crisis, the *Guardian* advanced a stronger case that the company had been right to proceed with its plan. Moreover, after the crisis, the *Guardian* was much more direct and assured in asserting that Greenpeace was wrong. The variance in the *Guardian's* coverage of the issue favoured Shell's case.

A favourable depiction of Shell

Conditions favourable to the promotion of Shell's arguments existed in the *Telegraph* and the *Guardian*.

During the crisis, the *Telegraph* had supported Shell's plan and immediately afterwards was critical of Shell for having abandoned it. The paper wrote that the situation revealed the 'failure of major companies to stand up to criticism' (June 22) and that it was a 'victory for multinationals over national sovereignty' (June 24). So, once again the

Telegraph reproduced the UK government's view of the situation. After a brief period of criticism for having changed course, the initial supportive framing of Shell, evident during the crisis, continued as the company was represented as having had little choice but to give in to Greenpeace, which, as before, was framed negatively. And, by the end of the year, the *Telegraph* reversed the criticism it had previously made of Shell:

> Faced with accusations of deception and environmental vandalism, firebombed by ecological terrorists and subjected to a consumer boycott, Shell capitulated and agreed to find an alternative method of disposal (September 7).

After a short period of reproach, the *Telegraph* held a more appreciative view of the decision to abort, as Shell was then, as at the beginning of the crisis, viewed with more sympathy and the company was presented as having responded well to a bad situation. The paper argued in a manner that favoured the types of arguments Shell made after the crisis.[13]

The *Guardian's* framing of Shell changed radically as the year progressed, and this change helped Shell's case. During the crisis the *Guardian* had criticised Shell for being unresponsive to public opinion and for not having conducted wider consultations before arriving at the sea disposal plan. After Shell terminated that plan, the *Guardian* still maintained this view. Subsequent articles, however, framed Shell as having learned lessons from the episode and, in doing so, framed Shell in the manner sought by the company. The first instance of this was when the paper covered a speech made by Shell UK's Head of Public Affairs, John Wybrew, in which he declared that the company must have better public relations and broader consultations. The paper also uncritically reproduced Shell's statements regarding its 'New Way Forward' programme for the Brent Spar. The *Guardian's* framing of Shell as having learned from the crisis might have been a reflection of the claims made by Shell as the company too maintained the same.

Towards the end of the year, when Shell held its 'Better Britain' awards (postponed during the crisis), the *Guardian* praised Shell for its environmental concern. Hence, by the end of the year, the *Guardian* reinforced what was questioned and threatened during the Brent Spar crisis – Shell's reputation for being environmentally concerned. The *Guardian* argued that the company's claims about its environmental activities were justified:

Shell's interest in the environment is no flash in the pan: the company was supporting initiatives in environmental education as long ago as the 1940s, and the campaign [Shell's 'Better Britain'] celebrates its 25th birthday this year (Nov. 22).

Whereas the *Guardian* had not supported Shell's claim about environmental concern during the crisis, after the crisis it reproduced Shell's desired image and presented the company's claims as justified. In short, the *Guardian* now framed Shell in a positive manner that helped the advancement of the company's case.

A critical press attention on Greenpeace and its campaign

Greenpeace obtained this type of press attention prior to the two events the organisation credits with prompting negative media coverage.[14] The press attention given to Greenpeace was a consequence of the papers' arguments about the crisis as having illustrated what they considered to be the true state of affairs. Their analyses were analogous to those promoted by Shell and similarly made problematic the type of actions that Greenpeace took.

The *Guardian* depicted Greenpeace not as a David fighting Goliath but as a key player in a battle between equals: 'BATTLE OF GIANTS' is how the paper described the past crisis. Greenpeace had fought an efficient campaign but lacked the scientific evidence to support its claims, the *Guardian* argued:

Although they [Greenpeace] have won the war they have not yet won the argument (June 22);

There are scientific doubts being raised about Greenpeace's arguments for not sinking the Brent Spar oil rig, but these are generally lost in the sea of publicity which has drowned out Shell and made heroes of Greenpeace (June 26).

The *Guardian* also framed Greenpeace as an organisation that was not quite what it seemed and represented the environmental group as being sophisticated, powerful and skilful in managing communications with the media:

Greenpeace ... feeds off images of the state or large organisations appearing to bulldoze aside people or new ideas ... (June 22);

... technology came into its own [in Greenpeace's campaign]. It may have been a traditional protest action, but the communications deployed were second to none ... the messages were kept punchy and simple and disseminated widely through press adverts and billboards. The campaign was even articulated in cyberspace via the Internet (June 22).

Like Shell, the *Guardian* also commented on the televisual qualities of Greenpeace's protest activities, arguing that Greenpeace knew how to gain media attention and secure public support for its campaigns.[15] By arguing in this way, the *Guardian* framed Greenpeace in a similar manner to that advanced by Shell and by the *Telegraph*. The *Telegraph*'s framing of Greenpeace, however, was much more critical and negative than that of the *Guardian*.

The *Telegraph*'s derisive framing of Greenpeace was unchanged after the crisis, e.g. 'GREEN FOR DANGER' (June 21). An interesting circumstance was that, whereas the *Telegraph* had not covered Greenpeace's claims about the environmental risks of Shell's sea disposal plan during the crisis it did so afterwards. This was done in order to question and discredit them – it was part of the *Telegraph*'s wider programme to cavil at Greenpeace's allegations. The *Telegraph*'s depiction of Greenpeace reflected what Shell maintained, and that portrayal was conducive to the promotion of Shell's view of Greenpeace:

Greenpeace's victory over Shell UK and the Government ... illustrates the capabilities of a highly organised and well funded international group ... One of the world's few environmental groups able to mount such an operation, Greenpeace marshalled a flotilla of boats, including two chartered ones, a helicopter and the latest video and photographic equipment. It also deployed consummate public relations skills in ensuring that the world knew about its attempts to prevent the dumping ... while its activists are out trying to stop commercial whaling or the dumping of radioactive wastes, there are many more staff running what has become a successful marketing, media and lobbying company (June 21).

The *Telegraph*, like the *Guardian*, also commented on the David and Goliath imagery, claiming that 'Greenpeace's strength is to be seen as the David against the corporate Goliath' (June 22). The paper gave critical attention to the public image of Greenpeace, arguing that, contrary to public perceptions, Greenpeace was not an environmentally concerned organisation but one that was more concerned about funding: 'GREEN-PEACE: A CAUSE DRIVEN BY CASH FLOW' (September 10). Greenpeace had campaigned against the disposal in order to boost its dwindling funds, the *Telegraph* maintained. That Greenpeace stood to gain financially from the campaign may have been true but it does not *ipso facto* invalidate Greenpeace's case, although that was the paper's implication:

> Top of the list of hypocrites comes Greenpeace, which decided to play silly games in wetsuits and helicopters not to save the environment but to reverse an alarming fall in their membership ... (June 25);

> ... reality had little to do with the choice of the Brent Spar as an issue for Greenpeace-style direct action. It presented a photogenic and winnable scenario, which would bring new members (and even greater financial clout to this multi-million pound global network) ... Reality consistently comes way down on Greenpeace's list of priorities' (August 13).

Greenpeace was frequently represented as manipulative, deceitful, powerful, unaccountable and irresponsible.

A negative framing of Greenpeace was manifested in the *Guardian* and, to a greater extent, in the *Telegraph* prior to the two developments that Greenpeace claimed gave rise to an antagonistic representation of the organisation. Whilst the nature of the framing of Greenpeace was not new, the developments helped perpetuate that existing (critical) frame.

The *Guardian* responded to the television executives' statement about Greenpeace in a manner that was consistent with the existing negative framing of Greenpeace as scheming and dishonest. The *Guardian* framed Greenpeace in a similar manner to that promoted by the news executives, i.e. as media savvy and technologically sophisticated, and as using sensational campaigning tactics to attract and manipulate media coverage. Albeit, the *Guardian* had on previous occasions discussed the proficiency of Greenpeace's campaigning tactics and, in particular, had elaborated on how the Brent Spar campaign had solicited and captured television coverage.

The *Guardian*'s response to Greenpeace's admission of a mistake also did not lead to a change in how the paper characterised the organisation, as Greenpeace claimed. The paper had previously framed Greenpeace's allegations as unproven and had cast doubt on Greenpeace's claims about the environmental risks of Shell's plan. In contrast to the development of a negative frame as a result of this admission, the *Guardian* outlined Greenpeace's claim as to how the mistake had been made and, in doing so, gave a sympathetic rendition that represented Greenpeace as having made an honest mistake.

Moreover, contrary to Greenpeace's claim that its acknowledgement gave rise to a critical representation of the organisation, a direct consequence of Greenpeace's statement was the negative representation of Shell and the UK government. In the first article on this subject (September 6), the *Guardian* not only framed government ministers as 'attacking' Greenpeace over this 'mistake' but also framed Shell as 'seizing' on this 'apology' in order to 'reopen the issue of the disposal of the North Sea installation' and 'turn the spotlight on alleged misinformation by influential pressure groups'.

However, a number of articles on the subject that Greenpeace needed to substantiate and prove the claims it had made about the Spar appeared in the *Guardian*. Although the paper had formerly constructed that subject, what was new was how often that view was expressed after Greenpeace's admission of its error. For instance, an article in October had the headline: 'TRUTH AS MUCH UNDER THREAT AS THE RAIN-FOREST'.

Also, in one instance, the *Guardian* did encourage the impression that Greenpeace had apologised for the whole of its campaign. This, Greenpeace claimed, was a common media misinterpretation of its apology for the oil-estimate error. But it was the only example I found. It appeared in its end of the year review: 'Greenpeace apologised for misleading the public' (Dec 30). It seems as though, in that one instance, a failure to highlight what Greenpeace had apologised for created that impression. Nevertheless, prior to that statement, the *Guardian* had always made it clear that Greenpeace has apologised for one mistake rather than for the whole campaign. This situation, I believe, again shows the self-serving nature of claims about media coverage.

The *Telegraph* presented the television executives' faultfinding claims about Greenpeace in a similar way to the *Guardian*, i.e. by reproducing their negative frame of Greenpeace as being manipulative. But that was also the *Telegraph*'s initial frame of the organisation.

The first article by the *Telegraph* on Greenpeace's admission of a mistake was quite reserved in passing judgement. Yet subsequent articles argued that this development indicated that Greenpeace had deliberately lied and misled the public, that Greenpeace had only admitted its slip because Shell would have soon found this out and that Greenpeace was trying to make a virtue out of the admission:

GREENPEACE FIASCO: Greenpeace's apology ... is an exercise in damage limitation rather than an act of contrition ... Three months too late Greenpeace has 'realised in the last few days' that its guerrillas were far more fervent than competent ... The misleading information was worthless to scientific analysis but invaluable to propagandists ... But the Brent Spar fiasco need not be wholly regrettable if the public learns the stark lesson it teaches; that single issue groups are often not unimpeachable guardians of society's best interest, but highly motivated and well-financed zealots who play fast and loose with the facts ... Greenpeace is a sophisticated organisation, adept at choosing soft targets to stir widespread concern. But its Brent Spar campaign has been irresponsible – a fact which should not be forgotten the next time it solicits money or tries to whip up public outrage (September 7).

Even though there was no change in how Greenpeace was framed (the paper still disparaged the organisation), the two developments were presented as though they confirmed the paper's initial criticisms of Greenpeace.

While the two developments may not have *fundamentally* changed each newspaper's view of Greenpeace, the developments did have certain consequences as more critical articles about Greenpeace materialised. But Greenpeace's contention that the two developments were pivotal in bringing about a negative representation of the organisation cannot be defended, as such a view already existed and had been propagated before the two statements. The existence of a critical view of Greenpeace (before the two statements), together with such a view being seemingly sustained by developments, meant that Shell's arguments about Greenpeace were reflected in what the newspapers wrote. Further, the manner in which the papers framed Greenpeace validated Shell's arguments as that perspective facilitated and lent a greater credibility to Shell's problematisation of Greenpeace, its campaign, and its strategies.

A view of the crisis as having displayed what the papers took to be truths about the *status quo*

This is illustrated in some of the quotations above. The newspapers had suggested a similar interpretation of the situation during the crisis but the articles then were more focused on specific events that were taking place.

During the crisis, the *Mirror* had urged Shell not to ignore public opinion, as public acquiescence was a necessary element. That was also a claim made by the *Guardian* in the presentation of its argument that companies operating in contemporary society required the acceptance of wider and external 'stakeholders' rather than just compliance with regulations. The *Telegraph* had maintained that the situation illustrated the agenda-setting power of pressure groups and the failure of major companies to stand up to the pressure groups' appeal to emotions in their arguments. These arguments mirrored those which Shell advanced after the crisis. After the crisis, all three newspapers elaborated on their earlier accounts.[16] Their respective claims about the *Zeitgeist* proposed a particular elucidation of the crisis.

All three papers argued that the incident was indicative of societal conditions. Their description of those conditions paralleled the claims made by Shell after the crisis and thus benefited Shell's case. It is perhaps within those observations that homogeneity with Shell's views is most clearly manifest, because those accounts accorded with Shell's identification of the three conditions the company classified as being problematic.

The *Mirror* was very critical of Shell and argued that the crisis demonstrated a necessity for companies to incorporate the wishes of the wider public. Shell's claim that it would listen, engage in dialogue with and enlist the acquiescence of its external stakeholders was similar to what the *Mirror* claimed was necessary.

The *Guardian* and the *Telegraph* also argued that companies had a wider responsibility to external stakeholders to whom companies were accountable. Thus their accounts also reflected Shell's arguments about the company's new commitment. The *Telegraph*'s identification of a dissipating public trust in big business was one that Shell had also recognised. In short, what all three papers said about Shell's approach was similar to what the company admitted and argued in the aftermath of the crisis.

As we have seen, a further aspect identified by both the *Guardian* and the *Telegraph* also resembled what Shell claimed, i.e. assertions regarding Greenpeace's campaign. The *Guardian* argued that the outcome of Greenpeace's campaign was 'an environmental own goal' (June 24) and that the campaign had been efficient but unfair. Likewise, the *Telegraph* argued that Greenpeace's campaign had been proficient but prejudicial. Such arguments accorded with Shell's claims. The *Guardian*'s and the *Telegraph*'s view of Greenpeace's campaign was the same as Shell's condemnation of it. They both argued that the campaign was a symbolic and televisual one that was more concerned with the presentational aspects that promoted a desired view rather than one based on an assessment of the actual risks of Shell's plan. The *Telegraph* reported:

> ... the importance of the Brent Spar was as a symbol of the pollution of the global commons by vested interests with short term objectives ... To Greenpeace's supporters this inexactness [of whether the sea disposal would damage the environment] does not matter ... (June 22).

Like Shell, the *Telegraph* viewed the situation as caused by Greenpeace's 'cavalier use of science' and its 'demonisation of environmental risks' (June 22).

The *Guardian* too, like Shell, identified the symbolism of Greenpeace's campaign and people's understanding of risks as problematic:

> ... we now feel that nature itself resides in the seas and the skies. It is a romantic notion – the sea may be hacked up into fishing territories and when one is sitting on a plane one hopes that air space is well regulated – but it is a powerful one (June 22);

> We are the Risk Society in the notable phrase of the German sociologist Ulrich Beck, composed of people constantly calibrating risks in our personal lives and with a deeply established expectation that the job of the political class is the avoidance or minimisation of future risk for the whole society, and the provision of compensation when this fails (July 1).

The article argued, like Shell, that the Spar incident had a great deal to do with perceptions of risks and expert assessments:

> The complicated relation between public perceptions of risks, expert assessments, and political calculations – demonstrated recently during the Brent Spar affair – seems to many to have become the most vital, and difficult, area in the politics of industrialised nations (July 1).

According to the *Guardian*, the Brent Spar crisis illustrated the new demands made on businesses and the rise of new societal conditions:

> [Shell's] climbdown ...is not a victory for the environment but for the politics of refusal (June 22);

The European consumer boycott of Shell ... mark a rejection of business and Establishment values as much as any direct protest against environmental damage ... The grassroots cry is for respect and consideration; the tendency is to reject power imposed without consultation ...(Nov. 15);

... what Brent Spar showed is that this new kind of politics is especially explosive when environmental anxieties are combined with national feeling against outside agencies, corporations or other governments (July 11).

Both the *Telegraph* and the *Guardian* maintained that the success of Greenpeace's campaign demonstrated that Greenpeace and other pressure groups commanded public trust and faith:

Environmental groups still retain the faith of the public. That is their main source of strength (*Guardian*, September 7);

The trump card in pressure groups' hand is easily stirred public sentiments ... people do not trust [governments and corporations] anymore. The consequence is that they accept no corporate governmental evidence unless they have been party to it from the start. That means [winning the public debate] early ... (*Telegraph*, June 24).

Both newspapers argued that Greenpeace's skill and effectiveness in publicising their claims also explained the crisis for Shell. In maintaining that, their accounts reflected Shell's claims:

[Greenpeace's] well-honed skills with helicopters and small boats make for arresting television. That in turn attracts the attention of a public that is becoming increasingly conscious of environmental issues ... But it is deeply regrettable that such a campaign rather than reasoned and informed debate has now won the day (*Telegraph*, June 21);

There is, one senses, a coming together of many issues around this particular campaign. What should never be underestimated is what a beautifully televisual campaign this was. A battered ugly man-made structure in the North Sea, being buzzed by a Greenpeace helicopter caught the imagination... We may know that Shell is a huge multi-national exercising enormous global power, but it is difficult to conceive what this might actually look like. Now we have an image to go with the concept (*Guardian*, June 22);

ROUGH SEA OF PUBLICITY; Shell took a battering in the North Sea ... But can big business ever compete with guerrilla PR? ... Corporate Goliaths like Shell have been slain by adverse publicity, not only by Davids such as Greenpeace, but by their own lack of crisis management ... Sadly, for a company with as comparatively strong an environmental record as Shell, this is a lesson learned too late. It is ironic that Shell's three year campaign of lobbying the British government ... was so successful ... they won the lobbying battle but lost the PR war (*Guardian*, June 26).

How might press coverage affect Shell's case?

Out of the three areas Shell made problematic (its own approach, Greenpeace's campaign and media coverage), the first two areas received greater press attention than the third, even though that too was discussed in a way that approved Shell's claim regarding the matter. All three papers were agreed that Shell's approach had shortcomings and the *Guardian* and the *Telegraph* concluded that Greenpeace's campaign was questionable. Nevertheless, Shell's claim that there were problems with the way in which the media described the situation did not receive as precise and in-depth an exploration as was given to the other two areas. And while much was made of television coverage (as can be seen in the above citations), what was significantly missing from both papers' accounts of media coverage was that pertaining to press coverage. And even though the *Guardian* had substantially changed its position, it did not retract or apologise for its earlier stories. Both newspapers claimed that how Greenpeace had used the media was problematic, yet these accounts were focused on television coverage, not press coverage. However, the notion that Greenpeace had unjustly but efficiently gained media attention and influenced media coverage was one that implicated the press as well as television. In advancing that notion, the papers supported Shell's arguments regarding media coverage.

The absence of commentary by the press on how press coverage might have affected the crisis is perhaps to be expected, given that self-criticism may not be advantageous, yet it is conspicuous for its absence. This was also the case with television coverage. A notable absence in television coverage was the television executives' admission of biased coverage. That development was not aired on *BBC*, *ITV* or *Channel 4*. Its absence in television coverage, and presence in press coverage, suggests that damaging information for television news (as the admission threatened impartiality, the canon of television news) was omitted. To state the obvious, this shows that television news is not always as impartial as it maintains it must be and that the press also protect their interests. An important observation is that, despite the expression of analogous views to that of Shell, both the *Guardian* and the *Telegraph* presented that outlook as their own. Perhaps this reflected the necessity and presumed gains of appearing objective, or perhaps it just happened to be the deduction. Whichever way it may have come about, accounts of the past crisis, especially when presented in an apparently independent way, bolstered Shell's case.

My study suggests that press coverage after the crisis was beneficial to the advancement of the types of arguments Shell made most forcefully after the crisis. What the press and Shell advanced after the crisis had consequences for how that crisis was subsequently viewed. As the newspapers expressed similar views to those of Shell, the company's arguments were repeated by them and this gave those arguments a greater credibility.

One of the main conclusions regarding media coverage after the crisis is that both television and, to a greater extent, press identified factors that were conducive to the promotion of the sort of arguments Shell offered (after the crisis) in order to manage the crisis. Television news did not argue in a similar manner to Shell, as the press did, but television news identified constituents that helped further the case the company subsequently made. Press coverage did specifically propound arguments that were similar to Shell's after the crisis. Hence, the conditions that prevailed within television and the press were favourable to Shell's case.

It is conceivable that these circumstances may have been a consequence of Shell's activities after the immediate crisis was over, as I showed earlier that the company took measures to address that damaging affair. It is also possible that Shell's retrospective interpretation, intentionally or otherwise, articulated existing news themes and, hence, received coverage. Fishman (1995) argues, in a study of news media dependency on the police for crime news, that the police's stories are more likely to receive substantial news play if they articulate a news theme. Fishman also maintains that the police are aware of that and deliberately play to existing news themes, publicising accounts that fit the formats of news discourse.

It is impractical to identify whether the news stories preceded or followed Shell's case. My investigation reveals instances where the news stories and Shell's case were constructed around the same time. For example, the *Guardian*'s coverage of John Wybrew's speech signalled the beginning of a change in how Shell was framed by that paper. The study also reveals that some news themes existed during the crisis but were later elaborated in a manner that reflected the types of arguments that Shell later made. Shell's arguments certainly encouraged and facilitated that elaboration. But we may never know which came first (the news stories or Shell's case). What we do know, however, is that there was a correspondence between them and that was useful to Shell.

Even if Shell expanded on pre-existing news themes in the media in proposing a favourable account, the very fact that the company did so would show that it was seeking to manage the past crisis by managing interpretations of what had taken place. And given that Shell did put great effort and resources into communicating about the past crisis and advancing a specific rendition, it is not unreasonable to suppose that its crisis management might have had some effect.

However, it is impossible to establish a cause and effect relationship, and this is a routine condition of social scientific study. It is difficult to produce this type of correlation because it is impractical to meet all three criteria for causality: (a) a relationship (b) time-ordering and (c) the elimination of all alternative explanations. I have, at least, confirmed a relationship. Further, the fact that I cannot show a cause and effect relationship, and that Shell's account gelled with existing news themes, should not detract from the situation I have demonstrated, i.e. that Shell proposed a beneficial account which was carried and delivered by the media.

Did Shell's activities after the crisis reflect the consultants' advice?

Much of crisis management, as defined by consultants, is about gaining acceptance of a standpoint. I have argued that Shell managed the crisis by communicating a particular outlook on what had happened. The actions Shell undertook after the crisis show that the company had indeed put some key recommendations into practice.

The consultants do not reject the possibility of engaging in crisis management after crises, but overlook, devalue and criticise that approach in favour of promoting crisis management during and prior to crises. The previous chapter showed problems with that approach and here a comparison of their recommendations and Shell's crisis management efforts after the crisis allows a further consideration of the consultants' preferred approach.

I have previously used an outline of the consultants' recommendations and again do so here.

- *Understanding and responding to public emotions and perceptions*

This notion structured Shell's response to the crisis, and the company also exploited this conception to further its interests.

In stating a new commitment to take into account perceptions the company demonstrated a greater appreciation of the consultants' diagnoses that perceptions are of vital importance and have consequences for crisis management. By making this pledge to be more considerate of perceptions and emotions Shell atoned for its past behaviour, created a favourable image of the corporation and solicited goodwill.

Not only did Shell apply this crisis management principle but it also reinvented the crisis in terms of faulty perceptions and the conflict between emotion vs. rational. By recreating the crisis in terms of mismanaged perceptions and misunderstandings Shell portrayed the opposition against the company (the crisis) as unwarranted. That also helped restore its desired reputation as being socially and environmentally responsible.

- *Cultivating knowledge of relevant audiences and communicating with them*

This notion is fundamental in crisis management, and Shell's actions after the crisis showed its incorporation.

As we have seen, to manage external communications better was a further promise the company made after the crisis. This was also in the company's interest because Shell communicated with varied publics not only because the crisis was topical and was of interest to them – which is how the company depicted it – but also because Shell sought to convince those publics of the merits of its case. Through communications, the company publicised and sought the acceptance of its views by publics who were also able to further corroborate its case. I have shown that external communication was the vehicle for propagating a specific account of the crisis and it is principally through that route that Shell managed this crisis.

Also, quite significantly, it is by utilising the argument that the company had previously failed to communicate and thus had mismanaged the crisis that Shell explained the past crisis. Hence, this idea was present and central to Shell's crisis management.

- *Understanding media requirements and cooperating with the media in granting information*

According to journalists' comments in a MORI survey about Shell's media relations having vastly improved since Brent Spar, Shell was clearly successful in this area.[17] Although I did not examine media briefings, it is my understanding that there were many such occasions. From interviews with the members of the media who attended the briefings,[18] and from an examination of the information Shell provided to the media (to which I had access), I found that Shell presented the same arguments to them as in the article and speech examined in this chapter. Furthermore, the exercise of having media briefings and releasing information to the media suggests that Shell was more accommodating of the media's interest in this case, as well as actively seeking to attract media attention.

The media can influence readings of the past crisis and hence also views of Shell. And, as I have said, media representations of the past crisis were amenable to the advancement of Shell's account of the crisis/its crisis management. This demonstrates that Shell could successfully handle the crisis after the end of the immediate crisis situation. That finding has repercussions for the consultants' proposition regarding the most efficient way in which to manage crises as the company appears to have better addressed and handled the crisis after it was technically over.

- *Responses have to be made and managed at an early stage as contentious issues arise*
- *Present and communicate the case clearly, quickly and succinctly*

The first of these proposals is the basis of the consultants' preferred line of an early response, and these recommendations are mostly significant prior to and during crisis situations. Thus, after the end of the immediate crisis Shell obviously could not be expected to follow these suggestions. Still, the broad principles behind these were applied.

Following the crisis, Shell was appreciative of the need to communicate and to allocate resources and time to discussing what had happened. Contentious issues had arisen earlier but they still remained after Shell ended the immediate crisis, and in then dealing with these controversial issues the company demonstrably responded to them. In that way, these two principles, mostly relevant in other phases of the crisis, were also incorporated after the crisis.

The examination of the emerging and the immediate crisis revealed that Shell had not incorporated the key elements of the consultants' advice and that it is difficult for an organisation to follow many of their recommendations during those periods. On that basis, I questioned the consultants' argument that the Brent Spar crisis demonstrates the importance of crisis management as a preventative measure. Having examined what Shell did after the crisis – and, in doing so, broadening the boundaries of this case – I have found that this case reveals factors consequential for what consultants say, not just with regard to this specific instance but also with regard to crisis management in general. Given what consultants said about this case, what I did not expect to find, but did, is that it demonstrates not why crisis management should be principally used as a preventative and early management of crises measure (as consultants would have it, and refer to this case as justifying that approach) but how crisis management can be engaged and beneficial after crises.

Conclusions

A key finding of this chapter is that Shell did not entirely mismanage the crisis, which is contrary to the consultants' conclusion. At the very core of crisis management is the construction and perpetuation of a desired view, and I have demonstrated how Shell did this. The route Shell took, reconstructing the past crisis in terms that were favourable to the company, is demonstrably possible and hence also available to other organisations seeking to manage their crises. We have previously seen the sorts of difficulties Shell had in handling the crisis situation and, in contrast to that period, in this chapter we have seen the company dealing with many issues that had also existed then. In showing the kinds of arguments the company proposed, and how media representations favoured the promotion of that case, I have argued that it is conceivable that Shell's communication efforts might have had an influence.

My consideration of Shell's handling of the various phases of this crisis suggests that crisis management, as formulated by consultants, might have been better achieved at this phase of the crisis rather than at previous stages. There were problems in instigating many of the consultants' recommendations about the early response to 'emerging' crises, and in this chapter I have demonstrated possibilities for crisis management after crises. These observations are consequential to what the consultants' regard as the best approach to crisis management because they illustrate problems in the consultants' position that crisis management should precede rather than follow crises.

This chapter also demonstrates that Shell heeded consultants' advice by embodying and utilising most of the principles of crisis management. From this situation, I see two main intriguing issues emerging.

The first is a question raised in chapter one: might individuals and organisations use a similar process, or a basic model, of interaction to manage impressions? That chapter argued that consultants upheld an interaction process that has affinities with symbolic interactionism's account of the process individuals are said to employ. I have now demonstrated that Shell did follow a course consultants recommend. What this situation reveals is that, at the very least, in this instance an organisation followed the recommended method of impression management and, in doing so, behaved in a similar way to that which Interactionism holds that individuals do. The generalisation that can be drawn from this is that individuals and organisations may have to account for virtually similar factors in interacting to manage impressions. Although this is an intriguing detection, there are limitations to that generalisation.

The second point is that Shell appears to have better managed the crisis at this stage, and did so following many of consultants' proposals, but why then do consultants not portray this case as one where crisis management initiatives worked and instead depict it as demonstrating the mismanagement of crises? It might be that consultants benefit more by portraying this case as emblematic of mismanagement, as that interpretation serves the promotion of their claim that crisis management must be engaged in regardless of whether or not a crisis is present. As we have seen, while they criticise the handling of the crisis situation, their principal criticism of Shell is for not engaging in crisis management measures prior to the crisis.

I believe that the consultants' version of this case reveals how important it is to further a particular line of reasoning. They use this case to endorse their argument about the importance of early response, an argument that requires this case to be labelled as one where a crisis was mismanaged, when they could represent it as one demonstrating the value of the other recommendations made. But it is more lucrative to argue that crisis management is *always* necessary rather than only required after crises. This once again suggests that the advancement and establishment of a particular formula might have more to do with these intentions, rather than addressing the problems to which that approach is presented as the solution. There is an apparent disregard for the availability of possibilities for crisis management through routes other than the particular one that is most eagerly promoted at the time. This suggests how professional fields are developed in a coveted manner and how the scheme known as crisis management is a very specific creation of consultants, who, in helping organisations pursue their interests, also attend to their own.

Conclusions

In many ways, the emergence and existence of this specialist consultancy practice, crisis management, attests to the explosion of the consulting market (Kieser 2002). I have demonstrated its historical roots and current home in public relations and that it deals with specific, restricted concerns. Yet it is inevitable that the ways in which practitioners seek to gain support for, and establish their authority are mirrored in the type of activities undertaken by consultants in the wider consulting industry. In that sense, the study of this one occupation is relevant to an understanding of others, specifically, how new professions come about, how they gain professional standing and how they are able to create a demand for their services.

From the outset, therefore, I was interested in examining the features whereby consultants gain support. That is not to say that their actions alone create a demand for their services. The business opportunity was undoubtedly there because there was an organisational demand for it, but it was exploited and shaped as crisis management grew.

What I find particularly remarkable is that the principal concept that consultants develop, the management of risk, is an object of public discourse. Two important issues arise out of this. Firstly, risk is a powerful notion to evoke in propagating actions that purport to control. Secondly, the very existence of that public discourse seemingly legitimises the measures advocated. Both aid the development of this field.

The consultants paint a portrait of the world as dangerous. It is a helpful impression because it creates fear and, in turn, a demand for measures to reinstall a sense of control. My study demonstrates how consultants not only promise control but also increase the fear of a loss of control. Kieser (2002) finds this to be a routine device consultants use to persuade people of the necessity of their counsel, arguing:

> To achieve control over events that impinge on the realization of one's plans can be regarded as one of the strongest human motives … Consultants … skilfully feed the fears of those who have not yet adopted the new idea … The expertise of the presenting consultant is also underlined … Often [that individual] quite openly makes it clear that intuition such as only an expert can have is indispensable (Kieser 2002: 173; 179).

Consultants feed clients' sense of uncertainty, Kieser observes, and they also contribute to creating more uncertainty because there is a constant flow of new concepts that 'always plant the seed for new, deep-reaching uncertainties' (2002: 175) and the cycle continues. In some respects, by the very condition that these consultants deal with crises/circumstances that seem to those involved to be disastrously out of control, their task of persuasion is made easier.

This book has pointed to the many ways in which consultants convince organisations of their way of thinking. With the aid of the Brent Spar case study, I argued that crises do not appear to be the manageable situations the consultants say they are, and I have identified some problems with their conceptualisation of proper responses. A principal problem is how complex processes are reduced to plain, neat situations and given the appearance of manageability. This reflects more of their practical competences than intrinsic features of the problematic situation itself.

Kieser's argument, that complexity is reduced because the advice then appears more appealing to clients, contributes to an understanding of why this is so:

> [Consultants'] concepts appear attractive if they reduce the perceived complexity of management and thereby contribute to the restoration of control (2002: 177).

Thus, we have witnessed in the crisis management consultants' account how there is a concentration on communications, and this is largely because that is the area in which the consultants have expertise and a wish to promote. But the consequence is that everything pertaining to crises and their management is related to communications, and that creates a one-dimensional comprehension of the character and control of such situations. It also points to how much impression management is the chief concern. But, in some ways, that may be to the detriment of a more genuine understanding of the conditions and processes involved.

Moreover, we have also seen how consultants present the principles of crisis management as being valid for all circumstances and organisations. This too simplifies and does away with the differences that may exist. The consultants focus on corporations but say that other organisations can also apply their knowledge. However, there is in fact very little indication of whether there are differences between, say, the public and the private sector. There is not only a lot we do not know with regard to what may be involved in handling the different crises of different organisations but there is also a lack of clarity. The impression I received was that the consultants intended to tackle the precise issues once they were hired. Kieser argues that consultants intentionally, and for their own interest, create this vagueness and ambiguity, and that these are normal characteristics of their approach:

> The consultant who presents a concept has to maintain a certain degree of vagueness – of mystification – so that getting his help seems advisable ... Ambiguity offers scope for interpretation. The reader or listener can project the problems she presently encounters in her organization onto the concept that is presented by the consultant and can thus interpret it as the solution to these pressing problems (2002: 178–9).

But it is not at all the case that clients respond in the desired manner. Kieser argues that consultancies have made managers 'marionettes on the strings of their fashions' (2002: 176), but he also points to studies indicating that some organisations exercise scepticism and develop a critical stance, even if they still buy into consultants' advice (see Engwall and Eriksson 1999). Indeed, Kipping and Armbruster (2002) discuss instances where clients resisted consultants' advice.

There are external forces that create a demand for the types of techniques consultants say they offer. It is not just that the consultants alone create a demand but also that their service appears to be a convincing solution to the practical problems organisations believe they face (Kieser 2002). What makes it so convincing? It is because the circumstances consultants point to and classify as risks are also ones organisations find threatening. The very existence of the risk discourse, for instance, is not just helpful to the consultants' case but also shows the existence of a wider concern with the type of areas they evoke. As I argued in chapter one, issues were now being thought about quite differently and that has consequences. In the case study, I demonstrated many of the conditions and circumstances that both the consultants and the risk thesis describe. Therefore, the consultants' claims can have resonance because of what organisations perceive to be true about the world. And those perceptions about the world are derived not just from what consultants say but from wider and, especially, leading discourses of the time that provide intellectual support and legitimacy for the consultants' case. I have said that responses to problems are structured by the existing dominant beliefs and rationales (Garland 2001). Yet the consultants' reference to these is also important in understanding and explaining how they are able to advance their field. There might indeed be a reciprocal relation between what consultants offer and what the organisations wish for and demand (Kipping and Engwall 2002).

The existence of crisis management clearly shows that risks have become commodities, and that it has become possible to trade services based on their assessment and control. But the very fact that this is viable reveals how much of a concern there is with managing conditions seen to pose risks.

If there is a reciprocal relationship between what consultants supply and what organisations demand, then organisations must perceive that there are problems with managing impressions. Crisis management consultants argue that organisations operate in a virtual reality constructed by the mass media. But, as the existence of crisis management indicates, the world is not just constructed by the media but also by the organisations attempting to influence that construction. My study shows that organisations strive to fashion their appearances and the contexts in which they are seen.

Crisis management is very much about exerting control over other attempts to define reality. It seeks to position organisations' interpretations as dominant because in this way they can benefit from favourable outlooks. The very fact that crisis is defined as a consequence of the proliferation of negative views shows the significance of this. It is really not surprising that the parallels I have pointed to between the consultants' account of social action and that of symbolic interactionism are there because both, under different positions and objectives, deal with how social reality is symbolically created.

Consultants cite the Brent Spar crisis because it is meant to reveal this and prove the validity of what they hold to be the best approach to crises. In examining that case, I largely agreed with their first argument and raised problems with the second.

This incident points to the fact that most things are open to interpretation. This explains both the organisational anxiety and the consultants' advice. And it does attest to many of the features of society that consultants point to. However, I argued that it also shows, contrary to the consultants' own argument, that it is more than a little difficult to control these circumstances. I especially took issue with their claim that crises can be prevented through the early management of issues, arguing that there are practical difficulties in applying this strategy.

With reference to the media coverage of this incident, I argued that organisations might play a restricted role in the 'presentation of self' (Goffman 1959), which is a finding consequential to the consultants' claim that organisations can govern that process. That is not to say that an influence cannot be exerted – sources seek to influence news, Ericson et al. (1989) argue, and I showed that crisis management seeks that objective – but there are constraints on this. There are not just other actors seeking the very same objective but also other processes involved, I argued, and their involvement curtails the particular impression that crisis management measures intend to create.

From what I have examined, it appears that it is not so much a single virtual world created by the mass media but several coexisting and often conflicting realities simultaneously sustained by the mass media, which certainly construct the world, producing their own and disparate meanings, but also reflect the designs and creations of external others.

This study centres on the construction of appearances and it points to how important they are held to be. It also demonstrates the type of problems that can be encountered in managing impressions. Yet, despite those problems, the existence of crisis management indicates that there are institutionalised attempts to control how organisations are viewed, and its consideration shows how such attempts might be organised, how they may at times fail and, at other times, succeed to an extent.

I described how the consultants' advice to create favourable impressions can be applied by examining Shell's crisis management after the crisis. What that consideration displayed is not just how this company used their advice and benefited from it but also how the broad principles behind the consultants' proposals can be applied differently from how they encourage. This in itself points to how particular types of reasoning can be utilised to develop a professional field in a preferred direction.

I have also argued that the citation of this case and consultants' specific rendition of it illustrate the importance to consultants of gaining support for a particular recommended approach and the measures that go into persuading clients to adopt the suggested course. By advancing a particular line of reasoning, consultants attempt to gain support for the strategy they endorse and that concern is, for them, key because it is that which directs and establishes their occupation.

The research also indicates that impression management is a concern operative at all levels of society, and it appears that it might operate in broadly similar ways at all levels. But just as the Interactionists pointed to the limitations involved in the individual's presentation of self, there are limitations for organisations. Consultants do not point to these limitations, I suspect, not because they are unaware of them but because it is not advantageous for them to do so. We should not assume that managers are naïve and wholeheartedly buy into crisis management. One reason for the adoption of crisis management must conform to what DiMaggio and Powell (1983) called 'rituals of rationality' – the way in which organisations comply, and try to be seen to comply, to what are accepted as rational, sensible management strategies, even if, on a cold appraisal, they do not actually contribute much to efficiency or effectiveness.

This examination of crisis management suggested two main interrelated explanations for its existence. Firstly, there is the active construction and promotion of it. Secondly, there are external reasons as to why crisis management appears desirable. What this says about new professions is that they do not simply arise in response to a need. That is an influential factor, but it is also the case that they exist because there are efforts taken to launch them and ensure their continued existence. Influential factors on that survival are wider rationales that sustain the profession, which are also helpful in creating an ostensible need for it.

It would be interesting to see how crisis management progresses in the future; whether consultants derive new concepts and what type of arguments they use in backing those. A topic for research I would recommend is to see how the consultants of the future would describe the Brent Spar crisis, whether that representation is different from their current rendition, whether that reflects the new reasoning and what that might reveal about how management concepts and consultancy practices change and evolve.

My study shows the social construction of reality and that there are conflicting and contested realities which vie for attention and dominance. It reveals that the mass media are not just important in creating social reality, and hence also important to the task of impression management, but also that they are seen as fundamental in society and as highly influential. However, there are many sources of influence on media representations. I have demonstrated how organisations are politically and ideologically motivated, how corporations as well as environmentalists have become media-sensitive and reflexive to the media and how that is a consequence of the importance of gaining public acquiescence and influencing public understandings. Consensus-building practices such as crisis management will undoubtedly gain in stature.

Certain features of globalisation – such as communication technologies, the ubiquity of the mass media and the weakness of nation states – are documented in this study but it also shows how globalisation is incomplete; there are differences between societies and the cultural nature of people's perception and judgment of risk. It shows responses to environmental issues to be complex and ambivalent yet also open to influence.

This study also found that it is by no means certain that a planned, strategic approach will have the intended results; that it will lead to the desired outcomes. The world is at times predictable and knowable but it is not always so. There is contingency, openness and unpredictability (Popper 1945). Yet the study also demonstrated that possibilities exist for capitalising on circumstances in order to gain acceptance of a particular viewpoint. There is inventiveness and creativity in seeking support for ideological positions.

I have pointed to how the concept of risk is central in the contemporary era. This book provides the risk thesis with an empirical experience to its largely theoretical observations and hence a response to the criticism made of the risk thesis for being overly speculative and not grounded (Lupton 1999). The study also shows how discourses such as the risk society perspective can not only be used as a tool to explain and justify an expertise, but can also help towards obtaining professional standing.

Appendix A: Notes on Method

My primary aim was a study of how crisis management consultants represented their world, their understanding of what the handling of crises should involve and the justifications they employed to argue how, in their view, their approach is necessary and superior. An interpretive methodological stand was the most appropriate for that task.

The principal research method, 'unstructured' interview (see page 244), was chosen because it was suited to the issue being researched: to explore the consultants' formulation of crisis management.

On access and respondents: How many subscribe to the view I chronicled as the crisis management consultants'?

At the very beginning of my fieldwork, in May 1997, requesting interviews, I wrote to the 16 London-based consultancies who were members of the Public Relations Consultants Association (PRCA), and listed 'crisis management' as part of the portfolio of services provided. I received four responses. One was a positive response (from Michael Seymour, Director of Crisis Management, Burson-Marsteller) and another was a clear 'access denied' response: 'Unfortunately, we are not able to disclose details of our crisis management work.'

Preserving client confidentiality is justifiably of paramount importance for consultancies. It is also the case that crisis management deals with sensitive, potentially damaging information and, perhaps more than other areas of public relations, is subject to a greater level of secrecy.[1] Naturally, this has an impact on gaining access. This may also explain why there was a reluctance to speak about it and why non-response was high. But there might also have been other reasons for this, as I explain later.

The two other responses I received stated that they did not specialise in crisis management and that I should contact Michael Regester, who did.

Surprised to have encountered such a low level of response, I once again wrote to the consultancies. Still no replies were received, although some telephoned to suggest I contact the firm Regester Larkin, who were experts in crisis management.[2]

I wrote to the Institute of Public Relations (IPR), whom I had previously consulted, stating my position and adding that an 'initial introduction from you to your members would greatly facilitate my research'. The Executive Director of the IPR, John Lavelle, wrote back suggesting that I contact 'the three IPR members shown below, mentioning the fact that I had given you their names, as they have all lectured at the Institute, written books and appeared on international stages on the subject of issues and crisis management'. They were: Michael Regester, Michael Bland (independent crisis management consultant) and Peter Sheldon Green (Managing Director of Sheldon Communications). Clearly, I was being directed not just to those seen within the field as experts (Regester had already been pointed out by others) but to those with a specific type of background. They might have been highly regarded and experienced practitioners but I was aware that they might also have been regarded as the type of people with whom an academic would wish to speak. It was also the case, as it later transpired in interviews with them, that these three people had books to promote.[3]

They all accepted my request to interview them and all offered unlimited time and access.

The account I give of crisis management and the views I ascribe to crisis management consultants are very dependent on what those people said in interview and what they wrote in their publications on the subject. My report is also supplemented by an ongoing effort to speak to other consultants and gain views on crisis management through other avenues, such as attending seminars on the subject.[4] Subsequently, I also gained access to some of the consultancies that had initially been hesitant about being questioned but it was very much the case that those consultants still said that they did not specialise in the area, and had I spoken to Michael Regester or Michael Bland?

I was glad that many cited those very people, Regester in particular, who had given me unconditional access.[5] Surely, this showed that what they had to say about crisis management was important and representative. At the very least, it showed that their peers and colleagues saw them as experts. Still, it would have been beneficial to have had a higher response rate from those who had described themselves (in the PRCA yearbooks) as being engaged in crisis management. However, as became evident from the reasons given for not participating in my study, and from what Regester said about obtaining referrals from other PR consultancies,[6] advertising the service of crisis management and actually engaging in it seemed to be two different things. I do not wish to suggest that those whom I interviewed were the only ones engaging in it, but clearly not all those who advertised crisis management actually practised it themselves. And, even though my respondents are small in number, they are the acknowledged experts and specialists in a small field.

I did not have much authority or capacity to reward and consequently was not in a strong position to elicit interviews. But I did do my utmost, repeatedly, to enlarge the scope of my sample. My research focused on what was possible. What I succeeded in doing was speaking to the acknowledged experts in the field and, in particular, the recognised leader and specialist. Certainly, it would have been valuable to speak to those who were less widely thought to be expert. I have, however, managed to conduct the first exploratory study of its kind and others may be able to enlarge on it later.

'Unstructured' interviews

In total I gained access to and interviewed eight consultants with whom 21 interviews were conducted. In addition, 34 interviews took place with public relations practitioners, journalists and in-house crisis managers. Although I had prepared some basic questions (see pages 246–7), as I had intended, the discussion often diverged from that template. The questions were used solely to guide what was essentially a conversation rather than a structured interview. The interviews were in depth, designed to encourage unforced narrative and focused on certain insights as they arose.

I interviewed for as long as I required, there was some restriction on the length of each session but not on the number of sessions.[7]

I used a tape-recorder, especially at the beginning. I wanted to give my full attention to what was said so that I could follow on from that rather than being preoccupied with taking copious notes. I was quite aware that in the absence of much literature on the subject, and given my objective to report the consultants' views, I was very dependent on recording what was said, not just for comprehension of the subject but also for later reference, citation and to register the consultants' own phrasing of their work. Nevertheless, as I gained in confidence and experience of interviewing, and as I wanted to see whether its absence would make a difference to what was said, the tape-recorder was put aside. Instead I took notes and this usually seemed to put participants at greater ease and yielded better information.

Although most interviews were face-to-face at the offices or, in one case, the residence of participants, some interviews were conducted over the telephone. In these instances, this was because of physical distance and because it was requested. Overall, I gained more information and more discussion in face-to-face interviews than in the telephone interviews, some of which were subject to interruption. In one case, an interview was arranged with a consultant on his mobile phone. I called at the specified time and, on hearing a disruptive background noise, enquired whether it was a good time to speak, gained a positive response and proceeded with the interview. But the connection was lost many times, the noise was not conducive to a seamless rapport; he was on a helicopter journey. Subsequently, he gave me another time when I could call him when he was in his office.

There are problems with the interviewing method that are routine and inescapable (Shipman 1997; Hakim 1987). Firstly, it is inevitable that the interviewees and I would act reflexively, both influencing the research situation. Both also make certain assumptions about each other and that, in turn, influences the interview. The principal assumptions I made about the consultants were that they were active, enquiring and brought to bear their personal, political and professional beliefs to give meaning to events and take action. And, I took it, as became later apparent, that they knew that their meanings were disputed by others and seek to defend them. I expected to receive sophisticated responses to my questions. The assumptions I made in part determined the questions I asked and the inferences made about answers. Further determinants were the particular aspects I wished to centre on.

However free flowing I had intended the interviews to be, there was a (justifiable and unavoidable) concentration on what I found interesting. The consultants too wished to highlight and elaborate on certain areas. For example, my interest in how crisis management is promoted inescapably led to a greater attention on that area. But it was also the case that my focus on this was also a response to the circumstance that I detected, that is, that consultants, in interviews and of their own accord, regularly identified and elaborated what they held to be the factors necessitating crisis management. Clearly, they too played a part in invoking particular topics. I wondered why consultants stressed the societal conditions they said made crisis management indispensable, and my conclusion was that it is principally in this way that crisis management is constructed and marketed. And, again, my questions directed them to elaborate on that. But it was also the case that they did not need much encouragement to do so, as they added to that description freely, citing past crises that lend justification to their case. Still, my account of crisis management is influenced by my own interpretations arising from how I saw the relevance and importance of what they said. That does mean that my account is limited to certain matters.

Further, a condition normally present in all interview situations is that the presence of the interviewer influences what the subject says. The interactionist position on this is that it is an inevitable part of every social interaction (Rock 1979). We should expect a lack of candour to be normal in all interviewing, interactionists argue, and they also hold that the answers to our questions are often those our respondents want us to hear. Or the reverse could also happen; people might find it hard not to be candid in face-to-face interviews. In both circumstances, the interviewees influence what researchers know, and researchers in turn exert an influence on the answers they receive. While that is a limitation, it is hard to see how it can be prevented. And, at times, it might not even be a limitation. In the context of my research interests it was, in fact, informative. My research was to do with how consultants wish to portray the world and crisis management, and if I had received (in interviews) information that seeks to convey what the consultants wanted us to believe to be true about the world, this circumstance is not necessarily limiting but enlightening. How respondents wish to depict things is, in itself, relevant and revealing.

Interview questions

These questions guided the interviews I conducted with the crisis management consultants.

- What does a crisis involve?
- What is crisis management?
- What factors, if any, differentiate crisis management from other types of public relations?
- How important is impression management in handling crises?
- What is the single biggest problem/threat in a crisis?
- Is there a big demand for crisis management?
- What is involved in your job?
- Are you called in once a crisis occurs or do you have a longer relationship with your clients?
- What role do you play in handling a crisis?
- Who else is involved in handling crises?
- Is there an integrated approach between all the parties involved? Is there a common understanding?
- Does crisis management differ in theory and in practice? How so?
- Edward Bernays described the role of PR as 'the engineering of consent'. What do you make of that description?
- What is being done to improve the efficiency of public relations?
- What would you say is the public perception of public relations?
- Has the PR profession evolved over the years? How? What have been the most significant changes over the last decade?
- Are there benefits and or constraints to being members of the PRCA?
- The IPR and the PRCA have professional codes of practice, are these useful? Do you have any informal codes of practice?
- What are the biggest challenges the PR profession now face?
- Do PR and crisis management perform a management function?
- Is there a danger that management consultancies will usurp the functions and services provided by PR/crisis management consultancies?
- What is a consultant's knowledge based on? What is the basis of your strategies? Do you draw on academic theories or research?

- How do you obtain clients?
- What do clients expect from you?
- Have there been changes in the way clients view public relations?
- Are clients generally receptive to your advice?
- Do client expectations change during the course of consulting/once they have had exposure to crisis management?
- Is there a discrepancy between client expectations of your services and what you can realistically provide?
- When clients approach you, do they already have plans in place to deal with crisis?
- How do clients rate the efficiency of consulting? How do you evaluate the efficiency of your strategies?
- Who are your clients?
- What problems faced by the consultant are the most difficult to explain to clients?
- Have you ever been asked to be economical with the truth? How have you dealt with this situation/How would you deal with this situation if it arose?
- How much of your job involves dealing with the media?
- Do you have contacts in the media? How important/useful/helpful are they?
- What do you think are the journalist's objectives in covering a crisis?
- What made you join this area of work?
- What did you do before?
- Can you recall what first attracted you to this field?
- How long have you worked in this profession?
- Do you know other consultants in this field? Who?
- Are there differences between your approach/strategy and theirs?
- How has the field of crisis management changed over the years? How do you see it evolving in the future?
- Have you ever thought seriously about leaving crisis management?

Case study

Interviews were also used for the case study, which was also drawn from unpublished and published material. Indeed, it was in interviews that consultants drew my attention to the Brent Spar crisis, which they, on their own accord, described as an instance that justifies their advice and claims about the world. My decision to focus on this case was taken on the basis of how often consultants cited and elaborated on this incident.

One of the advantages in examining the Brent Spar crisis was that there was a lot of accessible material on the episode. As I argue, characteristics of the management of this crisis were that it was extended and that Shell meant to influence how this incident would come to be seen.[8] Therefore, the company had a website on the topic of the Brent Spar crisis – launched in 1996 and withdrawn only in 1999 – and provided me with several published and internal materials pertaining to that situation. Greenpeace, the other main party involved in the crisis, also wished to explain and gain support for its perspective on the situation; a book about it was published by Greenpeace itself. So there was a fair amount of available information.

While that appears to be an advantage, it was also a difficulty. In the midst of attempts by Greenpeace and Shell to offer their own interpretations of what had happened, I had to be continually attentive to their attempts to convince and persuade. A lot of counterbalancing and a steadfast, critical stance were always required, but that is a routine condition that most researchers examining this type of dispute would impose.

A Shell director in charge of the Brent Spar decommissioning process and the press office at Shell UK provided much of the information that was not already on the website.

There was a sense, when I initially approached the company to request interviews and information, that this was a familiar request and that a referral to the website on the Spar was the routine response. There was neither surprise nor a refusal to assist. But this was part of its ongoing crisis management which involved a pledge to conduct 'open communications' about the Brent Spar disposal.[9] My request would have been also unsurprising; it had been a big story in 1995 and in 1997 – when I began my research of it – it was still a 'hot' subject, as a final solution for the disposal of the Brent Spar had not been reached.

In addition to the material provided by the company, I also gained valuable insight into the crisis and its management through four telephone interviews I had with John Wybrew, Director of Public Affairs at Shell UK at the time of the crisis, who no longer worked for the corporation. He was involved in handling the situation and had been central to the company's response to the crisis.

I approached Greenpeace several times requesting interviews with anyone who had been involved in the Brent Spar campaign but was turned down. The reason repeatedly offered was that they were too busy with their new and ongoing campaigns.[10] One of my attempts, however, coincided with the publication by Greenpeace of a book written on the incident by the Brent Spar campaign director and I was told that it put forward their opinion of the incident (*The Turning of the 'Spar*, Chris Rose 1998). I was sent it and a report published by the WWF (*Brent Spar*, WWF – UK 1995), where Greenpeace and Shell presented their cases. Principally, I relied on Greenpeace's book on the Spar for their perspective.

I also interviewed journalists and editors who had contributed to privately commissioned (by several oil companies operating in the UK) MORI surveys on the views of oil and energy journalists which discussed the incident.[11] They recalled covering the incident and their recollections were informative and provided a different perspective.

A case history published by the European Case Clearing House and written by Winter and Schweinsberg, two business academics, entitled *The Brent Spar Controversy* (1996) was also a useful reference and gave insight into the German media coverage of the dispute.[12]

The case study method was chosen because it allowed an in-depth examination of this crisis and its management. My assumption was that this method could provide useful insights because the aims were to understand what happened, how identities and meanings were constructed in this case and how particular people and groups made sense of it. This was as capable as any other method of illustrating what might be involved in a crisis and what might bear on its management. The case study facilitated reflection on the crisis management practice in the context of this crisis. It also allowed an examination of the consultants' claim that this case justifies their recommendations.

Appendix B: 'Spar Scene'

Greenpeace inflatable at Brent Spar. Water canon used by M.V. REMBAS and M.V. TORBAS at base of platform to prevent boarding. Copyright Greenpeace / David Sims June 1995

Notes

Introduction

1 The word 'consultants' refers throughout this book to the consultants I interviewed (see Appendix A, page 243) and the literature on crisis management
by its practitioners (Bland 1997; Bland 1998; Regester and Larkin 1997;
Seymour and Moore 2000) maintain this argument.

2 Ibid.

3 See page 67 for the total cost of decommissioning Brent Spar.

Chapter 1 'Crisis Management' – A General Outline

1 The management of crises and the consultants' methods of crisis management are two distinct things, as I will show, and I use the term 'crisis management' only to refer to the latter.

2 All the consultants interviewed described these characteristics, which are
also detailed in their publications, e.g. Bland (1997) (1998), Seymour and
Moore (2000), Regester (1987).

3 He is an author and lecturer on crisis management and an independent
crisis management consultant.

4 The consultants provided this description of their work in interviews.

5 Green is the author of *'Reputation Risk Management'* (1992) and the Managing Director of a public relations consultancy, Sheldon Communications.

6 These only go as far back as 1981. The primary objectives of the yearbooks
are to list members of the PRCA, the range of services they offered and to
publicise consultancies and assist organisations to choose between them.

7 These were outlined in the PRCA yearbook 1999.

8 Figures listed in the PRCA yearbook 2002.

9 These categories are from the PRCA yearbook 1999.

10 The quotations I use below illustrate this, e.g. the citation from Seymour
and Moore (2000) on page 17.

11 The consultants' argument is that key publics have to be identified and
communicated with. But one problem I will identify in my discussion of
Brent Spar is that the key publics may not always be evident.

12 Many consultants I interviewed mention this incident. It is also to be found
cited in texts on crisis management, for example, Regester and Larkin
(1997: 134–8).

13 I take it that the authors use this term to describe the effect of the reports
not questioning oil dependency. They suggest that because of that omission
the news reports presented oil use and dependency as given/'natural' rather
than problematic.

14 The concept of role here is not used in the sense used by Parsons and
Merton, i.e. in a structural sense to describe a set of expectations associated
with a given position in society. Interactionists hold that there may be cul-

turally derived cues for interpreting roles, but the actual process of role construction is an emergent, unstable and constantly negotiated activity. What is being described is a dynamic process.

15 All the following emphases in the quotations from Beck appear in the original.

16 Although the question of why such similarities are there is compelling, I am not confident that conclusive answers to the question of why are attainable – I have demonstrated *how* those similarities are there. One could, however, speculate and I have done so.

17 Andrew Grove, CEO of Intel, made this view quite clear in *'Only the Paranoid Survive: How To Exploit the Crisis Points That Challenge Every Company'* (Grove 1999).

18 On December 21, 1988, Pan American Airways Boeing 747 'Maid of the Seas' (Flight 103) crashed in Lockerbie, Scotland. The flight exploded as a result of a terrorist bomb, destroying 270 lives on the plane and on land in Lockerbie. Consultants have criticised the company for not demonstrating concern (as the CEO did not go to the site, did not apologise and did not attend the memorial services), for failing to communicate with the media and for concealing the truth that the airline, along with all carriers operating in Europe, had been warned about a possible terrorist attack.

19 See page 7.

20 *'Business and the Environment'*, an article by MORI published in *Green Futures*, November 1996.

Chapter 2 Brent Spar – Setting the Stage and the 'Emerging' and the 'Immediate' Phases of the Crisis

1 The terminology I employ to describe these two phases of the crisis, 'emerging crisis' and the 'immediate crisis situation', are similar to the consultants' description, but unlike them I am employing the terms with hindsight and not to imply, as the consultants did, that all crises can be expected to follow a foreseeable course.

2 This description of the Royal Dutch/Shell Group relates to how the multinational was structured at the time of the Brent Spar crisis (in 1995). Following the 2004 scandal over the misrepresentation of its proved oil reserves, on October 28, 2004, the Royal Dutch/Shell Group proposed to its shareholders the unification of the group of companies under a single parent company, Royal Dutch Shell plc. and instigated reforms in management and governance structure.

3 The figures are according to the 1997 Annual Report.

4 This term refers to the seven largest oil companies in the world.

5 These polls were conducted by MORI on behalf of several oil companies but because of their confidential nature, I am only allowed to state findings of the surveys pertaining to Shell as I gained access to the surveys with permission from Shell on condition that I used material limited to that company. I gained full access to the 1998 poll (from Shell) but only partial access to the 1995 poll (from MORI, which withheld material on the other participating oil companies).

6 At the time, this was referred to not as a 'disposal' but an 'abandonment' plan. Shell later changed the terminology. It is quite likely that the com-

pany eschewed using 'abandonment' due to its connotations, which reveals an attention to perceptions. I use the term 'disposal' because, as Shell might have also estimated, it is a value-free term, as Harre, Brockheimer and Mulhausler (1999) point out.

7 Shell launched this Internet site in 1996 and it was terminated in 1999.
8 This was the regulatory standard against which the UK government judged all licences for decommissioning oil installations.
9 After the Spar campaign he became the Executive Director of Greenpeace International and his promotion might further indicate Greenpeace's view of the campaign as having been an efficient operation.
10 Quoted in Winter and Schweinsberg (1996: Section A: 8).
11 In order to gain maximum media coverage, Greenpeace even carefully selected the activists who would 'occupy' the Spar from four different countries, argue Winter and Schweinsberg (1996: Section A: 9)
12 See chapter 3.
13 *Financial Times*, April 13, 1999: 14.
14 Ibid.
15 Ibid.
16 Greenpeace's case is obtained from *Brent Spar*, WWF (1995) and *The Turning Of The 'Spar*, Rose (1998).
17 Unless otherwise indicated, the following citations of Shell's claims are derived from '*Brent Spar – The Way Forward. Your Questions Answered*', a Shell UK publication, 1995.
18 Quoted in Winter and Schweinsberg (1996: Section A: 8).
19 The UK government was also criticised for allowing Shell to carry out the disposal.
20 Cited in Winter and Schweinsberg (1996: Section A: 7).
21 This is a reference to Shell UK's corporate environmental and social responsibility programme of the same name.
22 Shell's earlier terminology can be seen here.
23 Media coverage is assessed in chapter 3.
24 Chapter 3 tests the claim whether Greenpeace in fact succeeded in framing the issue in the media.
25 This and the following citations are from Shell UK News Release: May 16, 1995.
26 Chapter 3 asks whether television coverage of this did create a bias towards Greenpeace's position, as consultants and Shell later argued.
27 See page 79.
28 Kohl protested because he feared the loss of voters in the upcoming election, allege Winter and Schweinsberg (1996).
29 See chapter 3.
30 Source of Greenpeace's advertisement: Winter and Schweinsberg (1996: Section B: 13).

Chapter 3 Media Coverage and an Analysis of the Consultants' Interpretation of the Case

1 The next chapter also adds to that subject.
2 These assertions have been gathered from what has been publicly said in publications and speeches by the company's directors, as well as in interviews I conducted with John Wybrew.

3   As I argue subsequently, this was a condition of the company's crisis management after the crisis.
4   *Brent Spar*, a magazine published by Shell, 1995: 8.
5   See pages 190–1.
6   The following chapter will address this issue.
7   His argument is examined in the following chapter.
8   *Brent Spar*, a Shell UK publication, 1995: 8.
9   This was gathered from the Greenpeace publication on the Brent Spar campaign written by Chris Rose (1998), Greenpeace UK Campaigns Director, which addresses media coverage at length.
10 That focus might have been necessitated by Shell's crisis management efforts, which criticised Greenpeace's methods.
11 This survey was based on 40 interviews with journalists and editors. The following were the participants. From the national/weekly press: *Daily Telegraph, Financial Times, Guardian, Observer, London Evening Standard* and the *Sunday Telegraph*. From broadcasting: two sources who requested anonymity and the NorthSound radio. Several interviews were also conducted with specialist press e.g., *Petroleum Review, International Oil and Gas Journal*, and with periodicals and the wire service e.g., Reuters, Bloomsberg LP. In addition, seven freelance journalists were also included.
12 I later elaborate on Tuchman's outline of the conventions journalists use to suggest objectivity.
13 The account I give below derives much from McNair (1999).
14 In his study of claims-making in the Brent Spar controversy, Anders Hansen (2000) examined British newspaper coverage of the immediate crisis using much the same approach as I did. Unlike his study, however, mine deals with a longer period of time and with television as well as newspaper coverage.
15 That is from the beginning of press and television attention to the Brent Spar disposal until Shell's decision to relinquish the disputed plan.
16 I use 'text' to refer to both words and images, which were examined in the case of television news. Press coverage only examined the words as pictures are not included in the Lexis-Nexis database.
17 The paper was owned by Robert Maxwell's Mirror Group Newspapers, which, as a consequence of Maxwell's illegal financial dealings, was subsequently owned by the consortium.
18 The figures are for January to June 1995, and compiled by the Audit Bureau of Circulation. All the circulation figures I cite are derived from McNair (1999).
19 Tabloids consistently maintain higher circulation figures than broadsheets.
20 I employed the Lexis-Nexis search engine using the search term 'Brent Spar'. The Sunday editions of these papers are also included.
21 All the following capitals were in the original.
22 'Ton', the imperial measurement (equivalent to 1016 kg) and 'tonne', the metric measurement (equivalent to 1000 kg), both appear in discussions of the contents of the Spar. In citing Greenpeace's and Shell's statements (in all the chapters), I have used 'tonnes' or 'ton' when and where they do and have done the same for the citations from the press. With regard to the citations from TV reports, having had to rely on the verbal account, I have cross-referenced news reports' reference to Shell or Greenpeace's estimates and followed Shell or Greenpeace's terms. When TV news did not state the source of claims made, I have used 'tonnes'. The most important measure to

get right, as it played a main part in this crisis, was Greenpeace's estimate of oil contained in the Spar. Greenpeace and Shell consistently described that estimate as '5500 tonnes' and I have reproduced that.

23 This article represented the case against Shell's plan, and was followed by another article representing the case for that plan.

24 Throughout the crisis, the UK government supported Shell's plan and the *Telegraph's* reproduction of their frame was advantageous to Shell.

25 A list of the *BBC* programmes that covered the Brent Spar story was obtained from *BBC* Archives using the search term 'Brent Spar'. As *ITN* did not have a similar archive service to that provided by the *BBC*, the *ITV* and *Channel 4* news programmes on the Brent Spar were identified following an examination of all the news programmes in the period of my search and selecting the ones that covered the Spar story. All the news programmes were obtained by and viewed at the British Film Institute. I also transcribed the full dialogue of all TV news reports.

26 David Frost.

27 The reporter's statement duplicated Shell's news release (May 16) and later news releases that repeated that comparison. For example, see page 88.

28 See page 149.

29 At the same time as the Spar campaign, Greenpeace also opposed Shell on human rights and ecological issues in Nigeria – a crisis the company would face later that year when the Nigerian government executed Ken Saro Wiwa, a human rights campaigner. Incidentally, Greenpeace even made a 'satellite phone link…between the occupiers of the Spar and a demonstration concerning Ken Saro Wiwa, going on outside the offices of Shell International in London' (Rose 1998: 102).

30 This is a reference to the tax breaks offered by the government to the oil industry.

31 For example, Lezaun's (2004) study of the strategies developed by the British food industry to find the 'path of least resistance' to public acceptance of genetically modified foods showed that despite the concerted strategic preparatory effort, the marketing of GM foods still failed.

Chapter 4 Crisis Management After the Crisis

1 The 2004 controversy about Shell's misrepresentation of proven reserves contests Shell's conversion to greater transparency. The ensuing investigations into the firm's finances uncovered memos that suggested that people serving at the top also knew about the reserves cover-up (*The Economist*, August 14–20, 2004: 54, 'A Buyer for Shell?').

2 Cited in Shell's Website and Rose (1998: 158).

3 Cited in Shell's Website.

4 Wybrew said this in interview (November 18, 1999).

5 Chris Fay cited in '*Brent Spar*', a Shell publication.

6 Ibid.

7 This speech was delivered to a conference on the media at the University of Wales on May 20, 1996. It is quite possible that academic occasions such as this are chosen as they can furnish an appearance of authority to claims made.

8 A clip of Greenpeace UK's Science Director, Sue Mayer, making this statement was broadcast.
9 Both *Lunchtime News* and *News at Ten* covered the story.
10 Both programmes included a diagram of the Brent Spar with a visual and verbal explanation of how Greenpeace had made the measurement error by demonstrating how Greenpeace had inserted its probe into the wrong place.
11 Greenpeace had announced this on *BBC*'s *Breakfast with Frost* (June 18), but *BBC*, *ITV* and *Channel 4* ignored this until after Shell's decision.
12 Given that this paper referred to the Spar as 'Spa', I also used the search term 'Brent Spa' to see whether this would reveal more articles, but it did not.
13 This is further demonstrated below.
14 These were: Greenpeace's statement that its oil estimate was in error and television executives' claim that Greenpeace had manipulated television news coverage of the crisis.
15 The next section illustrates this.
16 This was more evident in the *Guardian* and the *Telegraph* than the *Mirror*, which was principally due to the premature end of the *Mirror*'s coverage.
17 See page 188.
18 These interviews were with environmental and oil and energy journalists and editors.

Appendix A Notes on Method

1 One of the very first questions the consultants who subsequently gave interviews would ask me was whether I intended to publish. They also refrained from naming names during recorded interviews. I also found that the consultants were more generous with their description of past incidents when interviews were not tape-recorded and, as happened twice, when the tape had run out and they had noticed but I had not!
2 Regester's name kept cropping up but it was absent from the listings in the PRCA yearbooks (Regester Larkin only became members in 1998).
3 Regester's book *Risk Issues And Crisis Management* (the second book on crisis management by a British author – he also wrote the first one) came out two weeks after my first meeting with him. Michael Bland was writing his book *Communicating Out Of A Crisis* and in our initial meeting told me that it was the first book that dealt with all aspects of a crisis. He also gave me draft chapters from it. Peter Sheldon Green gave me a copy of his book *Reputation Risk Management*. Until Michael Seymour's *Effective Crisis Management*, published in 2000, Regester's two books and Bland's book were the only ones by British crisis management practitioners.
4 Such seminars were organised by a company called Hawksmere which puts on one or two day seminars on various issues related to businesses. They are targeted at companies, attended by managers and directors and they were not cheap costing around £1000.
5 The Public Relations Consultants Association's '*Who's Who in Public Relations*' depicted Regester as 'a pioneer and an international authority on crisis management' (PRCA Yearbook 2000) and described his book on crisis

management (Regester 1987) as being 'regarded internationally as a leading work on the subject' (PRCA Yearbook 2000). That Regester Larkin was the only consultancy specialising in this line of work might have contributed to Regester's expert and pioneer status (Regester headed the crisis management division of the firm whilst his partner, Judith Larkin, headed issues management). Moreover, while the large consultancies generally carry out crisis management in specialised industries, (for example, although Burson-Marsteller had clients from various industries, its crisis management division specialised in the food and drinks industry), Regester Larkin specialised in crisis management and *across* the various industries. Their clients, for instance, included Shell International, American Airlines, AOL, Marks & Spencer, London Electricity and Vodafone (client list provided in PRCA yearbook 2000). Regester may also have been so often singled out as an expert because crisis management is a small field.

6 See chapter 1.
7 In particular, the largest number of sessions was with Michael Regester, Michael Bland and Michael Seymour.
8 See Chapter 4.
9 See Chapter 4.
10 This reflected the case made by Greenpeace that Shell continued to deliberate on this matter, trying to change the upshot of its campaign, while Greenpeace was busy with other matters (Chapter 4).
11 *Survey On The Views Of Oil And Energy Journalists* MORI 1995 and *Survey On The Views Of Oil And Energy Journalists* MORI 1998.
12 The European Case Clearing House is a facility for exchanging case material among teachers of business administration. It is a source of management case studies provided by individual authors and by management teaching establishments. Its declared objectives are to provide access to cases and to support authors by providing a mechanism for publication (www.europeancaseclearinghouse.co.uk).

Bibliography

Abbott, A. (1998), *The System Of Professions: An Essay On The Division of Expert Labor*, Chicago: University of Chicago Press.

Abercrombie, N. and Warde, A. (2002), *Contemporary British Society: A New Introduction To Sociology*, Cambridge: Polity Press.

Adam, B., Beck, U. and Van Loon, J. (2000), *The Risk Society And Beyond: Critical Issues For Social Theory*, London: Sage.

Allan, S., Adam, B. and Carter, C. (2000), *Environmental Risks And The Media*, London: Routledge.

Anderson, A. (1991), 'Source strategies and the communication of environmental affairs', *Media, Culture and Society* 13, 4: 459–76.

Anderson, A. (1997), *Media, Culture And The Environment*, London: UCL Press.

Barnes, J. (1994), *A Pack of Lies: Towards A Sociology of Lying*, Cambridge: Cambridge University Press.

Baudrillard, J. (1996), *The System Of Objects*, NY: Verso.

Beauchamp, T. and Bowie, N. (1993), *Ethical Theory And Business*, USA: Prentice Hall.

Beck, U. (1992), *Risk Society: Towards A New Modernity*, London: Sage.

Beck, U. (2000), 'Risk Society Revisited' in Adam, B., Beck, U. and Van Loon, J., *The Risk Society And Beyond: Critical Issues For Social Theory*, London: Sage.

Beck, U., Giddens, A. and Lash, S. (1994), *Reflexive Modernisation: Politics, Tradition And Aesthetics In The Modern Social Order*, Cambridge: Polity Press.

Beder, S. (1997), *Global Spin: The Corporate Assault On Environmentalism*, UK: Green Books Ltd.

Berger, P. (1963), *Invitation To Sociology: A Humanistic Perspective*, Harmondsworth: Penguin.

Berger, P. and Berger, B. (1976), *Sociology: A Biographical Approach*, NY: Penguin.

Berger, P. and Luckmann, T. (1966), *The Social Construction Of Reality: A Treatise In The Sociology Of Knowledge*, NY: Doubleday.

Bernays, E. (1923), *Crystallizing Public Opinion*, New York: Boni and Liveright.

Bernays, E. (1955), *The Engineering Of Consent*, Norman: University of Oklahoma Press.

Bland, M. (1997), *The Crisis Checklist – A Guide And Checklist To Help You Prepare For And Successfully Handle Crisis Public Relations*, Public Relations Consultants Association.

Bland, M. (1998), *Communicating Out Of A Crisis*, Basingstoke: Palgrave Macmillan.

Bland, M., Theaker, A. and Wragg, D. (2000), *Effective Media Relations*, London: Kogan Page.

Blumer, H. (1969), *Symbolic Interactionism: Perspective And Method*, Berkeley: University of California Press.

Blumer, H. (1986), *Symbolic Interactionism: Perspective And Method*, California: University of California Press.

Boden, D. (1994), *The Business Of Talk: Organizations In Action*, Cambridge: Polity Press.

Boden, D. (2000), *Worlds In Action*, London: Sage.

Broom, G. and Dozier, D. (1990), *Using Research In Public Relations: Applications To Program Management*, US: Prentice Hall.

Carr-Saunders, A. and Wilson, P. (1934), *The Professions*, Oxford: Clarendon.

Carey, J. (1989), *Communication As Culture: Essays On Media And Society*, London: Unwin Hyman.

Castells, M. (1997), *The Power Of Identity: The Information Age: Volume II*, Oxford: Blackwell.

Chapman, G., Kumar, K., Fraser, C. and Gaber, F. (1997), *Environmentalism And The Mass Media: The North-South Divide*, London: Routledge.

Charkham, J. (1992), 'Corporate Governance: Lessons From Abroad', *European Business Journal*, Vol. 4, No. 2, p. 16.

Charon, J. (1979), *Symbolic Interactionism: An Introduction, An Interpretation, An Integration*, New Jersey: Prentice-Hall.

Cohen, S. (1972), *Folk Devils And Moral Panics*, London: Paladin.

Cohen, S. and Young, J. (1982), *The Manufacture Of News: Social Problems, Deviance And The Mass Media*, London: Constable.

Cottle, S. (2000), 'TV News, Lay Voices And The Visualization Of Environmental Risks' in Allan, S., Adam, B. and Carter, C., *Environmental Risks And The Media*, London: Routledge.

Craib, I. (1992), *Modern Social Theory: From Parsons To Habermas*, London: Harvester Wheatsheaf.

Curran, J. (1989), 'Culturalist perspectives of news organizations: a reappraisal and a case study', in Ferguson, M. (ed.) *Public Communication*, London: Sage.

Curran, J. and Seaton, J. (1991), *Power Without Responsibility: The Press And Broadcasting In Britain*, London: Routledge.

Cutlip, S. Center, A. and Broom, G. (1994), *Effective Public Relations*, London: Prentice Hall.

Daley, P. and O'Neill, D. (1991), '"Sad is too mild a word": Press coverage of the *Exxon-Valdez* oil spill', *Journal of Communication* 41, 4: 42–57.

Dayan, D. and Katz, E. (1992), *Media Events: The Live Broadcasting Of History*, Harvard University Press.

Deppa, J. et al. (1993), *The Media And Disasters: Pan Am 103*, London: David Fulton.

DiMaggio, P. and Powell, W. (1983), 'The Iron Cage Revisited: Institutional Isomorphism And Collective Rationality In Organizational Fields', *American Sociological Review* 48, 147–160.

Douglas, M. (1966 [2001]), *Purity And Danger: An Analysis Of Concepts Of Pollution And Taboo*, London: Routledge.

Douglas, M. and Wildavsky, A. (1982), *Risk And Culture: An Essay On The Selection Of Technical And Environmental Dangers*, California: University of California Press.

Douglas, M. (1992), *Risk And Blame: Essays In Cultural Theory*, London: Routledge.

Dunn, J. (1993), *Successful Public Relations*, London: Hawksmere Plc.

Dyer, S., Miller, M. and Boone, J. (1991), 'Wire service coverage of the Exxon-Valdez Crisis', *Public Relations Review* 17, 1: 27–36.

Eldridge, J., Kitzinger, J. and Williams, K. (1997), *The Mass Media And Power In Modern Britain*, Oxford: Oxford University Press.

Engwall, L. and Eriksson, C. (1999), 'Advising Corporate Superstars: CEOs And Consultancies In Top Swedish Corporations', paper presented at the 15th EGOS Colloquium, Warwick University, 4–6 July.

Entman, R. (1991), 'Framing US coverage of international news: Contrasts in narratives of the KAL and Iran air incidents', *Journal of Communication* 41, 4: 6–29.

Ericson R. (1987), *Visualizing Deviance: A Study Of News Organization*, Toronto: University of Toronto Press.

Ericson R., Baranek P. and Chan, J. (1989), *Negotiating Control: A Study Of News Sources*, Toronto: University of Toronto Press.

Ericson R. (1995), *Crime And The Media*, USA: Dartmouth.

Ewen, S. (1996), *PR! A Social History Of Spin*, NY: Basic Books.

Fine, T. (1992), 'The impact of issue framing on public opinion toward affirmative action programs', *Social Science Journal* 29, 3: 323–334.

Fishman, (1995), 'Police News: Constructing An Image Of Crime' in Ericson R., *Crime And The Media*, USA: Dartmouth.

Fiske, J. and Hartley, J. (1978), *Reading Television*, London: Methuen.

Fiske, J. (1987), *Television Culture*, London: Methuen.

Fiske, J. (1993), *Introduction To Communication Studies*, London: Routledge.

Foucault, M. (1972), *The Archaeology Of Knowledge*, London: Routledge.

Foucault, M. (1976), *The Birth Of The Clinic: An Archaeology Of Medical Perceptions*, London: Tavistock.

Foucault, M. (1977), *Discipline And Punish: The Birth Of The Prison*, London: Allen Lane.

Foucault, M. (2003), *The Order Of Things*, London: Routledge.

Furedi, F. (1998), *Culture Of Fear: Risk Taking And The Morality Of Low Expectation*, London: Cassell.

Gamson, W. A. and Modigliani, A. (1989), 'Media discourse and public opinion on nuclear power: A constructionist approach', *American Journal of Sociology* 95, 1: 1–37.

Garland (2001), *The Culture Of Control: Crime And Social Order In Contemporary Society*, Oxford: Oxford University Press.

Gerver, I. and Bensman, J. (1995), *Towards A Sociology Of Expertness*, Basingstoke: Macmillan.

Giddens, A. (1991), *Modernity And Self-Identity: Self And Society In The Late Modern Age*, Cambridge: Polity Press.

Giddens, A. (1996), *In Defence Of Sociology*, Cambridge: Polity Press.

Giddens, A. (1998), 'Risk Society: The Context Of British Politics' in Franklin J., *The Politics of Risk Society*, Cambridge: Polity Press.

Giddens, A. (1999), *The Reith Lectures: Risk*, www.reith.bbc.co.uk/reith 99.

Giddens, A. (1999), *Runaway World: How Globalization Is Reshaping Our Lives*, London: Profile Books.

Glasser, T. and Salmon, C. (1995), *Public Opinion And The Communication Of Consent*, NY: Guidford Press.

Goffman, E. (1963), *Stigma: Notes On The Management Of Spoiled Identity*, Harmondsworth: Penguin Books.

Goffman, E. (1959), *The Presentation Of Self In Everyday Life*, London: Doubleday.

Goffman, E. (1969), *Strategic Interaction*, Oxford: Basil Blackwell.

Goffman, E. (1974), *Frame Analysis: An Essay On The Organization of Experience*, Harmondsworth: Penguin Books.

Graddol, D. and Boyd-Barrett, O. (1994), *Media Texts: Authors and Readers*, Clevedon: OU.

Green, P. S. (1992), *Reputation Risk Management*, London: FT/Pittman.

Greene, W. (1985), *Strategies Of The Major Oil Companies*, Michigan: UMI Research Press.

Grove, A. (1999), *Only The Paranoid Survive: How To Exploit The Crisis Points That Challenge Every Company*, New York: Doubleday.

Grunig, J. (1992), *Excellence In Public Relations And Communications Management*, New Jersey: Lawrence Erlbaum Associates.

Gusfield (1995), 'Professional Interests And The Mass Media' in Ericson R., *Crime And The Media*, USA: Dartmouth.

Habenstein, R. (1962), 'Sociology Of Occupations: The Case Of The American Funeral Director' in Rose, A., *Human Behaviour And Social Processes: An Interactionist Approach*, London: Routledge.

Hakim, C. (1987), *Research Design: Strategies And Choices In The Design Of Social Research*, London: Unwin Hyman.

Hall, S., Critcher, C., Jefferson, T., Clarke, J. and Roberts, B. (1978), *Policing The Crisis: Mugging, The State, And Law And Order*, London: Macmillan.

Hall, S., Hobson, D., Lowe, A., and Willis, P. (1980), *Culture, Media, Language: Working Papers In Cultural Studies, 1972–1979*, London: Routledge.

Hall, S. (1997), *Representations: Cultural Representations And Signifying Practices*, London: Sage.

Hansen, A. (2000), 'Claims-Making And Framing In British Newspaper Coverage Of The "Brent Spar" Controversy' in Allan et al., *Environmental Risk And The Media*, London: Routledge.

Harlow, R. (1953), *Social Science In Public Relations: A Survey And An Analysis Of Social Science Literature Bearing Upon The Practice Of Public Relations*, NY: Harper and Brothers.

Harre, R., Brockmeier, J. and Muhlhausler, P. (1999), *Greenspeak: A Study Of Environmental Discourse*, London: Sage.

Hartley, J. (1982), *Understanding News*, London: Routledge.

Haskell, T. (1984), *The Authority Of Experts: Studies In History And Theory*, Indiana: Indiana University Press.

Heath, R. (1986), *Issues Management: Corporate Public Policy-Making In An Information Age*, London: Sage.

Hobsbawm, E. (1994), *The Age Of Extremes: The Short Twentieth Century, 1914–1991*, London: Michael Joseph.

Holdaway, S. (1983), *Inside The British Police: A Force At Work*, Oxford: Basil Blackwell.

Hornig, S. (1992), 'Framing risk: Audience and reader factors', *Journalism Quarterly* 69, 3: 679–690.

Jackall, R. (1988), *Moral Mazes: The World Of Corporate Managers*, Oxford: Oxford University Press.

Jackall, R. (1995), *Propaganda*, Basingstoke: Macmillan.

Johnson, G. and Scholes, K. (2002), *Exploring Corporate Strategy*, Essex: FT Prentice Hall.

Kieser, A. (2002), 'Managers As Marionettes? Using Fashion Theories To Explain The Success Of Consultancies' in Kipping, M. and Engwall, L., *Management Consulting: Emergence And Dynamics Of A Knowledge Industry*, Oxford: Oxford University Press.

Kipping, M. and Engwall, L. (2002), *Management Consulting: Emergence And Dynamics Of A Knowledge Industry*, Oxford: Oxford University Press.

Kipping, M. and Armbruster, T. (2002), 'The Burden Of Otherness: Limits Of Consultancy Interventions In Historical Case Studies' in Kipping, M. and Engwall, L., *Management Consulting: Emergence And Dynamics Of A Knowledge Industry*, Oxford: Oxford University Press.

Koss, S. (1973), *Fleet Street Radical: A. G. Gardiner And The 'Daily News'*, London: Allen Lane.

Koss, S. (1984), *The Rise And Fall Of The Political Press In Britain, Vol. 2: The Twentieth Century*, London: Hamilton.

Lash, S. (2000), *Risk Culture*, London: Sage.

L'Etang, J. and Pieczka, M. (1996), *Critical Perspectives In Public Relations*, London: Thompson Business Press.

Levitus, R. (2000), *Discourses Of Risk And Utopia*, London: Sage.

Lezaun, J. (2004), 'Subjects Of Knowledge: Epistemologies Of The Consumer In The GM Food Debate', in Stehr, N. (ed.) *The Governance Of Knowledge*, New Jersey: Transaction Publishers.

Liebes, T. and Curran, J. (1998), *Media, Ritual And Identity*, London: Routledge.

Liebes, T. and Katz, E. (1990), *The Export Of Meaning: Cross Cultural Readings Of Dallas*, Oxford University Press.

Lippman, W. (1922), *Public Opinion*, New York: Macmillan.

Lippman, W. (1925), *The Phantom Public*, New York: Harcourt, Brace.

Lupton, D. (1999), *Risk*, London and New York: Routledge.

MacDonald, K. (1995), *The Sociology Of The Professions*, London: Sage.

Macnaghten, P. and Urry, J. (1998), *Contested Natures*, London: Sage.

Manis, J. and Meltzer, B. (1972), *Symbolic Interaction: A Reader In Social Psychology*, Boston: Allyn and Bacon.

McLuhan, M. (1964), *Understanding Media: The Extensions of Man*, Massachusetts: MIT Press.

McLuhan, M. (1999), *Understanding Media: The Extensions Of Man*, Massachusetts: MIT Press.

McNair, B. (1999), *News And Journalism In The UK*, London: Routledge.

McQuail, D. (1992), *Media Performance: Mass Communication In The Public Interest*, London: Sage.

Mead, G. H. (1967), *Mind, Self And Society From The Standpoint Of A Social Behaviorist*, Chicago: University of Chicago Press.

Mead, G. H. (1972), *On Social Psychology: Selected Papers*, Chicago: University of Chicago Press.

Merton, R. (1995), *Mass Persuasion*, Basingstoke: Macmillan.

Milliband, R. (1972), *The State In Capitalist Society*, London: Quartet.

Miller, M., Andsager, J. and Riechert, B. (1998), 'Framing The Candidates In Presidential Primaries: Issues And Images In Press Releases And News Coverage', *Journalism and Mass Communication Quarterly* 75, 2: 312–324.

Miller, M. and Riechert, B. (2000), 'Interest group strategies and journalistic norms: news media framing of environmental issues', in Allan et al., *Environmental Risks And The Media*, London: Routledge.

Mythen, G. (2004), *Ulrich Beck: A Critical Introduction To The Risk Society*, London: Pluto Press.

Neal, M. and Davies, C. (1998), *The Corporation Under Siege: Exposing The Devises Used By Activists And Regulators In The Non-Risk Society*, London: Social Affairs Unit.

Nelkin, D. (1995), *Selling Science: How The Press Covers Science And Technology*, New York: Freeman.

Neuendorf, K. A. (2002), *The Content Analysis Guidebook*, California: Sage Publications.

Noelle-Neumann, E. (1993), *The Spiral Of Silence: Public Opinion, Our Social Skin*, Chicago: University of Chicago Press.

Olins, W. (1989), *Corporate Identity*, London: Thames and Hudson.

Oxley, H. (1987), *The Principles Of Public Relations*, London: Kogan Page Ltd.

Pearce, F. and Tombs, S. (1998), *Toxic Capitalism: Corporate Crime And The Chemical Industry*, Aldershot: Dartmouth/Ashgate.

Plummer, K. (1975), *Sexual Stigma: An Interactionist Account*, London: Routledge.

Plummer, K. (2000), 'Symbolic Interactionism in the Twentieth Century', in Turner, B. S., *The Blackwell Companion To Social Theory*, Oxford: Blackwell Publishers Ltd.

Pollock, J. (1981), *The Politics Of Crisis Reporting: Learning To Be A Foreign Correspondent*, NY: Praeger Publishers.

Popcorn, F. (1992), *The Popcorn Report: Faith Popcorn On The Future Of Your Company, Your World, Your Lie*, USA: Harper Collins Business.

Popper, K. (1999), *The Open Society And Its Enemies*, Vols. I and II, London: Routledge.

Postman, N. (1985), *Amusing Ourselves To Death: Public Discourse In The Age of Show Business*, London: Methuen.

Punch, M. (1996), *Dirty Business: Exploring Corporate Misconduct – Analysis And Cases*, London: Sage.

Raucher, A. (1968), *Public Relations And Business: 1900–1929*, Baltimore: John Hopkins Press.

Regester, M. (1987), *Crisis Management: How To Turn A Crisis Into An Opportunity*, London: Hutchinson Business Press.

Regester, M. (1989), *Crisis Management: How To Turn A Crisis Into An Opportunity*, New York: Random House.

Regester, M. and Larkin, J. (1997), *Risk Issues And Crisis Management: A Casebook Of Best Practice*, London: IPR and Kogan Page.

Riechert, B. and Miller, M. (1997), 'Swamped in politics: News coverage of wetlands in three presidential administrations', paper presented to the Association for Education in Journalism and Mass Communications, Chicago, August.

Riechert, B. and Miller, M. (2000), 'Interest Group Strategies And Journalistic Norms: News Media Framing Of Environmental Stories' in Allan, S., Adam, B. and Carter, C., *Environmental Risks And The Media*, London: Routledge.

Rock, P. (1973), 'News As Eternal Recurrence' in Cohen, S. and Young, J., *The Manufacture Of News*, London: Sage.

Rock, P. (1979), *The Making Of Symbolic Interactionism*, London: Macmillan.

Rose, C. (1998), *The Turning Of The 'Spar*, London: Greenpeace Publications.

Rose, H. (2000), *Risk, Trust And Scepticism In The Age Of The New Genetics*, London: Sage.

Rosenthal, U., Charles, M. and Hart, P. (1989), *Coping With Crises: The Management Of Disasters, Riots And Terrorism*, Illinois: Charles C. Thomas.

Ross, I. (1959), *The Image Merchants: The Fabulous World Of American Public Relations*, London: Weidenfield and Nicholson.

Salmon, C. (1989), *Information Campaigns: Balancing Social Values And Change*, London: Sage.

Schlesinger, P. (1991), *Media, State And Nation*, London: Sage.

Schlesinger, P. (1994), *Reporting Crime: The Media Politics Of Criminal Justice*, Oxford: Oxford University Press.

Schlesinger, P., Tumber, H. and Murdock, G. (1995), 'The Media Politics Of Crime And Criminal Justice' in Ericson R., *Crime And The Media*, USA: Dartmouth.

Scott, A. (2000), 'Risk Society Or Angst Society? Two Views Of Risk, Consciousness And Community' in Adam, B., Beck, U. and Van Loon, J., *The Risk Society And Beyond: Critical Issues For Social Theory*, London: Sage.

Seymour, M. and Moore, S. (2000), *Effective Crisis Management: Worldwide Principles And Practice*, London: Cassell.

Schiller, D. (1981), *Objectivity And The News*, Philadelphia: University of Pennsylvania Press.

Schudson, M. (1978), *Discovering The News: A Social History Of American Newspapers*, NY: Basic Books.

Shibutani, T. (1970), *Human Nature And Collective Behavior: Papers In Honor Of Herbert Blumer*, New Jersey: Prentice Hall.

Shipman, M. (1997), *The Limitations of Social Research*, Harlow: Addison Wesley Longman.

Sklair, L. (2002), *Globalization: Capitalism And Its Alternatives*, Oxford: Oxford University Press.

Snow R. and Altheide, D. (1991), *Media Worlds In The Postjournalism Era*, NY: Aldine de Gruyter.

Snow R. (1995), 'Media And Social Order In Everyday Life' in Ericson R., *Crime And The Media*, USA: Dartmouth.

Swingewood, A. (2000), *A Short History Of Sociological Thought*, Basingstoke: Macmillan Press Ltd.

Tedlow, R. (1979), *Keeping The Corporate Image: Public Relations And Business, 1900–1950*, Connecticut: JAI Press.

Tuchman, G. (1972), 'Objectivity As Strategic Ritual: An Examination Of Newsmen's Notions Of Objectivity', *American Journal of Sociology* 77 (4): 660–70.

Tuchman, G. (1978), *Making News*, NY: Free Press.

Tumber, H. (1995), '"Selling Scandal": Business And The Media' in Ericson R., *Crime And The Media*, USA: Dartmouth.

Tumber, H. (2000), *Media Power, Professionals and Policies*, London: Routledge.

Tunstall, J. (1996), *Newspaper Power: The New National Press In Britain*, Oxford: Clarendon.

Urry, J. (2000), *Sociology Beyond Societies*, London: Routledge.

Urry, J. (2003), *Global Complexity*, Cambridge: Polity.

Vincent, R., Crow, B. and Davis, D. (1989), 'When technology fails: The drama of airline crashes in network television news', *Journalism Monographs* 117.

Wark, M. (1994), *Virtual Geography: Living With Global Media Events*, Indiana: Indiana University Press.

White, J. and Mazur, L. (1995), *Strategic Communications Management: Making Public Communications Work*, Wokingham: Addison Wesley Publishers.

Wilson, D. and Andrews, L. (1993), *Campaigning: The A–Z of Public Advocacy*, London: Hawksmere Plc.

Winter, M. and Schweinsberg, M. (1996), *The Brent Spar Platform Controversy*, Institute of Management Development, Switzerland.

WWF (1995), *Brent Spar*, WWF UK.

Index